Further praise for *Learni*

"A must read for all those who recogr̶ [illegible] ulta-
tion, in assessment, and in systemic w̶ [illegible] ...onal psychologists to re-engage with psychoanalytic [illegible] ...pening. Excellent theoretical
descriptions along with useful applicativ̶̶ns of the theory address the common arguments held regarding psychoanalysis and open your mind to the fact that perhaps
you have been using it all along – and if you haven't maybe you should. An essential
text, shining a light on what is unique in our contribution within education."
Dr Rhona Hobson, Principal Educational Psychologist, Halton Borough Council

"This book is a direct descendant of the work in psychoanalysis and education pio-
neered by Anna Freud, Susan Isaacs and August Eichhorn. Educational psychologists
need the Bionian quality of courage under fire, to be able to think when thinking is
impossible. The chapters in this collection explore what this means in an educational
context, providing insights into the 'emotional undertow' of teaching, and how to
make use of reflective supervision. The volume makes an important contribution to
the developing significance of psychoanalytical thinking in educational psychology
and is immensely useful to practitioners."
**Dr Kay Souter, Professor and Associate Dean (Retired) Australian Catholic
University**

"We need this book! We learn here about the roots of applied psychology in psychoanalytic theory, current applications, and the significant developments essential
to modern, accountable practice. Psychologists need to ensure that broad and relevant theory translates into practice, making sense of experiences and improving
outcomes. Work discussion, coaching, and newly developed relational models for
consultation and supervision exemplify how psychodynamic perspectives can be
integrated with other key perspectives, helping us support colleagues and service
users, increase depth of understanding, build rapport and reverie and achieve improved equilibrium."
**Dr Brian Davis, Deputy Head Of Psychology and Director for Professional
Doctorate Training in Child, Community and Educational Psychology, Tavistock
& Portman NHS Foundation Trust**

"*Learning from the Unconscious* is a unique example of a book that can completely change your view about things which seem to be obvious (like Psychoanalysis
itself!). It makes you think about the 'unconscious' elements of educational psychologists' interventions – working with emotions (including the emotions of the
psychologist!) – and understand their causes. This book will be of interest not only
for practitioners in educational psychology but also for educational scientists."
Dr Anastasia Sidneva, Faculty of Psychology, Lomonosov Moscow State University

"The experience of reading this book was like staring at the wrong side of woven cloth, seeing chaotic combinations of thread with colourful knots here and there. The book showed me that I had only to flip the cloth over to find a wonderful piece of embroidery design. It takes us through the application of psychoanalytic theory in educational psychology and anyone who works in the educational system will gain a comprehensive understanding of how thinking and feelings are linked to action in oneself and in the school system. The realisation that we are both a container for others and a collaborator in understanding this process can be an exultant experience."
Gracy Jebastina, Principal School Psychologist, Sukrut Therapy, India

"I welcome this publication aimed at supporting educational psychologists and others working therapeutically with children and young people. This volume brings together an impressive range of expertise across a number of related areas, all with a purposeful and coherent core, namely the application of psychoanalytic thinking. Presenting a range of diverse contexts, settings and emphases, the authors here have both benefitted from and contributed to the development of the profession and beyond. The blend of tradition and heritage with innovation and a contemporary lens makes this publication particularly welcome to coincide with the Tavistock Clinic's one hundredth anniversary."
Brian Rock, Director of Education and Training, Dean of Postgraduate Studies, Tavistock & Portman NHS Foundation Trust

Learning from the Unconscious

Psychoanalytic Approaches in
Educational Psychology

To the children and young people who have shown us the way.

Learning from the Unconscious

Psychoanalytic Approaches in Educational Psychology

Edited by
Christopher Arnold
Dale Bartle
Xavier Eloquin

KARNAC

First published in 2021 by Karnac Books, London, an imprint of Confer Ltd.

www.confer.uk.com

Registered office:
21 California, Martlesham, Woodbridge, Suffolk IP12 4DE, England

1 3 5 7 9 10 8 6 4 2

British Library Cataloguing in Publication Data. A catalogue record for this book is available from the British Library.

ISBN: 978-1-913494-23-0 (paperback)
ISBN: 978-1-913494-22-3 (ebook)

Typeset in Berling by Bespoke Publishing Ltd
Printed in the UK by Ashford Colour Press

Contents

About the authors

Christopher Arnold worked as a local authority educational psychologist in the West Midlands for nearly 30 years. He now is principal psychologist with psychologicalservices.gb ltd and a research tutor at the Tavistock and Portman NHS Foundation Trust training course for educational psychologists. He is also a research adviser for the UCL educational psychologist training course. In addition to his qualifications in educational psychology from Cambridge, Nottingham and Exeter universities, he wrote a PhD thesis on applications of chaos theory in children's learning. He is a past chair of the British Psychological Society's Division of Educational and Child Psychology and has contributed to a number of European projects related to reducing dropout rates among young people. He has contributed papers, books and conference presentations over many years.

Dale Bartle is co-director of the Doctorate in Educational Psychology Programme at Cardiff University and a research tutor at the Tavistock and Portman NHS Foundation Trust. He trained as an educational psychologist at the Institute of Education (University of London) and gained a doctorate in Child and Educational Psychology at the Tavistock and Portman NHS Foundation Trust. Currently, Dale has a varied teaching portfolio, which includes contributions to a number of doctoral programmes, primarily focusing on organisational psychology, group relations and research methodology. He is particularly interested in psychoanalytic approaches to applied psychology and research. Dale is actively engaged in knowledge generation, acting as an external examiner for a number of training courses across the United Kingdom, contributing to conferences, journal publications and various research communities.

Xavier Eloquin is an educational psychologist and organisational consultant with over fifteen years in the public and private sector. He completed his professional doctorate in Child and Educational Psychology at the Tavistock and Portman NHS Foundation Trust. He is a visiting lecturer to the Tavistock Educational Psychology training programme, with a focus on group and organisational dynamics. He has been a staff member at national and international group relations conferences. Xavier has a postgraduate certificate in Human Givens therapy. He has written several articles and chapters on subjects, including the salutary effects of Forest schools on adolescents and group dynamics in schools. He has worked in the UK, India and Qatar, offering consultancy, training and supervision to psychologists, teachers and other professionals.

Isabella Bernardo has worked in inner-city London as a local authority educational and child psychologist for seven years. More recently, she was seconded to a multi-agency children's services team as part of the government's Troubled Families programme. She has also worked in a Tier 2 CAMHS (Child and Adolescent Mental Health Service) team in London delivering a family consultancy service. Isabella also provides psychological services in Lisbon, Portugal, to families and schools. She has a special interest in supporting children with SEMH (social, emotional, and mental health) needs, providing both individual and family-based interventions, as well as supporting teachers and schools. Isabella is a member of the editorial team for the British Psychological Society *DECP [Division of Education and Child Psychology] Debate* journal.

Beverley Clarke's career encompasses history teaching and special educational needs (SEN) support as well as educational psychology. As an educational psychologist she developed expertise in social, emotional and mental health difficulties. She is an experienced supervisor and is listed in the BPS Register of Applied Psychology Practice Supervisors, and became a principal educational psychologist in 2000. She has held senior posts managing multi-professional teams, including integrated SEN/social work teams, as well as strategic leadership roles responsible for vulnerable learners, SEND strategy and service delivery. She received her doctorate in Child and Educational Psychology in 2014. She used psychoanalytic theories on the psychological functions of work to explore organisational restructure and its impact on senior managers, and trained as a coach in 2012, receiving her Postgraduate Diploma in Coaching Psychology in 2018. She runs her own consulting and coaching psychology business, provides leadership coaching for a national training charity and to leaders in education, alongside interim strategic support for SEND.

Gemma Ellis is a senior educational psychologist working in the south-west of England. She completed her doctorate at the Tavistock and Portman NHS Foundation Trust, researching the impact of domestic abuse on children from the perspectives of teachers. Her specialism is in reflective supervision of psychologists, social workers and school staff. This has also included working for a charity to facilitate work discussion groups with school staff and parents/carers. Alongside this, Gemma has worked as a research tutor and supervisor at the Tavistock. She has published articles in the *Educational and Child Psychology* journal and in the *Open Journal of Educational Psychology*. Topics include understanding the psychodynamic concepts of containment and denial in relation to domestic abuse and schools, and an analysis of professionals' understanding of sexualised behaviour in children who have experienced sexual abuse. She is a regular conference speaker and workshop facilitator.

Katharine Ellis is an educational psychologist. She initially trained as a secondary school history teacher and progressed to be an Assistant Head. Her roles in secondary schools encouraged an interest in Psychology and she began to study Psychology.

Katharine completed her MSc at the Institute of Education, University of London, followed by her doctorate in Child, Educational and Community Psychology at the Tavistock and Portman NHS Trust. Katharine has a particular interest in supporting school staff working with children and young people through training and supervision. Currently Katharine enjoys working both for a local authority and for an independent special school.

Lee-Anne Eastwood is a South African educational psychologist who has focused her career on her passion for assessment. Her master's degree at the University of the Witwatersrand introduced her to psychoanalytic theory, which she found to be a natural fit for her approach to clinical work. After her studies, she worked at Ububele, a learning centre with a focus on improving the emotional development and well-being of children under 7, their parents and other caregivers. In private practice, Lee-Anne started incorporating psychoanalytic approaches in assessments for children with additional needs. Over time, she became involved in training and supervising intern psychologists in this approach to assessment. Since relocating to the UK, she has continued to focus on assessment work and has assisted local authorities in providing assessment reports for statutory purposes

Caroline Keaney has worked as an educational psychologist in various local authorities, as well as in independent practice, for the past 15 years. She is currently undertaking clinical training at the Tavistock in child, adolescent and family psychodynamic psychotherapy. Her interests and areas of work include: working systemically with schools to support the needs of learners who have experienced developmental trauma, systems psychodynamic perspectives on relationships and behaviour in educational organisations, and developing a model of supervision for school staff.

Olivia Kenneally qualified as a primary teacher in 2000 in Ireland. She then completed a Higher Diploma in Applied Psychology at University College Cork, followed by an MEd in Educational Psychology at the University of Bristol. Olivia then completed her doctorate in Child and Educational Psychology (DEdChPsych) at the Tavistock and Portman NHS Foundation Trust, University of Essex. She has over 15 years' experience in this field. Olivia is an experienced cognitive–behavioural therapy (CBT) practitioner, having completed a Postgraduate Diploma in CBT for Children and Young People at the Anna Freud Centre, University College London. Olivia completed a Higher Diploma in Paediatric Neuropsychology at UCL, and practises in this field in private practice, the NHS and local authorities. She teaches on the doctoral course for child and educational psychologists at the Tavistock and Portman and contributes to doctoral courses in the UK and Ireland. Her research interests include: mental health, resilience, therapeutic approaches and paediatric neuropsychology.

Emma Kate Kennedy is the deputy director of the educational psychology training programme at the Tavistock and Portman NHS Foundation Trust and the manager of the Autism Spectrum Conditions & Learning Disabilities Team in the Children, Young Adults and Families Department. She is the organising tutor for the Trust's short course 'Supervision for Staff Working in Schools and Community Contexts: Working Relationally and Reflectively'. She also leads on the development of supervisory practice on the initial training course. She provides supervision to trainees and staff in her teaching and clinical roles, including teachers and senior leaders in schools. She has had a long-standing practice and research interest in supervision, as well as consultation, and leads consultation training on the doctoral programme.

Liz Kennedy worked for 26 years as an educational psychologist in north London authorities, where she was ultimately a specialist senior supervising across her service. Alongside her local authority role, Liz worked for 25 years as a course tutor on the Tavistock training, where she was both a consultant clinical psychologist in CAMHS and a trainer. At the Tavistock, Liz developed particular interests in partnership working, consultation and supervision; she ran the Supervision course for educational psychologists for ten years, and was part of the team training psychologists in consultation. She was course leader/co-tutor for the multidisciplinary training on Working In Partnership with Families of Children with Special Needs, which also ran for ten years. Liz trained as an adult psychoanalytic psychotherapist and currently has a private psychotherapy practice and a supervision practice.

Vikki Lee originally trained at the Tavistock and Portman NHS Foundation Trust as an educational psychologist and has worked in several London boroughs as a main grade educational psychologist and subsequently as a specialist senior educational psychologist for complex needs. She was instrumental in setting up and running Camden's Social Communication Assessment Service. Previously, Vikki held the role of deputy programme director on the Trust's educational psychologist doctoral training. She is now the psychology lead in a large CAMHS service at the Trust and continues to supervise trainee educational psychologists on placement.

Caoimhe McBay is a local authority educational psychologist working in London. She is a personal and fieldwork tutor who supervises trainee educational psychologists on the Tavistock and Portman NHS Foundation Trust doctoral training programme. Caoimhe is currently completing her Continuing Professional Development Doctorate in Educational Psychology at University College London and has a keen interest in researching the supervisory relationship. She has contributed to the training of helping professionals in the application of relational models of supervision.

Sara Reid trained at the Tavistock and Portman NHS Foundation Trust and currently works as a main grade educational psychologist at Redbridge Educational Psychology Service. Sara's particular interests include supervision models for educational staff and the embodiment of trauma.

Kay Richards has worked as an educational psychologist for 14 years. Prior to this, she worked as an English teacher in an inner-London secondary school, where she was first introduced to psychoanalytic theory as a member of a work discussion group facilitated by a child and adolescent psychotherapist. This experience ignited her interest in the application of psychoanalytic ideas to support growth and development in education settings and she subsequently trained as an educational psychologist at the Tavistock in 2006. As an educational psychologist Kay has held senior roles in a large local authority service. Her work is informed by psychoanalytic and systemic theory and she is interested in how educational psychologists can use ideas from psychoanalytic theory in consultation to increase capacity for creative thinking. She also works as a professional and academic tutor on the doctorate in Child, Community and Educational Psychology at the Tavistock and Portman NHS Foundation Trust in London.

Nicole Schnackenberg is a child and educational psychologist working for Southend Educational Psychology Service. She is also a trustee of the Body Dysmorphic Disorder Foundation, a trustee of the Give Back Yoga Foundation UK and a director of the Yoga in Healthcare Alliance. Nicole has authored books on appearance-focused identity struggles including *False Bodies, True Selves, Bodies Arising* and *The Parents' Guide to Body Dysmorphic Disorder*.

Chris Shaldon is a senior educational psychologist at Islington Educational Psychology Service and a professional and academic tutor on the educational psychologist training course at the Tavistock and Portman NHS Foundation Trust. Chris has an abiding interest in developing the practice and theory of supervision. His doctoral thesis explored trainee educational psychologists' (TEPs') experiences of supervision. Chris's current practice involves supervision of TEPs, educational psychologists and other professionals – individually and in groups. He has co-authored papers on supervision and multi-agency work.

Sinead Walker is an educational psychologist working for the London Borough of Bromley. Sinead has a particular interest and enthusiasm for the application of psychoanalytic thinking in educational settings, having spent five formative years at the Tavistock and Portman NHS Foundation Trust. Sinead completed the Postgraduate Diploma in Psychoanalytic Observational Studies before securing a place on the doctorate in Child, Community and Educational Psychology. She completed her professional training in September 2019.

Acknowledgements

The editors wish to thank a number of people in their support for this book. In particular, Brian Davis, course director for the doctorate in educational psychology at the Tavistock Portman NHS Trust, and Sean Cameron from UCL for their encouragement and comments in the early stages of the book, the numerous colleagues in a range of settings for their critical reading of early versions of the text. Christina Wipf Perry from Karnac Books for her trust and flexibility, Amanda Jackson, Carmel Checkland, Tara Cresswell, George Black, Jo-anne Carlyle, Todd Hinds, Liz Kennedy, Phil Stack, Oliver Wright, Amy Norris, Andrew Cooper and all those whose experiences have made this book possible.

Finally, thanks and love to our families for getting on with life while we were absent and getting on with the book.

A note on confidentiality
All identifying features in the following chapters have been changed to protect anonymity.

Odi et amo. Quare id faciam fortasse requires.
Nescio, sed fieri sentio et excrucior.

I hate and I love. Why I do this, perhaps you ask.
I know not, but I feel it happening and I am tortured.

Catullus (Poem 85, 84–54 BCE)

'*Then how long will it last, this love?*' *(in jest).*
'*I don't know.*'
'*Three weeks, three years, three decades …?*'
'*You are like all the others … trying to shorten eternity with numbers,*'
spoken quietly, but with real feeling.

Lawrence Durrell, *Justine* (1957)

Foreword

Dr Mark Fox

Taking a new step, uttering a new word, is what people fear most.

I felt privileged when I was asked to write this foreword. Having worked at the Tavistock and Portman Foundation NHS Trust for over ten years I was aware that considerable thinking would have gone into such a simple request – complexity compounding complexity. Behind this innocuous request I knew there would be layers of unspoken assumptions that connected with my career as an educational psychologist and, dare I say it, extended even further back into my childhood. I knew I had to deal with such fantasies and projections – before I began to write.

My earliest remembered encounter with psychoanalytic thinking was as an 18-year-old. My mother, a psychiatric social worker, was working with adolescents in care. She had taken me to a psychoanalytic conference hoping, I think, to stimulate my interest in psychology. In the evening the conference watched the film of the *Lord of the Flies*, which was followed by a discussion. I remember to this day the anger I felt as all these 'adults' enthusiastically endorsed the truthfulness of the film's portrayal of the adolescents' disintegration into anarchy and violence. I was too insecure to say anything – but I remember the anger.

Like many other undergraduates, I tried to read some Klein and Freud. I found Klein almost incomprehensible, but gained shards of psychological insight from Freud's single case studies – even though these stories about people with complex emotional difficulties seemed from a different era and more akin to literature than to science. I moved on to Erich Fromm's *Fear of Freedom* and his insights into the eight basic psychological needs. This led to Carl Rogers' humanistic psychology and Eric Berne's transactional analysis. So, my early experiences were eclectic but, unfortunately, I never had a warm and secure relationship with psychoanalysis itself.

However, like a distant and powerful uncle, I knew that psychoanalytic thinking – and, in particular, the centrality of our unconscious – was important, especially from a cultural perspective. The one thing I knew for sure, even then, was 'that the causes of human actions are usually immeasurably more complex and varied than our subsequent explanations of them'.

The question for me was, and still is, how can the complexity and power of psychoanalytic thinking be integrated into our work as educational psychologists

(EPs)? Gradually I learned, as an EP, that clients often did not want solutions to the problems they were initially presenting. More crucially, they also did not want to be told that they did not want solutions to their presenting problem. What they wanted was their story – especially their pain – to be heard. Only when it was heard were they able to think about what was behind the pain. Over the years I have heard people's anger that psychoanalytic thinking has ignored, rather than illuminated, their pain-filled reality. I felt it most sharply and powerfully when I worked at SCOPE. Managers and colleagues with a disability were deeply angry about their problems being interpreted from a psychoanalytic within-person perspective. First and foremost, they needed their experiences of the inequalities and unfairness in society to be heard before they thought about their own hurt. This was a similar anger to the one I had experienced when, as a teenager, 'adults' had attempted to tell me what was true, thereby denying me my own emotional experiences. I realised that for many of us 'To go wrong in one's own way is better than to go right in someone else's.'

And so to my ten years at the Tavistock and Portman Foundation NHS Trust, where I was fortunate to work with many of the authors of these chapters. My work here was not as a therapist, but as a teacher and supervisor of psychological research. Much of my thinking about evidence-based practice comes from this time, when I attempted to reconcile teaching on medically orientated courses at the University of Essex with the concept of research from a psychoanalytic perspective. I am pleased to see that some of this thinking is reflected in this book, where the issues of what is an evidence base for psychoanalysts is further developed.

I wrote at this time about the importance of practice-based evidence and of turning the evidence from the experience of professional practice into research, through the process of self-reflection and self-knowing. The three strategies that experienced professionals use to enhance their practice (as outlined by Dutton, 1995) can all be enriched by psychoanalytic thinking:

Pattern recognition: recognising familiar psychoanalytic mechanisms can help EPs make sense more quickly of an individual client's story.

Knowing-in-action: knowing-in-action is what gets the busy EP through the day – by not having to think through every consultation from first principles. The danger here, of course, is becoming locked unconsciously into repetitive ways of intervening, simply to keep anxiety at bay. Taking time to think, however, will help EPs reflect on our unconscious biases; for example, our projections onto others and the issues of transference and countertransference.

Naming and framing: framing a problem with a psychological theory gives us the language with which to communicate our assumptions to the client.

I have always been interested in encouraging EPs to use multiple frameworks that acknowledge the diversity of clients we work with. I would like EPs to stop ostensibly recognising, intervening and framing problems in the same way time and time again because they only have one way of seeing things. This book will encourage EPs to use psychoanalytic thinking as one frame – among the multiple frames – that we need to be effective.

For too long, much of psychoanalytic thinking has been lost to EPs. As this book acknowledges, part of the reason for this is that psychoanalysis has often been, or been seen to have been, defensive, privileged and elitist, for those with the time and money. Concepts can appear dated, obscure and wrapped in language that is unintelligible to the uninitiated. This book goes a long way to rectify these criticisms.

Paradoxically, the most important thing that I learned at the Tavistock was not about psychoanalytic thinking, but about another approach: narrative psychology. Narrative psychology gave me a framework into which I could then integrate psychoanalytic concepts. Narrative psychology is underpinned by the belief that we need to create a coherent story about our experiences to bring coherence to our own fragmented world. We each seek to develop a sense of order by arranging the episodes of our lives into stories.

We all have stories to tell – and stories we choose not to tell. Psychoanalytic thinking gives us a way of gaining new perspectives on these stories, so that we can tell new stories about our emotional reactions to innocuous situations, like watching a film.

> *In every man's remembrances there are things he will not reveal to everybody, but only to his friends. There are other things he will not reveal even to his friends, but only to himself, and then only under a pledge of secrecy. Finally there are some things that a man is afraid to reveal even to himself, and any honest man accumulates a pretty fair number of such things.*

A narrative approach seeks to question established narratives and to explore alternative narratives, which may at the present be unconscious. I think EPs have a responsibility to develop new narratives that allow the profession to take up new positions. Psychoanalytic thinking can do this – but it needs to do it in a way that is modern, open and transparent. It needs to do it with a warm and loving heart, rather than appearing like a distant and powerful uncle or cold, controlling aunt. This book provides a bridge to rebuilding a positive relationship with EPs and a way of opening up psychoanalytic thinking to a new generation.

I am sure that this book will put psychoanalytic thinking back into the daily practice of many EPs. But I also suspect that it will be ignored by some who want the profession to move to a reductionist, neurobiological narrative. This route led us, in the 1960s and 1970s, into radical behaviourism and a rejection of the importance, not only of the mind, but (crucially) of the unconscious, too. So, the book may also annoy EPs who do not wish to consider if there may be hidden stories behind their own masks. The world is coming out of lockdown – but are *we*?

Dr Mark Fox
June 2020

Note
All quotes in this foreword are from Fyodor Dostoevsky.

Introduction

This book owes its existence to a series of workshops and discussions among educational psychologists (EPs) interested in applying psychoanalytic thinking to EP practice. After a one-day workshop on just this topic at the Tavistock and Portman NHS Foundation Trust in 2017, a resolution crystallised: 'Let's get these ideas out there!' Thus began the slow, often crooked, path to the book before you now.

By 'there' is meant the vague and ever-changing (and expanding) territory of EP practice. And the ideas refer, of course, to psychoanalytic theory in its diverse forms. There is not, to our knowledge, a book like this for EPs at present and our primary aim has been to introduce readers to the numerous ways psychoanalytic thinking can be woven into the practice of an EP, working in hectic and preoccupied settings where need far outweighs the time available: a far cry from the cloistered tranquillity (or so it might be presumed) of the 50-minute analytic hour. And yet it is our belief, borne from experience, that psychoanalytic theory has a great deal to offer EPs.

Indeed, it is no bad thing, we argue, to hold on to the psychoanalyst W.R. Bion's encouragement, when in the midst of a tense consultation, to be able to 'think under fire' (as a former First World War tank commander, this was no casual metaphor), or to ask of oneself, when caught up in higher than usual levels of emotionality, *what is it about this case that hooks me*, or to return, given that EPs are 'skilled in the management of the moment' (Farrell, Woods, Lewis, Squires, Rooney and O'Connor, 2006, p. 72), to the here-and-now of emotional experience. In short, for the writers in this book, these ideas work. They have helped us to bring about effective change in complex cases and to support others to bear circumstances where change is not possible and where the chief source of strength and resilience is gained from a deeper understanding of the situation as it is.

In this book, psychoanalytic thinking has left the confines of the consulting room and demonstrates its utility in a range of settings. As

Kurt Lewin once observed, 'there is nothing as practical as a good theory' (Lewin, 1945), and for us, as applied practitioner psychologists, engaged with strong emotions in complex systems, this has proven to be the case. We have come back to these ideas again and again, not – as some might have it – as if seeking out the tenets of some faith, but as tools to fortify and expand our sense-making capacity in the face of forms of confusion and uncertainty (we write this in the midst of the coronavirus shutdown), which prove impervious to more reductive, rational and measurable approaches. These ideas make a difference. It is an emotionally rewarding and intellectually satisfying experience to work with a dynamic unconscious and engage with it in the lives of children, parents, teachers – and ourselves. To share this with others has been the chief impulse behind the writing of this book.

Aims of the book

As noted, we are psychoanalytically informed EPs, not psychoanalysts or therapists, and we are not proposing that EPs take up the stance of the latter – even if we could. Rather, we want to demonstrate the general practicability, based on practice-based evidence (see, for example, Hellerstein, 2008), of psychoanalytic ideas to the practice of EPs. Consequently, the aims of this book are as follows:

1.   To introduce readers to some of the key tenets and principles of psychoanalytic theory. While there are many psychoanalytic schools (see Lemma, 2016), this book draws primarily on Kleinian and post-Kleinian theory.
2.   To demonstrate ways in which EPs have used psychoanalytic theory and practice in their roles as EPs. The contributors of this book each bring a valuable perspective to approaching a number of recognisable EP activities.
3.   To contribute to the wider EP theory/practice discourse.

As practitioner psychologists, we are aware of the various discourses within educational psychology and assert that psychoanalytic and psychodynamic theories have a part to play in how the profession serves the individuals and institutions with which we work. We are well aware of the way psychoanalytic thinking is viewed by some of our colleagues and fellow EPs; we believe that psychology is more than able to hold divergent perspectives and discourses. Our use of these ideas in our thinking has been winnowed by applying a psychoanalytic perspective in the field and observing that they make a difference. They also serve to deepen our sense of what it is to be human and to relate to others, individually and in groups. If this book is in any way successful, we hope that part of that success rests in shifting perspectives with regard to how EPs relate to and use psychoanalytic ideas and practice in their everyday work.

What is psychoanalysis?

What, then, is psychoanalysis? Before moving into a theoretical overview in the next chapter, we thought it would be useful to outline and clarify our conception of psychoanalysis and psychoanalytic thinking. In simplest form, psychoanalysis holds that the human mind is comprised of a conscious and unconscious aspect and that many of our formative experiences and current mental processes operate outside of our present awareness. Furthermore, our personality, motivations and behaviours are shaped by these experiences and processes, in ways that are not easily accessible to introspection, as they are out of conscious awareness. Such is the nature of the dynamic unconscious that the past works on the present in countless ways, leading to distress and dysfunction at times, but also to creativity and wonder. This is an incomplete description but serves our purpose here. Expanding this general principle, Bell (2010) separates psychoanalysis into three broad categories: as a treatment, as a model of the mind and as an epistemology.

Psychoanalysis's inception was as a treatment and, for all the ensuing criticism of this nascent psychotherapy (see Chapter 1), there was something genuinely radical in Freud's determination that listening to his patients might lead to an improvement in their health and psychological well-being. Since Freud's time, psychoanalytic theory and practice as a treatment has progressed, developed, refined and diversified. There are now numerous psychoanalytic 'schools', but for all their differences they still had this initial conception of a dynamic unconscious informing, moulding and/or intruding upon one's present life.

From its therapeutic origins, psychoanalysis evolved a complex and multi-part theory of the human mind. We argue that its origins in therapeutic practice are a strength and not a weakness, in that psychoanalysis strives to engage with the totality of one's experience, including thoughts, emotions and unregistered (unconscious) processes that contribute to a complexity of motivation and relationship. The quote by Catullus in the epigraph captures this nicely How can one hate and love a person at the same time? Psychoanalysis offers a compelling reason for this, tracing these emotional torrents back to infancy, when the need for safety and satiety collides with a longing for freedom and independence. The psychoanalytic psyche is not one devised in laboratory tests, which have successfully hewn away all of the unnecessary mess of life.

Finally, psychoanalysis is an epistemology in its own right (Devereux, 1967), with a novel and compelling explanation for human motivation. It has moved beyond an account of individual functioning to be used as a hermeneutic device, a 'tool of cultural enquiry' that allows one to contend with the complex interplay of the self, the other and the world at large. Through society, culture and the institutions that are produced, these intra- and interpsychic tensions can be passed on to subsequent generations. For applied psychologists, psychoanalysis as an epistemological tool can be an invaluable methodology for understanding what might be going on and for exploring what forces might be at play when we engage in any of the challenging and emotionally loaded activities that make up our role.

We believe that, in this, psychoanalysis holds relevance for EPs as we go about our business. Put simply, we hold that there is a dynamic interplay between and within the conscious and unconscious aspects of an individual, as well as in groups and organisations, and it is this interplay that influences how people relate to themselves, others and the world at large.

Psychoanalytic or psychodynamic?

We have wrestled with this question over and over. Which term is suitable to our venture? The answer is not clear. Some hold that 'psychoanalytic' refers only to those ideas that originate with Freud, while all others (including Klein, Bion, Jung and their adherents) fall under the 'psychodynamic' heading. This seemed overly reductive and constricting to us. After much discussion, we have decided that, for the purposes of this book the two terms may be used interchangeably. We recognise and accept that this is an imperfect conclusion.

Chapter outline

The book has been organised into seven sections.

Part I, 'Orientation', presents an overview of the interrelationship of education, educational psychology and psychoanalysis. It looks at the shared history and subsequent divergence, and introduces the reader to psychoanalytic theory, chiefly Kleinian theory with its focus on object and part object relations. It discusses some of the chief criticisms that EPs level against psychoanalysis and also responds to these criticisms. Finally, it considers the issue of evidence and what it constitutes.

Part II is entitled 'Theory to practice' and its chapters consider the practical application of psychoanalytic thinking to the world and work of an EP. In her chapter, Olivia Kenneally explores the use of psychoanalytic concepts in EP practice. She begins with a discussion about the use of emotional data as a form of evidence, making links to evidence-based practice in the work of EPs. She then discusses how psychoanalytic concepts can be applied in educational psychology, with reference to several in-depth case studies.

In 'Thinking matters: how can Bion's theory of thinking help educational psychologists think about the task of formulation?', Kay Richards considers how Bion's work can help in exploring experiences with others. Gemma Ellis's chapter reflects on unconscious processes in the work of an EP, asking, 'What's yours and what's theirs? Understanding projection, transference and countertransference in educational psychology practice'. Bartle and Eloquin then illustrate some of the ways that psychoanalytic theory can help teachers, focusing on the ways in which emotional experience, when reflected on rather than reacted to, can provide powerful 'data' about what may be occurring in the inner worlds of their pupils. They introduce the concept of a classroom-in-the-mind, and consider the interrelated experiences of the inner world, external world and experience in role.

Part III presents two chapters that discuss the psychoanalytic applications of a central activity for all EPs: assessment. Elizabeth Kennedy and Lee-Anne Eastwood consider what a psychoanalytic approach can bring to an EP's assessment. As well as reviewing important psychoanalytic ideas, they discuss the dynamics implicit in an assessment referral, as well as the fact that assessment is also an interventional act. They go on to consider several examples of psychoanalytically informed assessment approaches. This is further taken up by Isabella Bernardo in her chapter, 'The use of projective techniques in educational psychology assessments'. She describes a number of projective tests that will be of interest and use to an EP and provides a historical and theoretical rationale for their use.

Part IV looks at how psychoanalytic thinking can inform consultation and supervision, two key EP activities. Emma Kate Kennedy and Vikki Lee examine consultation as a 'distinctive helping relationship' and provide 'historical and contemporary perspectives on psychodynamic thinking in consultation'. Xavier Eloquin follows this with an exploration of how psychoanalytic theory and practice allow for the use of self in the act of consultation, developing a model for how emotions, as part of the 'total situation', can be used as a form of information. In 'Feelings, relationships and "being held" – experience of psychodynamically informed supervision', Chris Shaldon and colleagues discuss the 'relational model of supervision for applied psychology practice' and reflect on the psychoanalytic aspect of this way of working.

Part V focuses on working in groups. Dale Bartle explores experiences of group facilitation in 'Reverie groups: space, free association and the recovery of thought', and Katharine Ellis describes a project in which she, as an EP, offered a series of work discussion groups for designated safeguarding leads from a number of schools in her area.

Part VI considers organisational perspectives. Beverley Clarke introduces the reader to a psychoanalytic approach to coaching school leaders. Drawing on her own experiences as a leader, an EP and an executive coach, she provides an outline and rationale for the use of psychodynamic approaches to coaching – and argues that coaching school leaders is an activity that EPs (properly supervised and trained) could contemplate taking up. Dale Bartle and Xavier Eloquin, in their chapter on social defences, provide an introduction to social defence theory and then present extended case studies to explore organisational defences to anxieties related to the task of the schools where they are located.

Part VII, 'Postscripts: widening the horizon', concludes the book, with Christopher Arnold offering an analysis of psychoanalytic ideas viewed through the lens of chaos theory. He describes phenomena found in complex and unstable systems and concludes that some of the criticisms of psychoanalytic theory are based on linear assumptions that are un-likely to be met in this field. Understanding elements of chaos theory can be very helpful in linking psychoanalytic ideas to more positivist assumptions and suggests new ways of gathering evidence and, ultimate-ly, methods of evaluation.

PART I

ORIENTATION

CHAPTER I

Psychoanalysis and educational psychology: context, theory and challenges

Dale Bartle and Xavier Eloquin

This chapter considers the relationship between educational psychology practice and psychoanalysis. Section I places the current relationship between the two in a historical context, looking at how psychoanalysis, education and educational psychology were at one stage far more intertwined. Section II offers the reader a general introduction to psychoanalytic theory, drawing mainly on Kleinian and post-Kleinian theory. It is not an exhaustive account, but seeks to introduce the reader to the theory and terms they will encounter in this book. Section III provides a critique and defence of psychoanalysis, focusing mainly on objections relevant to educational psychology. Section IV, the last of the chapters considers the issue of evidence from a psychoanalytic perspective and how this might be thought of in relation to a wider epistemological canon.

I

Psychoanalysis, education, educational psychology: a brief history

Psychoanalytic theory has had a significant influence on education almost from its inception (Hinshelwood, 1995), with educationalists keen to make use of a more benign therapeutic approach to working with the most disaffected. The Little Commonwealth, established by George Montagu (later the Earl of Sandwich) in 1913, was one of the earliest forms of 'therapeutic community' for boy, and then also girl, delinquents from as young as 9 months up to 18 years (Bazely, 1928). In the 1920s and 1930s, Summerhill School, set up by anti-authoritarian education-alist A.S. Neill, used Freudian and Reichian principles to underpin its radically different education philosophy (Neill, 1962).

In Austria, elementary school teacher August Aichhorn was tasked with setting up education centres for 'difficult' adolescents after the First World War (Mohr, 1966). Anna Freud encouraged him to enter analytic training in 1922 and he is recognised as a key founder of psychoanalytic education, which rejected contemporary forms of dis-cipline with 'wayward youth' (Mohr, 1966). Anna Freud, who also was a teacher before training as a psychoanalyst, applied and developed psychoanalytic theories of child development at the Hampstead War Nursery during the Second World War. It was here that her obser-vations on child stress and peer affection in place of absent parents were conducted (Young-Bruehl, 2008). After the war, she went on to oversee the Bulldog Banks Nursery, where a number of Jewish child refugees whose parents had been murdered during the Holocaust eventually resided. Freud's meticulous observations were able to show that the violent and aggressive behaviours they displayed were not a result of learning difficulty or psychosis, but an adaptation to the horrific environments they had grown up in (Freud and Dann, 1951).

Child and educational psychologists working with children and adolescents were also influenced by psychoanalysis at this time. Fritz Redl, like Anna Freud, trained first as a teacher before entering psycho-analytical training in Vienna in 1922. Working under Aichhorn, and then with Bruno and Gina Bettelheim, he applied his psychoanalytic insights to summer camps for socially and economically deprived stu-dents in Austria, before emigrating to the United States in 1936. There, in Detroit, he developed the Life Space Interview (Redl, 1966) at Pioneer House, a residential home for boys aged 8 to 12 with behaviour prob-lems. Eschewing conventional discipline and punishment for affection and compassion, his approach may be more in line with the demands of an EP role, where he advocated for 'therapy on the hoof' (Redl, 1966), engaging with young people in the midst of their lives as opposed to the formal and offputting environs of the 50-minute analytic session (Sharpe, 1985).

Susan Isaacs (1885–1948), a child psychologist and psychoanalyst, was a strong advocate for high-quality nursery care after her experience at the Malting House School in the mid-1920s (Isaacs, 1952). She later went on to become the head of the Department for Child Development at the Institute of Education, a training centre for educational psychologists (EPs) to this day. Her influence on child-centred practice and nursery development, rooted in psychoanalytic theory (she remained a practising analyst until late in life), is strikingly contemporary, and 'she probably did more than anyone else to integrate the increasing theoretical knowledge of child psychology with practical methodology in both education and child rearing practices' (Smith, 1985, p. 17). Certainly even the most avowedly anti-psychoanalytic EP would probably agree with her views on the importance of environment, play and adults in nursery education (Isaacs, 1971).

Even during the fallow years – as child and educational psychologists, among others, departed from psychoanalytic thinking (more of which below) – it still played a decisive role in educational and residential care settings in the UK and beyond (see Sharpe, 2007, for a fuller exposition), with the Mulberry Bush (a therapeutic residential school) a notable ongoing presence. Dockar Drysdale (1993), for example, developed Winnicottian ideas at the Caldecott and Cotswold communities. Sharpe (2007), drawing on thinking by Melanie Klein and Wilfred Bion, observes that psychoanalytic theory has much to offer, 'not only in the sense of explaining the psychodynamic processes at work, but also in informing how workers may help children'. While he writes with reference to children's homes, we share this view and believe that it is applicable to a range of institutions in which children and adolescents abide, and with which EPs work.

Psychoanalysis falls out of favour

In the 1960s, psychoanalysis began to lose some support. Behaviour therapy, advanced by Wolpe in South Africa and promoted by Eysenck in the UK and Skinner in the USA (Rachman, 2003), and its younger sibling, cognitive-behaviour therapy, demonstrated that a more targeted approach to mental health issues, with no reference to a patient's internal world, could produce remarkable change in a much shorter time period. It can be argued that psychoanalysis did not help its cause by disregarding calls for research into treatment effectiveness and outcome measures in the 1950s and 1960s. One result of this was that psychoanalytic theory removed itself – and was removed – from psychology departments, finding a more accommodating home in literature and humanities departments, where its explanatory lens was brought to bear upon all manner of aesthetic, literary and cultural phenomena. Moving out of psychology departments, psychoanalysis soon became cut off from innovation and current research (American Psychological Association, 2017). The argument that psychoanalysis is completely cut off from allowing research to influence theory and practice is perhaps overstated; for example, Bowlby's work on attachment in children had significant influence on the way drives were thought about.

Within educational psychology in the UK, the above issues were further compounded by the demise of child guidance clinics, with a consequent distancing among EPs, social workers and psychiatrists. While the latter tended towards a medical model when viewing child and family dysfunction, by the 1970s and 1980s EPs eschewed this in favour of more systemic approaches (Burden, 1978; Dowling and Osborne, 1994).

Educational psychology and resurgent psychoanalytic thinking

A review of more recent literature involving EPs and psychoanalytic ideas does reveal a resurgent interest. Just as psychoanalysis began to refine and develop its techniques, it moved on from rather reductive and generic accounts of 'penis envy' and 'Oedipal complexes' in the 1950s (Hinshelwood, 1994) to develop increasingly sophisticated accounts of psychotic and 'borderline' states of mind.

Since the new millennium we have seen EPs, among others, take up and engage with unconscious processes in various ways, and across a number of settings. Sutoris (2000) describes the use of a systems-psychodynamic approach to work with a secondary school with behavioural concerns. Greenway (2005) writes movingly of how psychoanalytic theory helped her make sense of her role as an EP responding to a critical incident in a school (following the stabbing of its headteacher). Dennison, McBay and Shaldon (2006) draw on psychodynamic theories to consider the contribution EPs can make to multi-professional teams.

In the last decade or so, this interest has accelerated, with EPs demonstrating increased application of psychoanalytic theory to their role and practice. Pellegrini (2010) explores the way that splitting, projection and projective identification can be observed and used in work with a difficult piece of casework and in the training of teaching assistants. These same processes, explored in more detail below, are taken up by Bartle (2015) in his account of supervising a trainee educational psychologist. Hulusi and Maggs (2015) have considered similar dynamics in work discussion groups with teachers, drawing further on Bion's conception of containment (described below) and unconscious group dynamics to argue for judicious use of psychodynamic practice in the supervision by EPs of teachers. Eloquin (2016a, 2016b) examines various orders of dysfunction in schools, using organisational psychoanalytic theory to explore how a failing school based its leadership model on an introjected version of a former 'tyrant' headteacher and several organisational defences deployed by similar schools to manage anxieties related to the task of engaging with and teaching adolescents.

This section has considered the interrelationship of psychoanalytic thinking, educational psychology and education in general. We turn next to a theoretical overview.

II

Theoretical overview

Psychoanalysis – inception

Psychoanalysis began with Freud's 'discovery' (Ellenberger, 1970) of the unconscious in his work with 'neurotics' and 'hysterics' in the 1880s. Through his work as a neurologist, he elaborated, over time, a tripartite model of human functioning – the id, ego and super-ego – that held that a considerable aspect of a person's felt experience was below conscious awareness: the unconscious. These three structures could have very different 'agendas' and relations to the external world, which might lead to intrapsychic conflict, as different parts of the psyche effectively wanted different things at the same time. The unconscious is the repository for difficult, painful and unbearable urges, drives and related experiences. While consciously forgotten, these experiences continue to influence current behaviour and feeling.

Central to Freud's theory of the unconscious is the concept of defence mechanisms. These are psychological processes by which one part of the mind prevents disturbing psychological material from being consciously apprehended: it is blocked and returned to the unconscious. Freud developed dream analysis and free association as tools to access unconscious content in symbolic form as a means of identifying, tangentially, what were the concerning emotional issues impairing a person's mental and emotional life. The 'latent' material acquired from dream accounts and the uninterrupted flow of free associations could be interpreted as 'references to the past, and to childhood sexual preoccupations. Those items in the patient's thought which came next to each other in the time sequence were deemed to have a linked meaning' (Hinshelwood, 1994, p. 12).

Klein and object relations theory

Building on and subsequently departing from Freud's thinking, Klein developed Freud's theory of 'object relations', drawing on her clinical work with very young children (Klein, 1935; 1946).* She developed ideas about how the external world is interpreted and symbolised through internal *objects* and part-objects (Waddell, 1998). These are not exact replicas of mothers, fathers, and carers but, rather, caricatures passed through the emotional lens of felt experience. A baby who has repeated experiences of being cared for and thought about will take in (introject) these experiences. As Waddell notes, 'as such experiences are repeated, the baby will feel that he has a source of goodness within, which he feels to be some kind of concrete presence, one which is part of him and not only something which is offered to him from without. He has a good relationship to a good object' (Waddell, 1998, p. 14). Thus, experiences of infancy and early years come to be represented unconsciously through 'good' and 'bad' objects in the mind.

Indeed, it was Klein's pioneering work with infants and children that offered a deeper insight into the inner world of the child, from infancy onwards. What was revealed was a rich, complex and sometimes savage world, akin to that of a fairy tale. Drawing on established psychoanalytic principles of the day, and learning from children through her revolution-ary play technique, she provided evidence of a complex inner world made up of conflicting emotions such as envy, fear, greed, aggression, love, care and gratitude. These insights help us to understand the depth and diver-sity of the emotional experience of even very young children. From birth, the infant (or even before) is in physical and psychological contact with a mother. How the infant's needs and wants are responded to will influ-ence what is taken in. In this way the inner world becomes populated with part-objects, entities in the external world reduced to the function they serve. These have a psychological correlate, which in psychoanalytic theory is known as phantasy. Phantasy can be thought of as the psycho-logical aspect of a physiological drive or 'the mental representation of an experience or need' (Lemma, 2016, p. 41). Over time, with sufficient quality of care, as the child develops he or she draws on a range of experi-ences, including his or her capacity to separate from the mother. There is a corresponding development in the inner world, where objects are taken in as resources that can be drawn on or as sources of persecution that can attack (for example, in instances of neglect, or perceived neglect). In this way we begin to see the dynamic nature of an internal world inhab-ited by symbolised forms, based on the child's striving for survival and experience of being cared for. Through repeated separation from and return to the mother the child discerns a sense of otherness: the child becomes aware that he or she is both separate from and dependent on the mother. The young child comes to see the mother as a whole being, inte-grating the good/providing and the bad, absent/denying as one and the same. This is the whole object to which the child relates – hence object relations. Careful observations of, and play with, very young children led Klein to postulate that these objects and the way they are related vary in different states of mind.

Klein distinguishes between these two discrete states – or, rather, positions – of mind that are developmental and sequential but are also contingent on emotionality and the type of care experiences a person has had (Hinshelwood, 1994). The first and most primitive mind-state is the 'paranoid-schizoid position' (Klein, 1946; Waddell, 1998). Here the internal and external objects are arranged, 'split', into extreme polarities – good and bad, for example – with no possibility of the two being brought together. The foundation for this is held to be in the infant's experiences of a 'good' present caregiver and a 'bad' denying/frustrating caregiver, who is assumed to be the cause of somatic discomforts such as hunger and cold by purposefully denying his or her presence – or, rather, an intentional absence. Splitting of this kind serves an important function for the infant, allowing her to conceive of important factors in her world as good, loving and caring, clearly separated from the causes of distress until the infant is ready to see both as one and the same person. With time and 'good enough' care, the infant is able to reconcile these polarities and recognise that both the 'good' present/loving caregiver and the 'bad' absent/denying caregiver are one and the same and, importantly, to experience some guilt about the rage the infant has experienced towards him or her. This is the second developmental position: the depressive position.

The depressive position is a state in which the mind can recognise and take responsibility for its own hateful feelings towards an object and tolerate the uncertainty of a life lived beyond the artificial comfort of binaries: no longer are things perceived as either/or, but as both/and. It is in the depressive position that the ego can achieve a form of psychological maturity and recognise the part it plays in its own drama. The world is no longer separated into good and bad; it is seen as a spectrum of experience in which one can be hurt but can, equally, hurt, and in which one must, to mitigate guilt and anxiety, make reparations, either in actual fact or symbolically. While there is a developmental scope to these states, it is observed that individuals at all life stages oscillate between the two states. In optimal conditions one might conceive of a developmental spiral, moving in and out of each position, rather than a linear progression from one to the other. It is through relationship with an attuned, thoughtful and caring other that the turbulence of the paranoid–schizoid position, and the fluctuation between it and the depressive position, can be tolerated in the service of psychological growth.

These two distinct states have a central task of managing anxiety. To this end, a variety of defence mechanisms, ways of warding off the intrusion of anxiety into consciousness, is deployed. A central defence from the paranoid-schizoid position is the multi-step process of splitting, projection and projective identification. This entails the separating (splitting) of some undesirable or unpleasant aspect of the psyche and 'exporting' or projecting this aspect out and identifying it in others. While defence mechanisms are intended to limit the impact of anxiety (Shaw, 2002), paranoid–schizoid defences do so in such an extreme way that in the long term they can be as disruptive as the anxiety itself. Depressive defences, like humour or sublimation, reduce the intensity of anxiety while still allowing the issue to be thought about. They can be seen as more sophisticated responses to anxiety.

A final point, with reference to projection, is its potential culmination in projective identification. This is a process with a range of functions: *as a defence against* unwanted feelings (by projecting them out of the self), a type of relationship (it links the projector and projectee) and as a form of communication, in which the recipient comes to experience something of the emotional state of the projector (Ogden, 1982; Moustaki-Smilansky, 1994; Waddell, 1998). This latter point is a difficult concept to apprehend at first, and yet has clear relevance for EPs. Gilmore and Krantz, writing as organisational consultants, observe that with projective identification 'the recipient ... of the projection is essentially inducted into the originator's scheme of things. He or she is subtly pressured into thinking. feeling and behaving in a manner congruent with the feelings or thoughts evacuated by the other' (1985, p. 1161). Given the pressurised situations in which EPs so often work knowledge of and attention to projected states of mind is important.

Transference and countertransference

Transference and countertransference are complex phenomena and are essential to understanding what takes place in psychoanalysis. In its simplest form, transference occurs when psychological material from the patient's past is projected onto or into the analyst in the present. Countertransference describes the emotional reactions evoked in the analyst by the transference: *how you [the client], bringing old feelings into this new [therapeutic] relationship, makes me [the therapist] feel.* We want to stress that this is a highly simplified description of highly complex processes. Initially the transference material was perceived in a reductive fashion, which culminated in rather repetitive transference interpretation: *you are angry with me because you think I am your father.* Over time transference came to be conceptualised as a passing over of a total experience, evoked in the analyst, if they are receptive enough, to allow for a sense of what the inner world of the patient might be like: *you are inducting me into your experience of what your object relating to your father is like (full of anger).* This conception of the transference as an aspect of the 'total situation' (Joseph, 1985) opened up psychoanalytic practice and allowed for a wider range of responses and interpretations.

Countertransference, too, has developed. Originally it was seen as an indication that the analyst still had emotional 'blind spots' that rendered them liable to emotional reactivity when transference material touched on something similar in their own past (the analyst's anger with their own father). This would mean a loss of neutrality and supposed objectivity, occluding the analyst's ability to correctly attend to what the patient brought. But it came to be recognised as a useful source of information about what was going on in the analysis (Heimann, 1950; Lemma, 2016); that if one knew well enough one's own psyche, then the way a patient made one feel in the moment offered insight into the mind of the patient: *the cold rage I, as a therapist, feel when you talk about your father and my desire to shame you for it becomes data about how intrapsychically your father keeps attacking and judging all that you do.*

For EPs, recognition of transference and countertransference allows for meaning to be found in the totality of an assessment or a consultation: how a child acts and what feelings he or she evokes in us, for example. But one must inoculate against wild speculation. How one is made to feel is a 'resonance' (Jacobs, 2001, cited in Lemma, 2016, p. 224), not a replication of the original emotion. We do not feel exactly what another feels, but if we are alive to our own emotional and somatic states, the arising of an unfamiliar emotion, allied with observable data and what we know about the client, can supply insight into the challenges they are facing – externally and internally – thereby deepening hypothesis creation. This underscores for us the importance of psychoanalytic supervision, consultation and training to shore against what Freud termed 'wild analysis' (Freud, 2002); feeling something in and of itself is not sufficient, nor is it psychoanalytic.

Contributions from Bion

Wilfred Bion is a name that continually arises in conversations among psychoanalytically informed EPs. His contributions to psychoanalytic theory are considerable and we cannot do them justice here. Furthermore, in this chapter we have limited our discussion of his theoretical innovations to aspects of theory that are present in the following chapters.

Container/contained

A concept central to many chapters in this book is that of the container/contained (Bion, 1963). Bion used analyst/patient and mother/infant dyads to present a model of how thought and meaning emerge – or do not (Symington and Symington, 1996). In both instances, infants/patients seek to rid themselves of discomfort or pain, manifested initially in violent projections (Bion, 1963). Through the containing (that is, thoughtful) presence of the analyst/mother's mind, these unprocessed sensory experiences can be made sense of, thought about and given meaning. Crucial to the concept of containment is the ability to tolerate uncertainty. In short, the conception of container/contained provides a model of how person can contain the somatic/emotional/psychic distress of another entity, allowing for thought and meaning to develop.

A theory of thinking

Building on ideas of containment, Bion elaborated an abstract theory of how thoughts and thinking develop. In the psychoanalytic encounter, it is the analyst's ability to contain unbearable 'facts' and render them bearable enough for the patient to face that leads to change: 'the mind grows through exposure to truth' (Symington and Symington, 1996, p. 3). Bion's abstract theoretical model supposes the existence of what he called beta elements, 'sense impressions devoid of meaning or nameless sensations which cause frustration' (ibid, p. 62). This is the persecutory emotional material requiring containment, the raw material that can be worked into thought, once a thinker can hold it. This capacity to think about and make sense of these impressions is termed 'alpha function': it is what a mind does to sense data to 'make sense' of them (Bion, 1962).

Groups, organisations and leadership

The application of psychoanalytic theory has transcended the original dyadic form. Ideas and concepts have been transposed from the therapeutic relationship to broader relational matrices. Bion was pioneering in integrating understanding drawn from analysis and work by Freud and Klein into the context of working with groups. The concept of the group-as-a-whole becomes fundamental in making a conceptual leap: from viewing a group as comprising its individual members to conceiving of it as an entity in its own right, which in turn influences the behaviours of its members. Such a formulation offers us deep and potentially illuminating insights into why groups may evolve ways of behaving in the service of their unconscious drives and their striving for survival. Bion (1961) observes the simultaneous existence of two potential groups in operation: a 'work' group, which is reality-based and task orientated; and what he termed a 'basic assumption' group, where the group's priorities shift, unconsciously, from the task at hand to ensuring the group's physical and psychological survival. An everyday example might be that of a multidisciplinary team that, contending with a case of overwhelming despair and futility, displaces a shared sense of impotence by focusing ire and blame on another service or discipline. This shift, which is often not observed at the time, having moved from problem solving to blaming others, provides the group with a spurious sense of unity.

This foundational work has been further developed and evolved to explore possibilities that may be open to exploration at the organisational level, which includes a curiosity about intergroup phenomena, the relationship between an individual and his or her organisation, and leadership as a boundary function, reminiscent of ego functioning in an individual psyche. Trist, Miller and Rice (in Fraher, 2004) explored the fusion between psychoanalytic theory and organisational life in their work with the Tavistock Institute of Human Relations, generating new ways of working in organisational consultancy and in promoting experiential learning events as theatres of ambitious creativity. This work continues, and we believe has relevance to EPs, traversing as they do multiple systems and subsystems in their day-to-day activities.

III

Psychoanalysis: a critique and a defence

Critiques and criticisms of psychoanalytic practice and theory abound (see, for example, Eysenck, 1991; Webster, 1995; Crews, 2017). It is interesting to note that much of the debate revolves around Freud himself, with many an evocative title asserting, denying or wondering if psychoanalysis is dead (Lemma, 2016) or at war (Gomez, 2005), or a cult (Pepper, 1992) or a pseudo-science (Cioffi, 1998) or … It is true that the psychoanalytic literature does quote Freud a lot, and often in a reverential and even unquestioning manner. To applied psychologists, for whom any research over five years can be considered 'old', this does seem strange and we think psychoanalysis does have a case to answer here. What gets ignored in this discourse, however, is that psychoanalytic theory and practice are not frozen in aspic. They have grown, developed and adapted to the times. Often, it seems to us, many of the criticisms of psychoanalysis are criticisms of a caricature at least 50 years out of date. Indeed, psycho-analytic researcher Drew Westen, commenting on the almost perennial Freudian obituary, observes:

> *However, the recent obituaries declaring Freud's demise share two central problems. First, they report the death of the wrong psychoanalysis. Critics have typically focused on a version of psy-choanalytic theory – circa 1920 at best – that few contemporary analysts find compelling. In so doing, however, they have set the terms of the public debate and have led many analysts, I believe mistakenly, down an indefensible path of trying to defend a 75- to 100-year-old version of a theory and therapy that has changed substantially since Freud laid its foundations at the turn of the century.* (Westen, 1999)

In the two decades since that statement was made, not much has changed in terms of the type of psychoanalysis that tends to be critiqued. Westen (1998; Westen and Gabbard, 1999, cited in Westen, 1999) also rebuts many of the critiques laid at the feet of *classical* psychoanalytical theory as being irrelevant to *contemporary* theory and he posits that there was much that Freud was right about, propositions that are central to more contemporary Kleinian theory:

1. Childhood experiences play an important role in personality development, the more enduring features of which 'coalesce', then shape, the way in which later social relationships are formed.
2. It is mental representation of self and other that informs interaction and relationships.
3. Mental processes themselves operate in parallel and simultaneously, including affective and motivational processes, some of which are in conflict with others and which can run outside of conscious awareness.
4. Identity development involves, among other things, learning

to regulate sexual and aggressive feelings, and a move from immature dependency to a state of mature interdependence.

5.   Much mental life is unconscious.

With the possible exception of point 5, we suspect that the above statements are something most EPs would agree with. In a shorter form, we argue that the critical elements of psychoanalytic theory – certainly for our purposes – are the existence of a dynamic unconscious shaped by early experiences, the defensive measures taken by the psyche to manage anxiety and the phenomena of transference and countertransference *as a means for deriving new information about what is going on in the here-and-now.*

Less is said about the development of object relations theory and Klein's discoveries concerning childhood envy and aggression or her pioneering work using play as a therapeutic medium. Or of further refinements and theoretical progressions in the 1950s, by thinkers such as Bion, Heimann and Rosenfeld. More recently psychoanalysts such as Steiner (1993, 2011) have introduced new perspectives, all within the Kleinian tradition, that have moved thinking and practice on in a number of fields with creativity and zeal. Kleinian psychoanalytic theory, we argue, has relevance, validity and, for us, applicability to ways of working outside of the consulting room. For this reason, we will limit discussion of criticism and critique to those objections raised by EPs.

It takes too long

EPs typically have limited time in the institutions they visit, and this is often held as an argument against taking up psychoanalytic thinking in their work. This is to misunderstand the issue and to conflate psychoanalysis *per se* (that is, treatment and its psychotherapeutic derivatives) with *working psychoanalytically*. While we may not have time to engage in longer-term therapeutic work (and this is not our role), a recognition of the existence of a dynamic unconscious, and how it can influence individuals, pairs, groups and organisations, is a powerful addition to an EP's conceptual repertoire. If for no other reason, the reflexivity it behoves helps one to consider why one may be feeling the way one is, and so limit the chances of *acting out*. Or, to put it another way, we are arguing that an awareness of unconscious processes in the here-and-now helps psy-choanalytically informed practitioners to better engage with and manage relationships in the moment.

The language and theory are impenetrable

Psychoanalytic theory is unarguably complex, and its detractors often level this as a criticism against it. Certainly, as Hinshelwood notes, Klein had a tendency towards 'occasional tendentiousness' (1994, p. 4), but such a nuanced and technical language is an inevitable result of an attempt to chart and describe mental processes not immediately available to con-scious awareness. The theoretical complexity of psychoanalytic thinking has its roots in its subject matter: severe psychic disturbances. Intrapsychic functioning does not conform to the more familiar and causal logics with which most of us are familiar, and so a deeper dive into a more associa-tive, non-linear mentation is required. If these ideas seem strange and, at times, alogical, it is because they track the strange and illogical function-ing of their subject matter: the human psyche.

This complexity is also a richness, one that allows for a nuanced and granular account of mental processes, in and outside of individual psycho-analysis. It is just this richness that offers practitioners a new vista on observable phenomena, from its use in assessments to accounts of why organisations might resist perfectly 'sensible' changes and reforms. Contemporary psychoanalytic thinking has come a long way from the Freudian tendency to reduce all behaviour to drives, and it provides an account of behaviour that presents the individual in all his or her complexity.

Similarly, psychoanalytic language and terminology is often regarded as dense and abstract. Terms such as 'paranoid–schizoid' and 'projective identification' can be initially offputting, but they are terms born out of rigorous clinical observation and an attempt to chart the occluded cur-rents of an inner world. Familiarity with such terms reveals a rationale that is rooted in a rather pragmatic attempt to use words that describe exactly the process they represent. 'Paranoid–schizoid', for example, is called just that because it articulates a position in which the infant (or anyone) who is feeling persecuted – hence paranoid – bifurcates the world and its experiences into starkly distinguished 'good' and 'bad': it is schizoid. Arguably, any discipline engaging with sophisticated processes has similarly complex language.

So what? It is high on explanatory power, low on action

EPs are, by one definition, practical problem solvers. Schools and other organisations turn to them when difficulties are encountered, such as with a child or adolescent who is struggling to learn or not conforming to behaviour expectations (to use the most prosaic of examples). A criticism of psychoanalytic theory is that it is high in terms of explanatory power, but rather weak when it comes to advising what to do next. By one reckoning, this is true. But this is to dismiss the power that an increased understanding has to increase capacity and resilience in the face of adversity. As Nietzsche said, 'If you have your why for life, you can get by with almost any how' (1997, p. 6). In some cases, just staying with a situation, and bearing the almost intolerable pain, sadness and intractability of it, is more powerful and effective than the understandable attempts to produce an array of fruitless or even counterproductive interventions (for an example of the latter, see Fox, 2002). Sometimes there are not problems to be solved, only facts to be accepted. It is through such acceptance that new attitudes can arise.

Psychoanalytic theory and practice offer more than this, however. Emotional containment, and the capacity to tolerate uncertainty, these are definite mental acts that, while not observable or quantifiable, lead to definite attitudinal changes which in turn inform both behaviour and relationships with others.

It has no relevance outside the consulting room

Psychoanalysis is a high-frequency, long-term treatment and the value of its insights and the application of these are sometimes conflated with its therapeutic praxis. If this were the case, then EPs would have well-founded reservations for not taking up this way of approaching psychological events. But, not long after its inception, it came to be used as an approach to study all manner of phenomena. Devereux argues that 'psychoanalysis should be seen as first and foremost an epistemology and a methodology' (1967, p. 294). Psychoanalysis, therefore, is not just a treatment but an epistemology in and of itself – a method for exploring and revealing unconscious processes with a repertoire of techniques specifically designed for this task.

This was already the case during Freud's lifetime, and he deployed it as a hermeneutic tool of cultural enquiry used to offer accounts of the everyday life, group behaviour, religion and civilisation (Freud, 1922, 1927, 1930). In the following century psychoanalysis has evolved as a tool for research (see Hollway and Jefferson, 2013, for example), consultancy (Obholzer and Roberts, 1994) and coaching (Newton, Long and Sievers, 2006), to name but a few activities. We argue that attention to the unconscious and the emotional undertow of the here-and-now is as relevant to EPs as to anyone.

It is not easily replicable

As a treatment psychoanalysis is not a structured or manualised approach. This in itself evokes tensions and anxieties: with no trusted framework to fall back on, practitioners pretty soon encounter their own frailties and flaws. As Lemma notes:

> the anxiety arises not only because the psychoanalytic approach does not have the reassuring structure found in CBT approaches, for example, but also because it is an approach that encourages therapists to address unconscious forces in their patients as well as in themselves – an undertaking that we all at best approach with a mixture of dread. (2016, p. 8)

EPs, while not engaging in long-term, high-frequency therapy, in the course of their work do encounter people and situations that are likely to mobilise defences against anxiety. Sometimes it can be a relief to have a preset rule of engagement, in the form of a specific test or questionnaire, that can manage some of these tensions. Psychoanalytically informed practice offers a distinct alternative to this, in which one's attitude and reflexivity is orientated around the emotional tone of the encounter. It is this that makes for a genuine and authentic relating between two or more individuals. As Bion, talking of psychoanalysis *per se*, observed: 'in every consulting room there ought to be two rather frightened people: the patient and the psycho-analyst. If they are not, one wonders why they are bothering to find out what everyone else knows' (1990, p. 5).

It ignores the impact of the external world

Freud's topographical model described the psyche in terms of conscious (that which is known), pre-conscious (that which can be known with some pondering) and unconscious (that of which we are unaware), with the latter two effectively constituting the unconscious. He recognised that such a model downplayed external influences and moved to his structural model of the psyche, the more familiar id, ego and super-ego (Freud, 1923). The super-ego, partly comprising of the dictates and pressures of society as represented through parental values and censure, then internalised, did allow for the external world to have a more dynamic effect on personality development, as the ego worked to manage the conflicting desires of the harsh judge of the super-ego and the unbridled desires of the id.

A similar charge is often levelled at Klein, with many contending that she neglected the influence of the external world in her theoretical model. Corvath (2016) disputes this, observing that in the last paper before her death Klein explicitly references the importance of the mother to the infant 'because in the first few months she represents to the child the whole of the external world' (Klein, 1975, p. 248). The external world, represented by the mother, is there from the start.

It can be argued that the unconscious, as the central tenet around which psychoanalytic theory revolves, can reduce an account of functioning to a solely within-individual lens. The counter to this, however – and the concept of object relations is helpful here – is that we do not react with our external world so much as we do to our representation of it (Moscovici, 1984; Hoffman, Singh and Prakash, 2015). Such an idea allows us to explore just why an individual, a group or an organisation may be acting the way they are. Might there be trace memories, or pattern matches of past people or events that have been triggered in the present, thus causing a seemingly inexplicable reaction? The obvious example here is of a child whose teacher reminds them of their parent in a certain way and thus earlier dynamics are played out in a new setting.

It has poor predictability

It has been noted that psychoanalysis is better at producing hypotheses than confirming them, leading to charges that it lacks the predictive power that most scientific theories possess. And it is true that wild analysis (which ascribes, willy-nilly, everything to the unconscious) does take place, with dismal frequency. But this is bad practice, not bad theory. While psycho-analysis does not conform to positivist conceptions of science in specific circumstances, it can demonstrate good levels of predictability. To give one high-profile example: Walter Langer, in his 1943 study of Adolf Hitler for the Office of Strategic Services (precursor to the CIA), predicted with great accuracy what Hitler would do if Germany faced defeat, identify-ing not just the act of suicide but its means, as well (Langer, 1972). The deep analysis of personality structures provided by psychoanalytic theory allows for accurate appraisal of how specific situations will stimulate specific defences. Social defence theory quite accurately predicts how groups and societies will react to crisis, including the current climate crisis. When dealing with complexity, predictability horizons diminish, but, as Arnold observes (see Chapter 15 in this volume), such short horizons do not lead us to eschew weather reporting as unscientific.

IV

Emotions as evidence: psychoanalytic contributions to enquiry

How do we know what we know? This question is central to the practice of educational psychology and underpins the way in which we work. This question influences the type of service we deliver, and ultimately, the way in which we help others. We believe that this question deserves our atten-tion and must be grappled with.

In a seminal paper, Mark Fox (2003) challenges the nature of evidence within educational psychology: 'Over the past few years evidence-based practice has become of central concern to health and social services in this country. The fundamental tenant [sic] is that there must be a clear link between professional practice and its research base' (p. 91).

Fox goes on to argue for the importance of understanding epistemological positioning, use of experience and acknowledges a tension between subjective and more objective forms of evidence. While not explicit in Fox's writing, we believe that psychoanalytic theory has a contribution to make in the development of this argument. Put briefly, we contend that emotional data can (and should) be seen as valuable evidence, which an applied psychologist can harness in the service of generating meaningful questions and insight.

In our experience, this form of evidence is often dismissed (as 'noise' or 'interference') and may be seen as antithetical to evidence-based practice. There is doubt and mistrust as to the validity and confidence with which we can privilege this type of information. Emotions are transient, nuanced and fluctuate. They do not fit easily into linear models of cause and effect. It may be a relief to diminish the status of this elusive and intangible aspect of human experience.

Questioning fundamental tenets of what constitutes evidence and how we know what we know may be perceived as threatening. The spectres of conflict and confusion are kept at bay at organisational, individual and interactional levels if we divert emotional traffic from our citadels of science. Perhaps the counsellors and therapists might be the repositories for such polluting material?

These quite understandable manoeuvres may, however, come at a cost. A vital human currency is devalued. Human understanding itself may be sacrificed in order to protect individuals and systems from the burden of human suffering and pain. Rational (*scientific*) approaches can become reified and ratified. A powerful narrative dominates the profession, where terms like 'scientist–practitioner' and 'evidence-based practice' reign supreme. Academic and political communities collude and enshrine doctrines which become social constructions and are taken for granted. This helps individuals and groups to navigate complex phenomena in ways that are defendable and defended. The place for ambiguity, uncertainty and instability is reduced. Rational and positivist perspectives offer refuge and resolution from conflict and confusion.

The seeds of deception

Bion (1976) commented:

> *The defects of verbal communication were clearly discerned about two thousand years ago by Plato: in the* Phaedo, *describing the trial of Socrates, he points out what a great disadvantage it is that in spite of the fact that Socrates and Phaedrus can apparently talk very accurately and precisely, they are actually using extremely ambiguous terms. I do not see that we have made much progress in that regard in the last two thousand years.* (p. 317)

This reflection connects with the notion of open textured thinking. The Austrian physicist, mathematician and philosopher Waismann (1968), used the term 'open texture' to describe the universal possibility of vagueness in empirical statements, which he argues solves the conceptual confusions of ordinary language. These ideas bring us to a point of interest in terms of epistemology. Fox (2003) speaks of the 'EP flip', in shifting from an espoused constructionist perspective to a defensive positivist positioning, when the EP is asked to justify their reasoning. Open textured thinking helps us to perform the EP flip.

We argue that this 'flip' can also be understood in psychoanalytic terms as a manifestation of a social defence (of which more later in this book), where the educational system, and mechanisms for resource allocation, can be seen to have evolved within a paranoid–schizoid system, struggling to manage the conflicts and tensions which emerge when there is evidence of failure and lack of progress. This systemic state of paranoia is understandable in relation to a perceived threat to the effectiveness of individuals and systems to promote change. The consequent schizoid 'split' seems to involve the medical model being reified as good (see the hierarchy of research evidence cited in Fox, 2003, p. 93) and more constructionist approaches as 'bad' – lacking robust evidence relating to reliability and validity. It follows that the concept of emotional experiences and feelings become split off in this mechanistic, open textured 'EBP' (evidence-based practice) construction.

This defensive manoeuvre may be thought of in relation to the concept of an epistemic fallacy. In essence, this involves making ontological statements (about 'what is') based on epistemological reasoning (what is known) (Bhaskar, 1975). This brings us to a fundamental schism, and an essential element of psychoanalytic theory. The unconscious.

It is argued here that, without exploration of the emotional world and the unconscious forces present in individuals, groups and organisations, it is likely that the applied psychologist is engaging in evidence-based fallacy, and epistemic confusion.

Arnold's chapter in this volume (Chapter 15) acknowledges the limits of models drawing on physics, and chaos theory in particular. It is argued that the predictive value of such scientific models has limitations, as also denoted by our careful reporting of statistical data in cognitive testing and the importance of confidence intervals. This brings us back to the notion of open textured thinking, which acknowledges that it is helpful to be aware of vagueness and the imprecise nature of language, in a way that can save us from the fantasy of precision and illusion of rigidity and stability in human behaviours and systems.

These ideas may also be related to those developing second-order cybernetics thinking in systemic family therapy (Dallos and Draper, 2000). An initial formulation of the structural approach to understanding a family system was of a mechanism to be depicted, where areas of dysfunction could be identified and 'fixed'. The evolution involved in second-order cybernetics shifted to viewing the system as interrelated elements, with mutuality of influence, and therefore the task was refocused – shifting from enquiries of how a system operated as it does, to why it operates as it does, with attention being paid to beliefs, relationships and behaviours. This change in perspective from *how* to *why* might also be argued as essential to psychoanalytic approaches, and in relation to the epistemic fallacy argument.

The EP who makes a reasoned argument for what 'is', based on the research and literature base of what is 'known', may have successfully defended him- or herself and colluded with a systems level defence, which avoids facing the ominous unknown. The unconscious aspects within the system and individual have been conveniently stepped over. The system and individuals are protected from coming into contact with undesirable aspects of themselves or others. The system and the practitioners have colluded (without necessarily intending to do so) in creating an incomplete picture, which paints a more certain image than is perhaps there. The structures seem robust, but somehow hollow.

Bion's idea of –K has relevance here. Hollway describes this as (2008, p. 10):

Bion's understanding of the difference between learning from experience and needing to know is one example (1962). He is sceptical of the kinds of knowledge that are stripped of emotional experience, whose raison d'être is to substitute rigid control of the world that can be thought (–K) for the uncertainty of being open to new experiences through thinking (+K). In pursuing the goal of a kind of knowing stripped of affect, the protocols of positivist science when applied to the human sciences resemble 'the aim of the lie' more than they resemble 'the aim of the truth'. (Bion, 1962 p. 48)

It may serve a protective (and relieving) function, to take up the role of 'scientist practitioner' in complex, confusing, messy, stuck and emotionally fraught situations – we may detect hints of this in statutory assessment work, policy documents and tribunal transcripts. This defensive engagement may, however, come at a cost, where the possibility of making meaningful contact in psychoanalytic terms might be lost. There is a body of evidence within this book that suggests to us that many possibilities for making links, generating insight and enabling transformation may also be lost.

Towards depth psychology

Therefore, if we might tolerate the possibility that our established ways of working serve a defensive purpose, and in turn may limit the potential contribution that we may offer to others, we might legitimately ask: what else might be considered?

Bion (1976) argues: 'I sometimes think that a feeling is one of the few things which analysts have the luxury of being able to regard as a fact. If patients are feeling angry, or frightened or sexual, or whatever it is, at least we can suppose that this is a fact; but when they embark on theories or hearsay we cannot distinguish fact from fiction' (p. 317).

Here Bion articulates a profound notion. I feel therefore I am. Emotion as evidence. As data. As fact. A form of evidence that we might value and use, not diminish or dismiss.

It is this radical idea that permeates this book. Different authors offer explanations of how they have used this fundamental concept in the service of their work. We argue that this way of taking up our role returns us to the human experience of engaging with others. We argue that this way of working can enrich and enhance our capacity to ask questions and to explore complexity with authenticity and integrity.

This brings us back to the essential underpinning element of our argument: *epistemology*, or 'how the status of the knowledge generation process is understood' (Hollway, 2008, p. 9). If we accept that we might use our own experience, of relating to others and engaging in our work and maintain curiosity as to what our emotional experience may reveal to use about the experience of others, then we have a fulcrum, which might help us with the heavy lifting involved in supporting others to change and transform.

This endeavour – to use ourselves in the service of others – is complex and requires careful attention, commitment and support from others. At a personal level, there is a need to strive for engagement, which requires a commitment to openness and receptivity. Keats (discussed by Bartle in Chapter 11) spoke of 'negative capability', the capacity to tolerate uncertainty in order to find something new. Bion speaks of attending to another 'beyond memory or desire'. Walt Whitman makes this commitment: 'I think I will do nothing for a long time but listen, And accrue what I hear into myself … ' (1855/2017, p. 71).

Each of these expressions share what may be seen as instructive. A dedication to attunement and the use of the self – as an instrument for exploration, and as a source of evidence.

There is, of course, a need for reflection and supervision, which is explored by various contributors. A common theme in this aspect of the work draws on the notion of the container/contained, which Bion considered foundational for the development of thought. This concept is described earlier in this chapter, and in subsequent chapters, which perhaps indicates to us the centrality of the concept. Hollway (2008) helps in pursuing why this idea might have such traction for us in our work (p. 9):

> *The container–contained relation provides an explanation for the affective development of our capacity for thought and it does so, not from the perspective of a unitary rational subject, but through unconscious, intersubjective dynamics, initially in the relation of mother and infant, where the mother functions as a container and the baby's projections are contained. This kind of unconscious intersubjectivity continues throughout life as we*

learn to use other containers (and parts of ourselves) to help us to think.

This quote captures an essential quality of how engagement in a psychoanalytic approach might be seminal to our work – the EP works within the relationships they form, and it is by valuing the relational and acknowledging the great power therein, which includes the potential to be liberated from the unitary and the rational, and open and curious about the unconscious intersubjectivity that is present in our day-to-day work. These dynamic tensions may hold both the origins and opportunities involved in our struggle with others.

Dynamic tensions and multiplicity

This emphasis on the virtue of learning from experience (and resisting defensive ways of practising) is a theme that runs through each chapter of the book. Contributors frequently offer vignettes, which – while offering illustration and insight – may also be seen as symbolic, in terms of the practitioners using themselves as tools and of drawing on their emotional experience as a resource and form of evidence.

Kelley, Woolfson and Boyle (2016, pp. 364–365) make the following comment, when reflecting on the professional practice frameworks of educational psychologists:

We need to ensure that we offer clients and stakeholders a distinctive contribution as psychologists – one that is different from the involvement of educational administrators, teachers and social workers. Although there is some overlap in the skills required across these professional groups, a range of effective practice frameworks (along with their conceptual underpinnings) secures the centrality of psychology and the distinctiveness of our contribution in our professional interactions with schools and families.

We argue that a psychoanalytic perspective has a powerful and distinctive contribution to make within educational psychology practice. In the second edition of their seminal text, Kelley *et al.* (2016) develop an argument for a critical realist perspective when considering philosophical developments that may underpin future practice in the profession.

They argue that this way of seeing the world (the nature of reality and of knowledge generation) requires that practitioners (p. 238):

- ensure that problems or issues are considered in an interpretative, collaborative context with those involved
- direct the gathering of different levels and types of evidence
- consider and guide resulting action in the light of psychological and psycho-social theory and evidence.

We agree with Kelley *et al.*, and argue that psychoanalytic perspectives can indeed offer us a fundamentally different type and level of evidence. This notion of levels is not, however, viewed as echoing EBP arguments about hierarchies of evidence. There are different forms and sources of evidence – not better or worse, but different. Slipping into the rhetoric of 'better' and 'worse' may be seen in relation to splitting (the 'good' and 'bad') and of artificial separations. Following this argument, one can conceive of the fundamental task of psychoanalysis as working towards a unification, or integration, where the separate parts are connected and embraced as they form a whole. If we shift our perspective from the psychoanalytic task to our task as practitioner-psychologist, we argue that the profession as a whole might be viewed in these terms. Consider, for example, the following reflection by Gameson, Rhydderch, Ellis and Carroll (2003, p. 100): 'On the basis of their collective experience the authors of this paper consider that current practice is often characterised by competing approaches that seem to be polarised, fragmented, too narrowly focused and inappropriately dominated by privileged or fashionable paradigms.'

The reader will be influenced by their own professional training, ongoing learning, beliefs, values and principles. This quote may hold a resonance. Asking 'What influences my way of working?' is likely to stimulate a multitude of responses. The point we are making here is that Gameson and colleagues appear to be echoing, at the profession-as-a-whole level, a sense of theoretical splitting (which is also inscribed in Fox's 'EP flip' involving idealising a positivist perspective).

We resist the temptation to be drawn into this splitting, and resist attempting the elevation of psychoanalytic perspective and marginalisation of other perspectives. We suggest that a psychoanalytic way of working can offer a valuable contribution, which may be integrated into eclectic practice, befitting the diversity of activity that EPs engage in. A historical reluctance to integrate a psychoanalytic perspective within the profession over time has been considered in earlier parts of this chapter. We argue that this might be understood in terms of a social defence (see Chapter 14): why would a profession that engages in the painful experiences of children (and those working with them) wish to attune to this emotional experience? It makes sense, at a meta-level, that the theoretical perspective that embraces such contact might become split off – cast out and even denigrated, in the interests of self-protection.

It is recognised that a social defence (hypothesised above) emerges from a social milieu. Educational psychologists work within such a milieu and require theory that accommodates this reality. In returning to the notion of different types of evidence (Kelley *et al.*, 2016, p. 364-365), psychoanalytic ways of working require an interpretation of different types of evidence, including, for example, the use of emotional data and observational data. This may be thought of in terms of a binocular vision – where the inner world and outer world are simultaneously attended to. This curiosity towards the external and internal world may also be thought of in relation to a particular conceptualisation of what might be meant by the term 'psycho-social'. There is a body of literature that offers a psychoanalytic perspective when considering 'psycho-social' experience (see Frosch, 2003; Hollway and Jefferson, 2013). The hyphen becomes a point of interest here, and can be conceptualised as a third space, where the social and the individual co-construct a reality, shaped by the unconscious. Frosch (2003) comments (p. 1553):

> *The psychoanalytic concept of fantasy is perhaps the most potent theoretical expression of the interpellation of the subjective into the social, in that it suggests (at least in its Kleinian form), particularly when combined with the notion of projective identification (Hinshelwood, 1991) that fantasy is not 'just' something that occupies an internal space as a kind of mediation of reality, but that also has material effects, directing activities of people and investing the social world with meaning.*

We argue that this has relevance for the educational psychologist, working across multiple systems and multiple realities, which are constructed at the conscious and unconscious level within and between people.

Concluding thoughts on evidence

Fox (2003) encourages us to consider our epistemological positioning, and how this might influence our work. We value this challenge and, with recourse to Bion, suggest that a radical alternative to evidence-based practice is a core tenet of this book. Experientially based practice, where emotions are seen as a meaningful form of evidence, provides us with the opportunity to explore what is going on in the moment. We have argued that this form of evidence is often disregarded for defensive purposes. We further argue that concerted curiosity about our internal and relational experiences can inform our work in profound and illuminating ways. We believe that, when this form of evidence is integrated into an EP's repertoire, alongside more conventional information sources, a whole new understanding emerges. Our hope is that the following chapters might offer the reader some insight into how these ideas can be operationalised in practice.

Note

*It should be noted that there are other psychoanalytic theorists, notably Fairbairn (1954), who have taken object relations theory in different directions. In this text we focus on Klein's work only.

PART II

THEORY TO PRACTICE

CHAPTER 2

The use of psychoanalytic concepts in educational psychology practice

Olivia Kenneally

This chapter aims to provide a comprehensive account of how psycho-analytic concepts can be used successfully in educational psychology practice. It will describe how using psychoanalytic concepts can add a depth and richness to educational psychology practice. In doing so, research on the applicability, effectiveness and reliability (or not) of such approaches will be considered. This will be followed by a brief introduction to key psychoanalytic concepts and how they can be used within educational psy-chology practice, and then moves into specific application of such concepts through case studies. Reflection on, and conclusions around, this way of working will be drawn.

Emotional data as evidence

Evidence-based psychological therapy has long been viewed as an es-sential component of educational psychology practice. Evidence-based practice and high-quality research are often described synonymously, with the notion of randomised control trials being recognised as the 'gold standard' of research (Fox, 2003). This begs the question of feasi-bility within the therapeutic world, where each individual may require a unique and bespoke approach appropriate to his or her needs, contexts, environments and experiences. Mychailyszyn *et al.* (2011) recognise the individual, and indeed community-based, elements of therapeutic practice, pointing towards the reality of real-world contexts which are messy, with many elements being difficult to control. Swisher (2010) goes further to recognise the importance of interventions being responsive to need, personalised to the client and his or her individual circumstances. This suggests the importance of an evolving therapeutic model which does as Swisher (2010) suggests, and responds to personalised need and individual circumstances. It therefore raises the key concept of emotional data and how this is used as evidence, in an evolving fashion, considering the said and unsaid, to further inform practice, intervention and outcome.

In considering emotional data as evidence, one is drawn into the realm of experiential learning and emotionality, with Bion describing emotionality as being at the 'psychoanalytic heart of things' (Bion, cited in Waddell, 2002, p. 113). As educational psychologists (EPs), being concerned with children's learning, educational environments, family units and communities, application of psychoanalytic concepts and use of emotional data does not stop at the individual therapeutic relationship. Instead, a systemic approach is taken whereby emotional data is considered within all the above contexts – leading one directly into the messy context of real-world research. Indeed, the impact of unconscious processes in learning are described eloquently by Mintz (2007), who illustrates how understanding and application of psychodynamic concepts can lead to differences in how teachers respond to stressful events in the classroom, thus changing the outcome. Surely it follows that having a good understanding of unconscious processes and emotional data will support one to respond to situations differently, possibly providing one with a more accurate and reflective account of behaviour as a communication, as opposed to working with surface behaviour only?

The benefits of using emotional data in EP practice is raised by Kennedy, Keaney, Shaldon and Canagaratnam (2018), particularly in relation to supervision. They describe the Relational Model of Supervision for Applied Psychology Practice (RMSAPP), postulating the position of the central place of emotion in human experience. In particular, they recognise transference and countertransference as tools in the supervisory space, and posit that, given effective use, these tools may support the supervisee in using emotions as data in his or her work with others. Pellegrini (2010) demonstrates how he uses his feelings as data and articulates how this is triangulated by complementary feelings in the audience when training.

Pellegrini highlights how awareness of emotional data through projective processes, when combined by other data such as cognitive data, can lend to richer hypotheses, so adding to the jigsaw puzzle.

Evidence-based practice

As EPs, our varied role calls for the use of many different psychological approaches, such as consultation and solution-focused brief therapy (to name a few). Engaging in such approaches, along with the reality of real-world research inherent to our role, means that epistemological standpoints within the context of evidence-based practice require consideration. At one end of the scale lies the epistemological standpoint of social constructivism, which Fox (2003) describes as where 'people or cultures construct how objects in the world are represented' (p. 97). It follows that a key element of practice becomes the developing and evolving understanding about oneself and how one constructs the world, where interactions, feelings and behaviours are all understood better within the socially constructed context in which they are experienced. Pellegrini (2010) describes EPs at this end of the scale to be possibly more likely to move towards a psychodynamic approach as an alternative approach to interpret human behaviour, due to the parallels between them. While Pellegrini posits this as a possibility for educational psychology practice, when one conducts an online literature search there is a dearth of psychoanalytic research specific to EPs.

A question is therefore posed. Can psychoanalytic approaches be successfully applied within educational psychology practice, in light of the need for evidence-based practice? Evidence-based practice has long been a dominant discourse, with Fox (2003) describing the need for clear connections between research and practice. It is interesting, then, to consider this in relation to the place for psychoanalytic approaches of the EP. Fonagy (2003) suggests that much literature highlights a lack of psychoanalytic outcome research, with many of the psychoanalytic approaches to research being of a qualitative nature, and being criticised for what Midgley (2006) described as the data problem, the data analysis problem and the generalisability problem. So can an approach such as this be of use to the practising EP?

The debate between psychology and psychoanalysis, and indeed clinical psychology and education, therefore continues, and is again described by Fox (2003), who asks whether we as EPs wish to embrace the randomised control trials of clinical psychologists or align ourselves more with education research. Fox (2003) gives some objections to the former way of working, which include an objection to the research hierarchy, described as being inappropriate for educational psychology practice, with quantitative analysis described as being a dehumanising style of research. This opinion may very well depend on one's epistemological stance, with arguments against a positivist experimental research perspective in favour of a constructivist one (described in Fox, 2003). Here professionals are described as reflective practitioners, with every situation differing, and thus there are many different ways of seeing things in each situation.

Midgley (2004) supports this view, and astutely outlines that, by buying into one approach (such as the scientific realm of evidence-based practice), one risks losing the distinctive elements of the psychoanalytic approach. He goes on to try and strike a balance, advocating the use of a methodology that avoids the pitfalls of the traditional case-study approach, providing one with a more systematic and structured approach to data analysis, while still retaining the distinctive emotional and experiential aspects of the therapeutic process. Indeed, Midgley's dilemma is one close to the hearts and minds of EPs, with the qualitative/quantitative debate forging for many years. The issue remains for EPs: how can an approach that does not purport to make use of systematic qualitative approaches, but focuses solely on the traditional case study – which, as Midgley (2006) describes, poses difficulties in respect of validity, subjective use of materials, retrospective writing, subjective focusing on material in analysis and lack of generalisability – be incorporated as a useful aspect of educational psychology practice? On the other hand, Pellegrini (2010) raises interesting questions around some EPs' strict adherence to evidence-based practice and problem-solving models, which he muses could be 'defences against using one's feelings to understand another person's experience ... this requires sensitivity to one's emotional experience as well as the emotional states of others' (p. 258). His point is interesting, as the cognitive, behavioural and emotional response to casework is raised, with him querying the preponderance of some practitioners to the cognitive/behavioural aspects of casework to the detriment of the emotional response. In any case, increased research has been undertaken to prove the usefulness of psychoanalytic concepts and the increasing use of emotional data and emotional response in education settings – for example, Kennedy *et al.* (2018), Eloquin (2016), Hulusi and Maggs (2015), Bartle (2015), Pellegrini (2010), Soloman and Nashat (2010), Diamant (2009), Maltby (2008) – along with the usefulness of qualitative approaches for research, such as Midgley (2004) and Rustin (2003), which feature the case study.

As EPs, qualitative approaches play an important role in our work, bringing opportunities for use of emotional data with them. The qualitative approach is described favourably by Midgley (2004) as one that does not treat the subject(s) as purely a set of variables but focuses on the discovery of their understanding of their world and experiences. Some of the difficulties with this kind of research are described well by Darlington and Scott (2002, p. 1), who capture it as the 'swampy lowland of practice', where 'there are rarely control groups, where operationalising key constructs in behavioural terms is highly problematic, … where the politics of the setting are often overwhelming and where values and ethical issues are critical and complex'. Midgley describes this as being synonymous with places of work of the child psychotherapist. EPs, also, may resonate with this qualitative approach to research, and the possibilities and pitfalls it can bring. One way of approaching this is suggested by Fonagy (2003) and Soloman and Nashat (2010), whereby the usefulness of joint working, insight and experience between disciplines, together with a therapeutic presence in institutions, are highlighted as possible ways to engage in more robust research models. The application of psychoanalytic concepts within the social constructionist, consultative, solution-focused role of the EP may, in light of Fonagy's (2003) and Soloman and Nashat's (2010) suggestions, therefore provide a useful vehicle for further research.

Practical application of psychoanalytic concepts

Having considered arguments for and against the evidence base behind psychoanalytic ways of working, along with research surounding the role of unconscious processes evident in the learning environment, attention is now turned to the practical application of psychoanalytic concepts in the daily work of an EP. Two case studies that portray psychoanalytic concepts in action will be considered. The first case focuses on the use of a longer-term therapeutic assessment, comprising six weeks' assessment with a view to this informing a long-term intervention plan. The second case focuses on a longer-term intervention, and looks at the application of specific concepts along with a psychoanalytic understanding to development. All names have been changed for reasons of confidentiality.

The case that follows below is about a boy called Zane and depicts how providing containment both for the pupil and for staff can support engagement with difficult emotions, make sense of experience and behaviour and support engagement in intervention that is more appropriate and conducive to change. Extracts from practice are reported in italics to give a flavour of the application of psychoanalytic concepts. Four psychoanalytic concepts are exposed through this case. Containment forms the first concept introduced, and is described by Segal (in Lanman, 1998) as:

> *a mother capable of containing projective identification unconsciously processes those projections and responds adequately to the infant's need. When this happens, the infant can reintroject his projections, modified by understanding, and he also introjects the breast as a container capable of containing and dealing with anxiety. This forms the basis of his own capacity to deal with anxiety.* (p. 466)

Bion described this as the mother's capacity for reverie. The mother takes on the idea of container, with the infant's fragmented emotions and overwhelming anxieties being the contained. The role of the EP/learning mentor/teaching assistant (TA)/teacher/parent as 'container', all before the psychic withdrawal of the learner (Price, 2002), cannot be understated, and it is the container–contained relationship that can often enable learning or, in this instance, psychological growth to take place.

Projection weaves a thread throughout the case, and is described in Copley and Forryan (1987) as 'the omnipotent phantasy of splitting off parts of the self and projecting them onto or into another object' (p. 161). It is usually concerned with the projection of unwanted parts of oneself – such as overwhelming anger/anxiety that is projected into another person's mental state, where it is then denied, allowing for a sense of tension relief in the person projecting. Knowledge and awareness of these unconscious processes and how they are played out can enable the EP to get to the heart of the communication (as evident in this case), with intervention following naturally from this.

Transference and countertransference feature repeatedly, shedding light on the case and highlighting the importance of emotional data, emotional connection and self-reflection. 'Transference' from previous relationships and experiences is recognised in many papers, including Fraiberg's (1980) 'Ghosts in the nursery', and can be conceptualised as the space where clients bring past feelings from an earlier experience into the present. New relationships can be experienced or even subject to distortion on the basis and experience of earlier relationships and may involve a re-enacting of earlier relationships in the present that are inappropriate to the present. Salzberger-Wittenberg (1970) refers to countertransference as involving the feelings stirred up in the worker as a result of contact with the client, and as a result of them being receptive to the clients' communications, which often gives clues to the client's unconscious processes. One has to be mindful, however, and consider whether feelings experienced in the countertransference are a result of the worker's own past experience or of receptivity to the client's projected feelings, as illustrated in the case excerpts below.

Case 1

Zane was an 8-year-old boy and lived with his mother, younger brother and older sister. He attended primary school in a city area. His twin brother had been put into care. Social services were involved throughout. Zane was white British.

Zane was referred to the educational psychology service by school due to:

- poor engagement in tasks
- difficulty regulating emotions
- 'outbursts'/'temper tantrums'
- craving negative attention.

Involvement was negotiated whereby five therapeutic play/assessment sessions to support Zane to process and engage with emotion were carried out, along with consultation with teacher and observation in class.

Consultation with teacher

> During initial consultation with the teacher, I recall feeling a
> sense of anxiety, along with anger and feelings of worthlessness.
> I considered these as I watched her facial expression and body
> language, which seemed stilted and rigid. Having managed to
> contain my own sense of being overwhelmed, I wondered
> aloud if she perhaps felt frustrated and possibly even angry at
> the situation? At this, she broke down in tears, confiding her
> distress to me. I gently tried to hold her emotions, labelling them,
> normalising feelings, and delivering them back in more tolerable
> forms.

Through providing a containing environment, the teacher was able to be supported in being able to think about her emotions in useful ways and consider how they may have been a communicative aspect of Zane's behaviour. The containment provided seemed to play a key role in changing her perceptions of Zane's behaviour, and thus interaction with him, and she spent the rest of the session thinking and taking in thoughts and ideas. This can be likened to a client who, having been able to process emotions and make more sense of experiences, could think about them differently. Bion refers to this as something that can be 'transformed into thoughts capable of growth and accretion of meaning' (Bion, in Copley and Forryan, 1987, p. 194).

Observation

Two weeks later, interesting observations were made as the teacher was checking work. When she checked Zane's, she immediately highlighted a mistake:

> Zane clenched his fists and pulled his arms close into his side, as
> if pulling in his whole body and holding it together, for fear if he
> didn't that it might fall apart. I felt myself take a sharp intake of
> breath and hold my stomach. I considered this in relation to Bick's
> notion of holding oneself together or 'second skin defence'.

A second skin defence is an interesting psychoanalytic concept, and can be described as a means of holding oneself together or even holding one's personality together externally through muscular, vocal or sensory means. This can develop in early infancy in the absence of internally secure psychic holding (Bick, in Waddell, 2002, p. 108).

> I felt there was a projection of anxiety and fear, which went unrecognised by the teacher, but was experienced by me a few feet away. He looked away, rubbed his face with both hands, and looked back while the teacher explained her point. As she walked away, he looked after her with a hurt and vulnerable expression on his face. I continued to feel anxious and had an urge to try and make things better. I considered the countertransference in respect of his projection of emotion into me and my own countertransference relating to my own experiences and 'need' to get things right.

A good example of observable data interacting with emotional data is evident here, where the trigger for and subsequent projection of strong emotions could be easily observed, interacting with reflection on and awareness of countertransference. Holding oneself together, or 'second skin', seemed to emerge as a theme for Zane. In the first session this was apparent, seen by him holding his sleeve over his hand and keeping this hand over the covered one. He seemed to engage in 'holding together' when he may have been overwhelmed by emotions, or possibly a 'nameless dread', a term coined by Bion (cited in Waddell, 2002) for unlabelled emotion.

The notion of projection and containment featured very strongly in the second session, where one could see the temporary relief Zane derived from splitting off or expelling emotions through therapeutic play. It also portrayed the notion of the session and worker having a containing function, supporting Zane to then label an experience (as opposed to experiencing a nameless dread). Strong emotions were portrayed in the second session, where they were processed and reflected on through play. These emotions were taken out on the goat, who had hurt the cheetah (which Zane had chosen to represent himself), as portrayed in the following extract:

> Zane wrapped wire around the goat's neck. I wondered if this was a communication of somehow needing to take air/goodness away from the goat or if it was a projection of how he actually felt himself – without goodness/air/basic things needed to survive/his

> twin? He enacted the pig urinating on him and I pondered silently
> if this was his way of expelling overwhelming or unwanted feelings.
> I commented that the pig seemed to want to get rid of something
> from inside him, maybe something that was paining him and
> wondered aloud if it was maybe an angry or worried pain (feeling a
> sense of anger mixed with anxiety). He looked at me, smiled, saying
> 'Yeah, it's the two pains', gave a small laugh, with his shoulders
> dropping. I felt immediately more relaxed.

Copley and Forryan (1987) discussed the concept of expelling as being not only a physical method of evacuation but also a mental channel of evacuation at the most primitive level. They describe it as being an evacuation into a container and thus a form of communication.

> Reflecting on this made me wonder if he viewed me and our
> sessions as the container into which he could expel unwanted
> feelings, then being able to think about them together.

The session continued:

> I commented, 'I wonder does the pig feel a bit better now', to
> which he responded that the pig 'didn't want to go toilet any
> more'. I pondered silently if it was a communication of relief
> after release of anxiety. The fire engine drove over the goat, then
> spraying water on him – I found this interesting, as it seemed to
> suggest a shift from a paranoid–schizoid to a depressive state, in
> using the fire engine to harm and then to save, recognising that the
> thing that can help can also hurt.

The above extracts portray the strength of emotion that is projected outwards, or expelled, through the most primitive forms of evacuation. It highlights the usefulness of a containing environment in which to expel this, with temporary relief being experienced through this containing presence and process. Two differing states of mind are evident within the above extract: the paranoid–schizoid position and the depressive position. Klein (in Hinshelwood, 1994) described the paranoid–schizoid position as a splitting of the world into 'good' and 'bad' by the infant, who experiences unmet needs such as hunger as an attack by a 'bad' carer, subsequently projecting and locating strong emotions such as hatred outside of the self. This is in sharp contrast to a more reflective position, whereby the infant can both acknowledge these projected emotions as their own and bear to think about them, feeling guilt and need for reparation. It moves away from a polarisation of things into 'good' and 'bad', instead recognising the capacity for the coexistence of differing and polar qualities within a whole person – the one who frustrates also being the one who loves, for example. Positive development regarding these states of mind are noticed at the end, where Zane is able to make a move from what seems to be a paranoid–schizoid state to a more depressive state of mind, highlighting the importance of the experience of a containing other in the development of one's own internal object. The ability to move between these states may have implications for classroom interaction and behaviour.

Ending and separations are key concepts to be thought about, within both the therapy room and the classroom, as highlighted by Maltby (2008). The following extract conveys some of the difficulty Zane seemed to experience with endings, and portrays how the presence of a containing adult can support:

> As I reminded Zane about the session end, he broke the toy ambulance into bits and I felt tense. I wondered silently if he was communicating that abandonment and anger were making him feel like he was falling apart. I tried to contain the feelings of anger and anxiety I felt in the countertransference, normalising and labelling these feelings and reassuring him I would hold him in mind. He turned and gave what seemed to be a genuine smile, with his shoulders dropping, his arms becoming looser and picked up the ambulance pieces, starting to fix it, allowing me to help. I felt an ease of tension in myself and urge to hold him. I wondered if this may have been a realisation that he can think about and express overwhelming emotions and expect the other person will be OK and there.

There were a number of consultations with the head and teacher after the sessions ended, around containing environments. Zane's behaviour had improved dramatically and he was reported to be able to take in learning. It was interesting to wonder if this was due to him being able to process some overwhelming emotions and digest them, leaving room to take in positive experiences and engage with emotionality. This seemed to have improved in the classroom, with Zane being able to engage with aspects of himself that could be thought about usefully with another instead of being projected outwards. This was evident in sessions togeth-er, with him visibly and verbally expressing relief when feelings were held and thought about. His difficulty in taking things in previously, instead almost 'spitting things out', may have been an infantile response to some-thing that was too overwhelming to be processed – instead, projecting at the expense of a separate self and other, leaving the body to be the mouthpiece when there are no words for it.

Case 2

The second case, while demonstrating application of psychoanalytic con-cepts, provides a window into the application of psychoanalytic concepts with respect to child development. EPs make use of child development theories as described in respect of how a child functions, and these can often be used to plan interventions. The application of psychoanalytic con-cepts to stages of development provides a psychoanalytic underpinning to child development according to age, stage and experience, and aims, as Waddell (2002) suggests, to make sense of a child's inner life. Waddell describes a psychoanalytic concept of development as being synonymous with the concept of 'states of mind', which she describes as encompassing the past, present and future, as an individual oscillates between these states throughout his or her life. Waddell (2002) describes the psychoanalytic stages of development as infancy, early childhood, latency, adolescence and adulthood, with the latter part of latency (pre-puberty) being described as a relatively 'quiet' period, without major or novel upheaval. This is in stark contrast to the early part of puberty/adolescence stage, when internal structures are challenged by internal conflict and anxieties, with regression towards infancy being noted, among other defence strategies (Waddell, 2002). During latency (typically referring to the primary school period), an internal identity that supports, and is required for, social interaction that is beyond the family unit. Waddell (2002) describes the latency child as enjoying a sense of management of his or her environment, a large part of which includes the school environment, which focuses on tasks requiring knowledge and skills. Maths, for example, is attractive to a latency state of mind, given the order and controlled knowledge that underpin the subject.

The following case study portrays the application of psychoana-lytic concepts, describing and discussing some of the key aspects of development in adolescence through work with Mary – a 14-year-old white British girl who lived with her father and older sister.

Mary was referred to the educational psychology service for an eight-week therapeutic intervention by school for 'acting out' behaviour, theft, poor engagement with abstract ideas and feelings, and regular conflict with her father. Mary had had a difficult childhood, experiencing inconsistent care, as both parents were alcohol and drug users. Mary's father now abstains from these and is the main caregiver (her mother left years ago to live in another country).

Adolescence is a time that represents progress for some, but also loss. One can sometimes see the adolescent clinging to latency states of mind, which was noticeable in Mary. In session one, she described her favourite subject – maths – a subject based on figures and formulas, and therefore would appeal to the latency child's mind due to the focus on order, knowledge and skill during this stage (Waddell, 2002). As one progresses through the latter stages of latency into the early stages of adolescence, one sees a shift from facts and accumulation of knowledge to more abstract ways of thinking about one's opinions, feelings and thoughts (Youell, 2006). In session one, Mary appeared to be 'stuck' in her development, still focused on facts and figures. Her teachers described her as doing well in these subjects and encountering difficulty in those requiring engagement with thoughts and feelings. Indeed, according to staff her relationship with teachers in these classes was compromised. Mary described this:

> they know I have a reputation … they just pick on me … their classes are boring … they are boring.

There may have been some defensiveness and anxiety here about moving from a latency state of facts, to thoughts and feelings. There also may have been a splitting of objects (or teachers) into good and bad, which is characteristic of the adolescent and infant states. Splitting and projection are essential elements of adolescent development and parents and teachers often feel worn out by constant projection. What Mary may have been doing was projecting her anxiety of engaging with abstract thoughts/feelings into her teachers, leaving them as they described: almost incompetent and anxious.

Copley (1993) suggests that adolescence is a time when young people experiment with identity, becoming part of a group, which becomes a place for them to acquire containment, test identities or project anxieties. Her group appeared to be fairly homogeneous with similar ways of dressing, which can be seen (according to Copley and Forryan, 1987) as a type of holding-to-gether skin. School had highlighted 'acting out' behaviour as a concern and adolescence is a time where there can be an increase in risk-taking behaviour. Her teachers described her group's behaviour as being similar to that of tod-dlers, with an obvious manner of engagement in it, meaning that they would be 'caught'. Behaviour like this is typical of adolescence and often expresses a need for boundaries and rules similar to latency states (Youell, 2006).

Engaging with thoughts through writing was highlighted as an area for development, with Mary being described as 'refusing to engage'. In session three, when faced with this, a sense of hostility and anxiety was felt and the author wondered silently if she was projecting her anger at having to engage (with overwhelming emotions) and anxiety about not knowing what she contained. Salzberger-Wittenberg, Henry and Osbourne (1983) wrote: 'producing work faces us with the anxiety about what we contain. Are we empty? Full of mess?' (p. 76).

The following excerpt illustrates this:

> I commented gently that she appeared to be finding it difficult and she said, 'I don't know.' I replied, 'It's OK to find it difficult and not know.' I picked up my book, letting her know I was there for her, and she began. This provided some containment as, when I articulated that it was 'OK to not know', I felt some relief and she subsequently began. I felt there had been possibility for growth. She also presented as more able to engage when I took attention away (to my book), which may suggest she found the prospect of needing adult help daunting, and may be suggestive of some patterns of avoidant attachment, maybe linking with the idea of lack of containment in infancy, maybe feeling 'Why would adults help her?'.

Adolescence is a time when young people find themselves in vul-nerable positions due to the myriad changes that are occurring: psycho-logically, socially, biologically, physically and developmentally. Some adolescents take up positions of power as a defence against vulnerability, dependent on how they feel vulnerability within themselves (Briggs, 2008). Mary seemed almost afraid of thoughts, linking them with de-pression, and seemed to view them with little compassion, commenting in session five:

'Anyway, it's depressed people who think about their thoughts a lot and feel sorry for themselves.'

I wondered silently if she found it hard to engage in thinking about her thoughts, because she was unconsciously terrified of being depressed.

In the final session, as we explored feelings around something that made her happy that week, she placed herself within a paranoid–schizoid state. However, she displayed growth in that she could move into a depressive state with appropriate containment, which is needed in adolescence:

MARY:	I hate answering those questions … I hate the sessions, as I don't think about my thoughts and I hate thinking about my thoughts.
PSYCHOLOGIST:	It's OK to hate doing something and it's OK to find it scary to think about your thoughts, but it's good to hear you expressing your feelings.
P:	And look … everything is still all right … it's OK to face your feelings – nothing bad has happened.
M:	Well, I don't hate you – I like you, I just … I barely know you and find it weird to tell you my thoughts.

Mary seemed to push away her thoughts, wanting me to take them on. I considered the communication, wondering if the feelings of irritation I felt in the countertransference were my own or if she was herself experiencing unconscious feelings of anger/irritability/hatred (maybe for me) which she wanted to project into me. At the end, she appeared to have moved from a paranoid–schizoid state into a depressive state and appeared to be concerned for me at this time, and I felt a sense of warmth and vulnerability. I felt she had been able to introject something good from the containing process of being supported to acknowledge her confused and painful feelings, have this held and expressed back in a manageable form. She also seemed, in doing this, to have reached a point where I as the 'psychologist mother' was both a hated and a liked person, as a whole. This is reminiscent of the depressive position and shows growth on the client's part.

As one can see from the above, a psychoanalytic approach to development can provide a window into the past which helps make sense of the present, and can allow one to think about possibilities for the future. As an EP, reflection on development and behaviour within the context of adolescence, underpinned by a psychoanalytic approach, highlighted the unconscious processes that came to play in Mary's interaction and behaviour, along with the feelings she brought out in adults around her.

Conclusion

The application of psychoanalytic concepts within educational psychology practice, education and learning is described throughout this chapter. Increased understanding and change are described through specific casework examples and add to the practice-based evidence literature. Evidence-based practice, however, cannot be forgotten, and Eloquin (2016) also highlights the importance, when hypothesising, of making use of other data, including interviews and observations, alongside emotional data. In light of this, the importance of supervision and reflection cannot be understated, with Eloquin capturing the importance of a thoughtful and curious space whereby inviting reflection from all forms a cornerstone. Indeed, theoretical knowledge, reflection, engagement with (and deeper awareness of) emotions, both of oneself and of the client, can be applied in all our work – giving a different perspective of the journey.

When one considers the varied applications of psychoanalytic concepts, opportunities abound for EPs in working as a consultant, with a psychoanalytic eye and ear. The role for EPs here, not only in relation to knowledge of systems approaches, but also through knowledge and application of psychodynamic processes as described, can change understanding, interaction and interventions, supporting a system to develop the reflective function of staff, manage feelings and thoughts, and recognise – as described by Billington (2006) – the 'umbilical connection' between learning and emotion.

CHAPTER 3

Thinking matters: how can Bion's theory of thinking help educational psychologists think about the task of formulation?

Kay Richards

That thinking would be of interest to psychologists is, perhaps, no surprise. As educational psychologists (EPs), ostensibly we spend much of our time engaged in thinking about other people's thinking given our involvement in the complex tangle of roles and relationships with ourselves, each other, our clients and the systems in which we live and work. When requests for involvement come our way, a great deal of thinking has usually already occurred. Yet what we're often asked for – and, as psychologists, are perhaps uniquely able to offer – is a different kind of thinking which results in a formulation or hypothesis about a situation, sometimes referred to as 'the psychology' of our work. But what does it mean for us and our clients (usually parents, children and members of school staff) when thoughts about the situations clients find themselves in encounter our professional minds? What follows in this chapter are some thoughts about this question, using Bion's (1962a) theory of thinking as a guide.

I believe that communication between people is both heard and, fundamentally, felt. Alongside what is articulated to us verbally, further communications find their way into our work that are hidden from view, but at times make themselves known in how we feel about our work. Over the years, I have wondered how this dynamic may play into the link between ourselves as practitioners and our clients in the context of one of our main roles: to help make sense of other people's thinking in our hypotheses and formulations. In this chapter I aim to describe how I have thought about this dynamic, using Bion's (1962a) theory of thinking as a grounding for exploration within the context of formulation or hypothesising about the needs of children, their schools, families and carers. There are undoubtedly tensions to be acknowledged in working as an EP in a transparent way, while also exploring and focusing on these communications to develop my own thinking about the work that I do, as well as considering my own professional growth and development. Consequently, there is a further question we might ask. What are the resulting issues to consider if we are open to working in this way?

This chapter started life, as much writing does, as a half-formed thought; a sense of something intriguing but unexplored. For me this was repeatedly met with a feeling of frustration from attempting, and failing, to catch traces of early ideas in motion. As anyone who has tried to write will know, half-formed thoughts are as dust in air, and they do not stand still to catch hold of for long. Nevertheless, what has returned is the sense that at its core psychological formulation links thoughts between two thinkers; our own and our clients'. While developing my own thoughts about formulation in the context of Bion's theory of thinking (1962a) I've experienced that feeling many times. However, now I've come to understand it as speaking to something of the experience of thoughts and thinking that the theory itself offers. This chapter offers the possibility of engagement with this theory. It doesn't offer any firm conclusions, but rather poses some questions and considers what it is like to sit with the ideas that reading the text prompts. Finally, it explores where these ideas have taken me in my practice as an EP.

Bion's theory of thinking

Reading Bion's writing is like running on sand. It feels like you're not getting very far and after a while you start to wonder if it is worth the effort at all. But, like running and similar activities that challenge and exert us, there's ultimately something to be gained from putting one foot in front of the other to see where you might end up. It is not within the scope of this chapter to give a detailed summary of the theory and there are, as I hope the reader will come to appreciate, persuasive reasons not to do so. However, if some key ideas are offered, it might help elucidate the treatment of the theory in the context of thinking about formulation.

In attempting to define the development of thinking, Bion (1962a) describes two interrelated developmental phenomena: the thoughts themselves; and the 'apparatus' to cope with them, which he terms 'thinking' (p. 111). Bion (1962a) offers a description of 'thoughts' as realised when 'pre-conceptions' meet with a 'realisation' (p. 111). In psychoanalytic terms, Bion (1962a) describes that this is best viewed as analogous with the philosopher Kant's notion of an 'empty thought', whereby the mind processes sense data, but also creates intuition and drives. The empty thought in Bion's (1962a) theory is therefore the baby's innate expectation of a breast from birth. Upon receiving the breast, the empty pre-conception has been met with its expected realisation and the result is a conception of the breast itself as a concept that can be known. However, the advent of thinking is different and develops when a pre-conception is met, not with its expected realisation but with frustration, which the baby has to manage. Bion (1962a) details that babies who are able to tolerate the frustration of an absent breast are able to modify their frustration so that the absence becomes a thought in its own right, which enables the baby to develop a capacity for thinking and, ultimately, learning. Infants who are unable to modify frustration in this way risk a limited capacity to develop thinking and may come to depend upon a negative form of knowing driven by omnipotence.

Bion (1962a) recognises Klein's (1959) concept of projective identification as vital to this early capacity for thought. An attuned mother who is able to cope with the primitive projections of sensation and confusion can modify these frightening 'beta' elements (p. 115) so that they can be internalised and made tolerable for the baby. Bion (1962a) proposes that the development of an 'alpha-function' (p. 115) occurs between mothers and babies in healthy relationships where the baby's projections are tolerably returned to them. It is this alpha-function that enables the mass of sensations which overtake babies to be converted into useful 'alpha-elements' (p. 116) that are available to infants as a platform for thought. Waddell (2002) describes this phenomenon as the mother 'actively holding the baby's mental state' (p. 37) and in doing so she creates and develops a capacity for thinking. Thinking in Bion's (1962a) theory is therefore a dynamic process, the origin of which is found in the deeply connected emotional experience between mother and child, and which paves the way for the growth of the baby's capacity to think as he or she develops.

In *Learning from Experience*, Bion (1962b) further clarifies the relationship between mother and baby, offering a description of the 'contained' nature of the projection within the mother, or 'container' (p. 90). The symbiotic relationship between mother and infant within the 'container–contained' dynamic is described as creating growth for both the mother and baby, and through this repeated experience the baby learns to internalise the experience of his or her distress being engaged with and develops a capacity for managing frustration. Fundamentally, it is through this emotional connection between the mother and baby that Bion (1962b) locates the genesis of thinking as born from the attuned relationship between mother and baby, rather than a singular process that the baby develops alone (O'Shaughnessy, 1981).

Formulation as a core skill for EPs

At its heart, Bion's theory describes thinking as a dynamic and emotional experience between two minds, and this speaks to the core function of psychological formulation as a process of sense making between a psychologist and a client (Johnstone, 2014). Formulation is one of the pillars of practice as a psychologist, regardless of theoretical orientation or practice framework. The British Psychological Society (BPS, 2017) highlights formulation as one of five 'core skills': assessment, formulation, intervention, evaluation and communication in the guidelines for practising psychologists, regardless of the professional context or division in which they work (p. 9). Formulation is defined as a summary of the client's needs. It is integrative and rooted in psychological theory that guides future planning of options and interventions. The Health and Care Professions Council's *Standards of Proficiency* (HCPC, 2015) refer to formulation in eight standards for practitioner psychologists, and two specific to the work of EPs. There is particular guidance for EP doctoral training courses in England, Northern Ireland and Wales, which specifies the integrative and collaborative formulation skills that trainees are expected to demonstrate by the end of their training courses (BPS, 2010). Although not aimed specifically at EPs, the British Psychological Society published *Good Practice Guidelines on the Use of Psychological Formulation* in December 2011 (Division of Education and Child Psychology). These guidelines are aimed at clinical psychologists and explain that formulation can be conceptualised as both 'an event and a process' (p. 2), with the emphasis placed on the meaning making of the individual or consultee, which is constructed in collaboration with professionals. Across these documents – which both guide the practice of psychologists and hold it to account – emphasis is placed on the link of formulation, psychological theory, the psychologist and the client in crafting a story of the situation in which the client finds him- or herself. Since the publication of these best-practice guidelines, a further significant document has also been published: *The Power Threat Meaning Framework* (Johnstone and Boyle, 2018), which places the psychologist squarely in the foreground of collaborative meaning making through formulation constructed with clients.

It prompts the question, then, that if our professional guidance positions thinking with (rather than about) our clients as a fundamental part of the service we offer, what does formulation look like in educational psychology practice? Within this, we also need to ask what expectations service users might have of the 'psychology' of our work and how we can use our understanding of thinking in relationships to develop meaningful formulations that offer something useful to our clients.

Formulation within executive practice frameworks for educational psychology

Educational psychology practice has developed 'executive practice frameworks' to support practitioners to think about coherent ways in which psychological theory can be applied in complex problem situations (Kelly, 2008). Although it is not the purpose of this chapter to analyse these in detail, the most well-known among EPs are perhaps the Problem-Analysis Framework (Monsen, Graham, Frederickson and Cameron, 1998) and the Constructionist Model of Informed and Reasoned Action (COMOIRA) (Gameson, Rhydderch, Ellis and Carroll, 2003). Available for use with different theoretical perspectives, a cornerstone of executive practice frameworks is the mapped route they offer, enabling EPs to approach the diversity and complexity of initial problems systematically, and in a way that leads to robust and evidenced formulations and interventions (Annan *et al.*, 2013; Wicks, 2013). Practice frameworks have much to offer educational psychology practice, arguably due to the clarity of their steps, which offer a secure route through the murky problems we are so often given to think about. In some sense they encourage us, as practitioners, to leave no stone unturned. But I often find myself wondering about those stones we don't see, but nevertheless might detect in our shoes as we are working with, and walking through, problem situations with our clients. Practice frameworks afford a degree of visibility to our processes that arguably supports critical evaluation on the part of both the EP and his or her consultees (Annan *et al.*, 2013). However, if we agree that there is a relationship within which we relate to our clients, and a core part of our role is to think with them about their experiences in the context of this relationship, we also need to think about how our interactions operate. In thinking about our working relationship from a psychoanalytic perspective, then surely we also need to consider the possibility of dynamics between us and our clients that might get in the way of the formulations we are able to construct.

Consultation as a constructivist endeavour

Consultation is a widespread model of educational psychology service delivery that aims to facilitate joint problem solving between EPs and consultees and is a key part of executive practice frameworks. Although no singular definition of consultation exists, it is frequently described across literature in educational psychology practice as a collaborative model involving two or more individuals who come to work together to create change in relation to a perceived concern regarding a service user or client, often a child or young person (Wagner, 2000; Sandoval, 2014). Consultation is inflected with a constructivist epistemology which describes the world as dependent upon our own view, which is itself dependent upon our interactions with our environments and situated in a historical and cultural context (Denicolo, Long and Bradley-Cole, 2016). Consultees, usually parents and school staff members, tend to arrive at consultation meetings with both a problem (as they see it) and a hope that by the end of their involvement with an EP some way of managing the problem will be found. Even consultees who arrive to consultation meetings stating 'I have no idea what is going on' do have ideas, but they are often disparate and difficult to hold onto, leaving the consultee feeling that there is nothing coherent for him or her to build upon.

We could say that for a consultee entering into a consultation with an EP the 'problem' is a painting with any number of contributing elements, and that, depending upon their view, it may feel elusive, abstract or incomplete. Enclosing the painting is the picture frame representing the consultee's view of the world and, therefore, their understanding of the problem. Our role as EPs is to relate to our consultees in a way that enables us to look together at the problem, and its frame, and bring together a formulation that offers a way forward. Practice frameworks acknowledge that all involved will have a perspective on the initial problem, including what and who might be helpful (Annan *et al.*, 2013). Sometimes this is clearly articulated, including the extent to which they think the practitioner might be helpful, which may depend upon prior experiences, such as the consultee's past involvement with services, beliefs about education, interactions with other professionals and the extent to which a person feels able and ready to engage in a helping relationship. I argue that not only does the consultee have a perspective on the problem, but, arguably, also on the role of the practitioner involved and the extent to which they might be helpful, and that this network of relationships is brought to the EP within the context of the problem. Some of these hopes, beliefs, fears and concerns about entering into the working relationship are communicated outside of conscious awareness but nevertheless get inside professional relationships and can affect how the practitioner and consultee can relate to each other. Described as transference and countertransference in the psychoanalytic literature, Gillian Ruch (2018) writes about this dynamic in the context of contemporary social work practice, and notes:

> *These deeper levels of communication mean thinking about the process as much as the content of interactions, and often involve trying to make sense of the tensions between the surface and the depths, and the intertwining between feelings associated with the past and the present, as well as the ways in which these tensions can influence or distort our behaviour and experience.* (p. 42)

Making the link

Sandoval (2011) describes how, within the process of consultation, there is opportunity for growth for both the consultee and the consultant, who learns not only about the world view of the client but also what it is to be human. The consultee enters the consultation with a pre-conceived story about the issue which is rooted in their interactions and experiences, and the consultant's job is to explore this with the consultee to see how the story fits together, what theories about the situation it depends on, and where in the story there are gaps where the story doesn't make sense for the client. As EPs working in consultation, it is our role to find these narrative cracks and open them up to new ideas and thoughts. In returning to Bion's (1962a) theory, we could perhaps think of these fissures in the story as pre-conceptions that meet with absence. The consultant's role in formulation is to think with the consultee to enable the frustration that accompanies these incomplete thought traces to be verbalised and explored, in the hope that, together, a story can be formulated that throws light on the dissonance. This shift from something frustrating to something that can be explored and tolerated is crucial. These are the links that (perhaps) on their own the consultee hasn't yet made, but with the support of the EP is able to explore.

Linking the divergent pieces in the space that is found within these two minds seems indicative of the acceptance, emotional holding, active exploring and sense making that Bion's (1962a) theory has at its heart. Thinking in Bion's writing is, therefore, dependent upon a relationship where sensations are modified into something that can be tolerated, but this is not a process taking place in the mind of one individual alone. There needs to be another person with the capacity to attune, receive and tolerate the tangle of senses that can't be managed, and to modify and return them so that they can be taken in (Waddell, 2002). It is the links between pre-conceptions and their realisations that both satisfy and frustrate, and a capacity to manage frustration, that are fundamental to thinking, learning and growth.

At this point, it may be helpful to consider the chapter's key message through a case study, which highlights how the theory helped me to make sense of a difficult consultation and how thinking about it supported my formulation.

Case study

Of the many cases I have been involved in, this one stays in my mind. It was a situation where I felt my own thinking challenged by feelings so strong that they seemed to seep into my ability to take up my role and to formulate an understanding of a young person's needs.

I received a request for a consultation meeting regarding a young person who had been permanently excluded from a secondary school. Despite the exclusion, the young person was subsequently reinstated after a meeting of the school governors, who felt that the exclusion couldn't be upheld. I suspected this would be a difficult meeting and was warned by school staff that the family had completely lost trust in the school and the local authority. Similarly, some members of staff at the school felt strongly that the decision to reinstate the young person was not the best outcome for anyone involved.

The meeting felt long and draining. I had never met the family before, yet soon felt their powerful distrust in my role as an employee of the local authority, the organisation they believed to be responsible for the failure of proper processes, which had resulted in the young person's needs not being recognised. I soon felt under attack by the parent. She had memorised exact dates, which she fired at both me and the SENCo (Special Educational Needs Coordinator) to evidence when and where the school had failed the young person, misled the family or misreported situations. I felt overwhelmed, intimidated and unable to think. It was difficult to retain a space for thought in the face of such powerful feelings and I caught myself imagining a police interview. I felt defensive and as though I had to justify my presence, my role and my competence to carry it out. I have since come to think of these feelings as intense projections from the family of their distress, which I became overly identified with. I felt that my only option was to try to reflect back what I'd heard, recognising the emotional impact the situation had on the family and the distress they had experienced. I tentatively wondered if the parent had memorised the dates because this was perhaps the only way she could think about such a difficult situation and gain some sense of control over it. Relenting slightly, the parents agreed with this, describing how she had to hold it together like this, otherwise they'd all be lost. I found this a very powerful description and offered that, in hearing this description, I could feel something of the family's feelings of sadness, loss, anger and distrust. I now wonder if being able to name these feelings signalled my capacity to cope with the anxiety, confusion and frustration from the parent and to offer some initial ways of connecting the emotions. The remainder of the meeting was difficult and it seemed impossible to focus on the future until the parent's feelings had been voiced. However, next time I met with the parent at the school we were able to come to a point of thinking about what the family wanted for the young person and what she needed from the school to enable this to happen. Together, we were able to write some 'future hopes' to reflect this and agreed on a further meeting in school to discuss next steps.

What could we say about this situation? In the moment, I can certainly remember feeling that something had overtaken my capacity to retain a grip on my own sense of myself as a professional and I felt preoccupied with the guilt, shame and incompetence that the encounter had left me with. In writing about Bion's (1962a) theory of thinking, Edna O'Shaughnessy (1981) reflects that, at its heart, Bion presents thinking as a 'human link' (p. 181) and through this link another mind (the mother, in Bion's writing) is able to 'pay attention, to try to understand' (p. 182). This speaks to my experience of this consultation, where it was so difficult to think, but in the face of strong emotions it is the attempt to engage that remains important. Sandoval (2011) describes that, through the process of consultation, the consultant learns not only about the world view of the client, but also what it is to be human. I've learned that sometimes a situation can't be simply explained, but it is the engagement with the felt emotions in consultations that may provide a way forward and allow thinking to be possible. Sometimes, though, barriers of one kind or another prohibit this kind of reflection on our work and we may displace these feelings elsewhere, perhaps by describing children, parents or carers as 'difficult' or schools as 'unsupportive'.

Linking the theory to ourselves

As EPs, we venture into the unknown and the 'not-yet-thought' each time we attempt to make meaning from another person's experiences, whether this is a child we are working with, a parent or a member of school staff. There are links here to the experience of reading Bion's writing, which is itself an emotional experience. Thomas Ogden (2004) describes the experience of reading *Learning from Experience*, noting that 'What it is to learn from experience (or the inability to do so) will be something for the reader to experience first-hand in the act of reading this book' (p. 286). It is inscrutable, at times frustrating and, Ogden argues, purposefully so. As readers we're knowingly led into a fog which may indeed confuse and frustrate us, with only our own thoughts and connections to find our way out. So why, then, continue? What is there to be gained from the confusion that arises when something unknown is struggled with? Of the attributes ordinarily thought to support effective learning – persistence, creativity, motivation, curiosity, to name but a few – confusion is least likely to be welcomed in. We don't invite it, yet still it arrives, like an unwanted guest at a party that we have to tolerate, hoping it soon gets the message that no one wants it around. Judith Edwards (2015) describes the process of learning (and teaching) Bion's theory where the experience of 'turbulence' signals that there is potential for growth and, by managing the uncertainty in ourselves as readers, the ideas can become 'pegs to hang your thoughts on' (p. 378) as our practice in using the theory develops.

Look before you leap

The central argument of this chapter is that EPs have something to gain from using Bion's (1962a) theory to support the development of their own thoughts about formulation. By doing so, EPs can develop shared meanings in their work and support their own growth. In considering the use of psychoanalysis away from the traditional analytic setting, Frosh (2010) explores the extent to which concepts may throw light upon encounters where 'something happens' (p. 4) and, ostensibly, seems to be suggesting that, if people are interacting in a situated space, there is both an embodied self and a less visible but nevertheless influential 'betweenness' which could be illuminated by psychoanalytic concepts in accounting for what goes on. However, there is also something of a warning offered here, which cautions the risks of using ideas with a focus on a perceived explanatory power where concepts become calcified, masking the fluidity and instability of the dynamics that they help to describe. Frosh suggests that these tensions need not inhibit the application of ideas, as long as reflective consideration of the 'leaps' being made is acknowledged.

If there is a metaphorical and theoretical 'leap' to be made, what lies between for EPs? What might we need to acknowledge when using ideas from this theory to develop our own thoughts about formulation? One consideration might be how, as EPs, we can remain focused upon the dynamic nature of formulation as an evolving narrative which offers the necessary flexibility that the guidance cited earlier indicates, but recognising the pressures and challenges of the context in which many EPs work. With a continued role in statutory assessments of young people's needs – which have increased year on year since 2010, and an 11 per cent increase seen since January 2018 (Department for Education, 2019) – EPs face continuing pressures that impact on how they are able to carry out their role. A possible driver that poses a 'risk' in the context of uncertain financial contexts in schools is a desire for certainty for young people and those who support them, by way of a detailed and legally enforceable identification of needs provided by the statutory assessment process. So how do EPs who wish to use these dynamic ideas work with the tentative and shifting nature of the unconscious, on the one hand, and the prescriptive certainty offered by the processes implicated in their working practices, on the other? There is potential for our theoretical legs to be overstretched in the possibility that we may become tourists, who take in the main conceptual landmarks of Bion's complex theory without spending time experiencing the benefits of getting lost and finding our own meaning, as Ogden (2004) suggests. Claudio Neri (2015) similarly describes this risk, using the metaphor of a theoretical 'slogan' (p. 18), that well-meaning practitioners might adhere to their practice in a way that denudes the ideas of meaning.

As EPs, what responsibility are we left with, then, and how might we go about achieving a balance that feels authentic to us and, fundamentally, purposeful for the people we work with in our roles? Collaboration with clients doesn't necessarily mean that there's a balance, and, as Newman and Rosenfeld (2019) highlight, the factors affecting equilibrium in a helping relationship are complex. The idea of exploring what might lie between the consultant and the client, the EP and his or her thoughts is, I think, vital if we are to surface and manage the 'leap'. We cannot ignore that when we are professionally involved with the lives of other people – whether they are children, parents, carers, members of school staff or colleagues – we are relating to them for the time of our involvement and, perhaps, in their (and our) minds for some time thereafter. This is at the heart of our work and if formulation links our thinking as psychologists to the thinking of our clients in joint aims to understand, untangle and make sense, there needs to be further thinking in our profession regarding what this actually means for us.

EPs who have been trained in different theoretical approaches and may be curious about the use of psychoanalytic concepts in their work can access supervision, peer support, reading groups or further training to find out more. The current publication will hopefully go some way to supporting this, yet over the years I have found that the ideas described here only really become catalysts for my own thoughts when they are shared with another's mind through supervision and discussion, and in this way in my own practice I am able to guard against stretching the ideas too far. Perhaps we might look to other disciplines, social work practice being one, where the tension between using psychoanalytic thinking and the 'leaps' involved in doing so have been more broadly explored to take our lead.

CHAPTER 4

What's yours and what's theirs? Understanding projection, transference and countertransference in educational psychology practice

Gemma Ellis

- What happens when you feel someone is expecting something of you in a meeting that you were not expecting?
- How does that make you feel?
- Have you ever left a meeting not feeling the same as when you went in?
- What can you do about it?

This chapter will explore these questions in relation to the psychoanalytic concepts of projection, transference and countertransference (as well as introducing parallel process and projective identification). This way of thinking can help psychologists to make sense of the work that they do and the impact it has on them. It is the intention of this chapter to conceptualise each concept in relation to educational psychology (EP) practice. This means that illustrations are presented as if in a situation where it would be easy to see which concept is at play and define it. However, as we know from EP work, nothing is quite so straightforward. We are complex human beings with our own 'stuff' – which influences how we feel and behave on each given day. In the EP role, we (as ourselves in role) are the key tool to the job. However, we are also working with other human beings with all their 'stuff' going on – the parents/carers, the children/young people, the teachers/teaching assistants/special needs coordinators and other staff. They all have their own stories, those that they share with us and those they do not (those that they are conscious of and those that they are not). It is always a muddle. Using several short case studies, this chapter will present each concept and its relationship to EP practice with slightly less muddle, while acknowledging this is not how interactions always work.

Sigmund Freud elevated pre-existing descriptions of the unconscious, highlighting its importance in understanding how people function. As Trowell describes in her explanation of key psychoanalytic concepts:

> *The unconscious reveals its existence in our dreams and in all the slips and mistakes we make, in which our real thoughts or wishes emerge. Experiences that are unacceptable to ourselves or in the social world are located in the unconscious and kept there by a censoring process … When these thoughts are too conflicting, anxiety takes over and to protect ourselves, people use 'coping mechanisms or defences'.* (Trowell, 1995, pp. 12–13)

The concepts discussed within this chapter are all unconscious defences, used as a way to cope with feelings and thoughts. Projection is the expulsion from the self of feelings and qualities unacknowledged by the subject and so located in another person or thing. Early theorists saw projection as a phenomenon associated with transference, where the patient transfers their past experiences, conflicts and trauma into the relationship with the practitioner; later developments on transference saw it as a re-enactment which led to an understanding that such re-enactments in children were not from the far-gone past, but from phantasies linked to their immediate present (Klein, 1959). Similarly, countertransference is generally understood as including the whole of the psychotherapist's unconscious reactions to the person they are seeing, rather than limiting it to the unconscious processes evoked in the psychotherapist by the patient's transference.

Either way, feelings in the practitioner can give a good indication of the other person's state of mind. These unconscious dynamics are usually present in one form or another in EP work – sometimes they can help, and at other times hinder, the interactions and the work that we do.

This chapter is based on the understanding that by bringing these unconscious dynamics to light and developing our sense of self we will be more reflective practitioners with an awareness of ourselves and others. This is the idea of 'using ourselves', as explored by Andrew Cooper in his work. As he says, 'concepts like transference, countertransference, projection, and splitting can seem daunting, but they describe powerful processes that will destabilize our best intentions to practise effectively if we cannot track them and work with them as they are occurring' (Cooper, 2018, p. 19).

Projection in EP practice

By projecting oneself or part of one's impulses and feelings into another person, an identification with that person is achieved ... [with projection] the identification is based on attributing to the other person some of one's own qualities. Projection has many repercussions. We are inclined to attribute to other people – in a sense, to put into them – some of our own emotions and thoughts; and it is obvious that it will depend on how balanced or persecuted we are whether this projection is of a friendly or of a hostile nature. (Klein, 1959, p. 295)

Projections are a common defence mechanism that people use when they feel overwhelmed with the feelings that they have. As an EP, we encounter projections regularly in our interactions with those we work with – if we are able to recognise them as that. As we present ourselves 'in role' as a professional psychologist, we can be seen as a blank slate onto which a variety of emotions can be presented.

Case study 1: Melanie and Becca

Melanie walked into Ryland School to meet with Becca, a young person who was struggling to engage in lessons. As she walked in, the girl slumped further down in her seat and said, 'Oh, another person who hates me and thinks I'm stupid.'

This is a common response, particularly from adolescents with whom we work. In this case, Becca may have been feeling overwhelmed with her feelings of anger towards the adults around her. She then projected those out to Melanie, stating that it was Melanie who hated her and was judging her. How aware Melanie is of using herself in role will depend on how she reacts and interacts with Becca after that comment.

A common response when we are called into schools is feeling that we have been placed in the role of the 'expert', the one who knows. This idealised projective phantasy can set us up in an impossible position where nothing that we offer will be the 'solution' that the 'expert' can or could give. This can often be felt alongside feelings of uselessness and inadequacy.

Case study 2: Jessie

Jessie was feeling stuck. She was trying to contract a piece of work with a school to help them to think about strategies to support an 8-year-old, non-verbal pupil to stop screaming and scratching themselves. She had looked at the referral information and had an initial meeting with the parents and the teaching assistant. When she walked out, she felt completely inadequate; she could not think of anything that could be offered. During supervision, she was able to think about how helpless and hopeless the school and parents felt with this situation. Jessie realised she had been placed in a position to 'fix' and 'answer' the 'problem' of these behaviours and that she was then left feeling that was impossible. Indeed, it was impossible to 'fix' this pupil, and during supervision she was able to think of the skills and strategies that she had to offer some advice about support in the classroom, as well as providing a space to talk about the emotional grief and despair that occurs from working with children/young people with profound and complex needs.

Case study 3: David

David was facilitating a discussion group about Eddy, a child in one of his primary schools. The child had considerable attachment needs and could be aggressive in his interactions with staff. The staff group were struggling to know how best to meet his needs. The teacher and special educational needs and disability coordinator (SENDCo) had wanted him to carry out an individual cognitive assessment with the child, but he had felt that a number of group discussions with the staff would be more helpful to the child and the school. He walked into the room and was pleased with himself for remembering to bring biscuits, as it was an after-school session. Everyone sat down and he handed around the biscuits. The first teaching assistant looked at him and the group, and said, 'We would really rather have fruit.' David felt silly suddenly and wondered how he could have got it so wrong. As the discussion progressed, David continued to feel stuck and helpless with the situation, struggling to feel that he was contributing anything helpful and doubting his decision to not carry out a cognitive assessment. He left the meeting with a terrible headache. In between that session and the next discussion group, David had supervision and fortunately his supervisor was trained in relationship/reflective supervision and was able to think with David about what might have been happening in the group. In the next session, David was able to 'wonder aloud' to the group and share some of his ideas as to what might have been happening. He talked about the range of feelings that working with children like Eddy can provoke and how sometimes they can feel overwhelming and difficult to acknowledge. The feeling within the group shifted at this point and the members began to talk about feeling angry with Eddy when he hurt them and then feeling guilty and sad for him. They said that they had felt David just didn't understand what it was like, and they had wanted answers for what to do, not biscuits. David was able to think with the group about the feelings they had and acknowledge them and hear them. They had projected their feelings of anger and incompetence and uncertainty on to David, leaving him with a terrible headache.

It is not uncommon within a group that we are presented with a minor issue such as the snacks, or car parking, which become the focus for all of the irritations or tensions or anxieties the group are holding. Group dynamics are complex, and defence mechanisms including those discussed in this chapter can be heightened in groups. By thinking with the group, David was able to allow and acknowledge the feelings that can be provoked when working with children with additional needs. In a group, you are trying to make sense of a variety of individual defence mechanisms, as well as how groups can work together (unconsciously) to make sense of what is happening in and out of the room.

Transference in EP practice

The way we can be made to feel by someone can be linked to what they have transferred onto us from their own unconscious. As Trowell highlights, '[Freud] described how our conflicts, feelings and expectations linked to past experiences of significant figures could be transferred on to other people in our lives – *the transference*' (1995, p. 14, emphasis added).

Using the quote above might help us to create a slightly clearer understanding of the difference between projection and transference if we think about generally projecting feelings on to other people, and with transference we are transferring specific feelings we have about someone else from the past on to this new person in the present.

Case study 4: Sunita

> Sunita was in a meeting with [15-year-old] Zain's mother and Zain's head of year [who was also the maths teacher]. Sunita felt the meeting was productive as they discussed what support could be put in place, but when she looked around, she noticed the mother had physically shrunk back in her chair and was looking upset. She asked the mother if she would like some water and a minute to think about what was being discussed. The head of year left the room to get the water and the mother turned to Sunita and said, 'Did you see how much they don't like Zain and think he's naughty and will never pass any exams? They just want him to fail, I know that.' Sunita was surprised, as this was not how

she had taken the meeting. She wondered what else might be happening for the mother when the mother said, 'It's just like what happened to me at school. I found maths difficult and no one ever supported me.' Sunita realised that the mother had transferred her experience of a maths teacher in the past on to the head of year in the meeting and was experiencing the staff in the school as she had experienced them when she was at school. Through not processing her own experience of school, it was taking over that of her son. Sunita was able to carefully explore this with the mother over subsequent sessions, which allowed a space to think about Zain's own needs in the present as separate from his mother's from the past.

Sunita's experience is not uncommon. We are often working with a child or young person as the 'focus' and, of course, this means working with all the adults around them. These adults will have had their own experiences with schools when they were children, which are then reactivated when they have to be back in the school meeting the EP. Greenson (1967) highlights the role of people from the past in transference: 'The experiencing of feelings, drives, attitudes, fantasies and defences towards a person in the present which do not befit the person but are a repetition of reactions originating in regard to significant persons of early childhood, unconsciously displaced on to figures in the present' (Greenson, 1967, quoted in Mattinson, 1975, p. 33).

Countertransference in EP practice

Countertransference is a development of the concept of transference. As Trowell highlights, 'Freud also experienced the countertransference: that is, he became aware that his patients were stirring up inside him feelings, reactions and thoughts from his own background' (Trowell, 1995, p. 14).

Case study 5: Donna

During a piece of work with a parent to focus on her interactions and relationship with her child, Donna, the EP, found herself noticing a lot of negativity. Through reflection, Donna was curious about whether the mother was projecting her feelings of discomfort on to her child and therefore finding it hard to like her own daughter. In response, Donna found herself really disliking the mother and worked hard in supervision to explore this. She thought carefully about whether the countertransference feelings she was having were picked up from the mother and child relationship or from her own background. Donna's supervisor was a trained psychotherapist and psychologist and asked Donna some curious questions, to think about her own childhood. Donna was able to reflect that her relationship with her mother had been fraught with negativity and that this had been stirred up again in the interaction at work.

As Donna's example highlights, it is essential that we have a clear knowledge of ourselves before we step into our role. In order to understand what is 'their stuff' we have to know what is 'our stuff'. If we can be aware of these feelings, we can become more effective and helpful in our work.

Being aware of countertransference highlights the power of the projections to which the analyst is exposed. The more disturbed the patient, the more pressure there may be on the analyst to identify with the patient's projections and be pulled into action, losing his capacity for containment ... Countertransference is, in fact, the tool with which one knows what is to be contained. (Box, Copley, Magagna and Moustaki, 1981, p. 163)

Parallel process and projective identification

Before ending this chapter, it feels helpful also to briefly explore two further associated concepts. Parallel process is a concept introduced by Searles (1955/1965), and describes the dynamics that he saw being displayed during supervision with therapists. He found that difficulties that the therapist had worked through with the patient were then replayed in the supervision session. It was a development from the idea of the countertransference; Searles' (1955/1965) concept of parallel process was an expansion of the patient/therapist dyad. He noted that aspects of the patient–therapist relationship emerged as a re-enactment in the dynamics in supervision.

Case study 6: Sarah and Ben

Sarah had spent the morning in a nursery with a child who had been exposed to domestic abuse from birth and recently been placed into foster care. When Sarah arrived into supervision late, she could not find the notes she had made and proceeded to empty her bag all over the table, feeling more and more stressed that she could not find what she was looking for. As she tried to then describe the visit in the morning, it was hard for Ben (her supervisor) to find a flow and a thread to what she was talking about. The narrative jumped around from different cases to different settings and issues, and it was hard to pinpoint what Sarah wanted to talk about and how to best support her. Sarah felt that Ben didn't want her to be there and she was a burden to him and had failed in supervision. She said, 'Oh you've probably got better things to be doing and don't want to see me today, anyway.' Ben asked Sarah if she felt that she was recreating some of what she had witnessed that morning. Sarah instantly felt calmer and realised that she had been holding on to all the distress and mania she had observed, and acting it out in the supervisory relationship.

Another form of unconscious process is that of projective identification. This concept is a complex one, and for the purposes of this discussion Bion's (1959, 1984) development of the idea is highlighted. In this understanding it may be seen as a mode of projection where the analyst acts as 'a container for the patient's intolerable experiences' (Hinshelwood, 1991, p. 256). An example of this form of projective identification would be when a teacher finds him- or herself feeling hopeless and overwhelmed when working with a pupil, and where this feeling does not link to the teacher's life. The projection is identified with and acted out by the person who has received it. This is when we feel 'taken over' by a feeling that does not relate to our own lives or how we might have felt before. Cooper explains projective identification as a situation 'In which one person succeeds in exporting a state of mind more or less directly into someone else who then comes to experience this state of mind as his own while simultaneously being aware that something has ambushed him internally' (Cooper, 2018, p. 24).

Case study 7: Sasha

Sasha had just picked up the phone to one of her SENDCos, who was demanding that Sasha come in immediately. The SENDCo told her a parent was being very aggressive and they must have the child assessed immediately, as there was to be a meeting about the child in two weeks' time. Sasha said that she was not able to get into the school and provide written feedback within that time. She found herself unable to structure her thoughts enough to think with the school about other ways of working. After the phone call she was left feeling stressed, incompetent and confused. When she made it into the school the following week, she met with the 'aggressive' parent and found the parent was very anxious about how the child was presenting and told Sasha that a close relative was poorly and she had recently been made redundant. She told Sasha that she felt that the school were not giving her the time she needed to explain everything that was happening at home. The parent's anxiety had been translated into aggression, which in turn had been transferred on to Sasha, leaving her feeling anxious, stressed and incompetent.

This case study demonstrates the projective identification experienced by Sasha in terms of taking on the anxiety of the school and the parent as her own feelings and acting them out in her behaviour (not being able to think, feeling incompetent). It also highlights how one unconscious communication can be read as another when we do not take the time to understand and hear someone (and to know and use ourselves). Sasha's SENDCo had labelled this parent as aggressive as opposed to anxious. This is not an uncommon 'misreading', particularly among children/ young people and parents we work with. See the work of Winnicott (1982) for more on how anxiety can present as aggression.

It is therefore helpful to make sense:

of the experience we all share when for no obvious reason in our-
selves we find that we are thinking, feeling or doing something
which is not how we ourselves were before the meeting. When we
become angry or enraged or depressed or hopeless and yet a little
while before we were all right, it is helpful to consider 'Am I in touch
with something the other person is communicating unconsciously.'
(Trowell, 1995, p. 20)

Projective identification links to the work of Klein on splitting. This is where the 'good' and the 'bad' are split off from each other. When such splitting is put on to someone else, that is where projective identification comes in. This process is clarified by Mollon: 'According to Bion, the child's transmission of anxiety is by projective identification – a process that Klein described as a phantasy of locating part of the self in the object, but which Bion elaborated as an actual communication' (Mollon, 2002, p. 68).

Another way in which we see these unconscious processes of projective identification and splitting is when we work with children and young people who may 'hold' all of the negative feelings and are 'bad' in order to keep their parent or teacher as the 'good' object. This idealised view of the teacher is not sustainable or realistic and can create difficult dynamics for the teacher to understand.

What can we do with all this?

Having a clear understanding of what is ours and what is not in any given situation will help us to make better sense of what might be happening in an interaction. When we end an interaction feeling something that we do not feel is ours, we can use that understanding to help make sense of what might be happening unconsciously for the other person. The defence mechanisms that we have explored in this chapter provide a way of highlighting the internal conflicts and difficulties of those with whom we work (and, indeed, in ourselves). By better understanding these mechanisms, we can open further hypotheses about what might be happening for those we work with. If you feel confident doing so, and feel it would be helpful, you could name what you think is happening in an interaction and then explore that together within the consultation. However, this is not always appropriate, and sometimes just having an awareness of the dynamics can be more powerful to the work:

> *Understanding something about the transference relationship does not meant that the … worker always needs to interpret this to the client. In many situations an interpretation is quite inappropriate and a lot of good casework is done when the transference is never actually mentioned. But it is probably helpful to the worker to know quite clearly in his own mind when a client is displaying a strong transference reaction, and when he is not. If he fails to do this, he will grossly underestimate the reactions, feelings and fantasies of those clients who are operating on this basis.* (Mattinson, 1975, p. 34)

Not only is it important that we as practitioners have an ability to understand ourselves, and therefore what is not 'ours', but also it is important to have this understanding in our own supervisory relationships. Therefore, in supervision it is vital that there is reflection on practice and what might be being played out in the interactions we have in our work role.

Defences are a way of managing and help us to cope in the world. They are not to be judged or seen as a 'problem' if we can understand them and use them to help those we work with. The more that there are clear systems in place and we are clear about our role and the purpose of our task in any given work situation, the clearer we can be about what might be happening in these situations. Mattinson, in her work on the reflection process in supervision, talks about boundaries, and understanding and creating one's own boundary when working with others (Mattinson, 1975). If we, in our role, cannot hold onto the unconscious thoughts and feelings we are picking up and effectively make sense of it, then we are creating an 'attack on linking' and on our thinking (Bion, 1959, p. 308).

Through recognising who we are and using reflective supervision to support us to understand the 'use of self', we can protect ourselves as well as support our clients:

> *it concerns a capacity for attunement to our emotional experience of ourselves in relation to others, an attunement to the flow of emotional transactions between ourselves and our service*

users and colleagues which are occurring constantly whether we choose to recognize them or not. This is why the use of self is so important ... Equally, understanding how to recognize, track, and make sense of the emotional dynamics that are always alive in our work deepens our practice, improves our performance and our effectiveness and decision making, and helps protect us from the sometimes psychologically damaging impact of the work we do. In other words it is a core professional skill, perhaps the most central skill we need to develop, sustain, and hone. (Cooper, 2018, pp. 19–20)

Bion's concept of containment has been mentioned earlier, and it is central to how we manage to feel supported enough to 'use ourselves' in role, as well as how safe and secure those we work with feel. In Bion's work (1959, 1984), he writes about the container/contained concept. In the first instance, this concept describes the way that the main caregiver holds onto the baby's upsets and frustrations. The caregiver then returns them in a more manageable way when the baby is ready – for example, providing words or reassurance or sustenance for his or her difficulties. To feel contained, therefore, is to feel safe in the knowledge that something or someone else is holding onto the unmanageable (Bion, 1984). As Cooper expands, for us as workers:

The steps involved in the containment process are first emotional receptivity, then tolerance of the suffering and confusion that ensues, and then an effort to think and make sense of these experiences, and finally 'returning' the experiences to their originator in a new form that the person finds 'digestible', meaningful, and helpful. (Cooper, 2018, p. 25)

Containment is something that we offer to those we work with. It is also an aspect of reflective supervision that is essential if we are to better understand the self in role. Having another 'thinking mind' can help us to process and create meaning from the feelings that have been provoked or felt by us (Cooper, 2018, p. 26). It can also be the tone used in supervision as opposed to what is actually being said that can alert one to any unconscious processes and communications and how the supervisee might be feeling about the client (Howell, 1992).

As mentioned in the introduction to this chapter, it is rarely clear or obvious from the way someone presents what they are unconsciously feeling, especially the more they are struggling. Bion describes the way that those we work with can create 'attacks on linking' (Bion, 1959, p. 308). Mollon explains this concept in relation to patients in analysis, and I feel it can also be used to explore our work with a range of 'clients':

> *Some patients may talk endlessly, but in such a way that it is extremely difficult for the analyst to grasp any underlying links between the diverse topics of the narrative. Meaning does not gradually emerge and organize around themes and anxieties, in a way that it does with other patients. There may be a kind of scattering of meaning, so that the analyst's experience is of having to gather together the scraps of dispersed emotional communication and piece them together like fragments of code.* (Mollon, 2002, p. 68)

As EPs, our role includes exploring what is happening 'under the surface' helping to create the linking and thinking between all the 'scatterings of meanings' that we are given (Mollon, 2002, p. 68). As the case studies in this chapter illustrate, we can be deterred from this role with attacks on linking when people feel most psychically vulnerable and defensive. If we are unable to make sense of this, and use ourselves and this awareness in our work, we are missing an entire possibility of connecting and linking the clues that we have been given.

Concluding thoughts

This chapter has explored the concepts of projection, transference and countertransference and how they are relevant to our practice as EPs. Parallel process and projective identification have also been introduced. The idea of understanding and using ourselves in role has been central to the chapter. This way of working can feel outside of conventional models of formulating hypotheses and following known frameworks for 'understanding people'. It is the premise of this chapter that we can improve our practice – and, in turn, the impact we can have on those with whom we work – if we can use the 'information' we are being given through the unconscious communications as well as the conscious ones.

Reflective supervision that includes the utilisation of understanding psychoanalytic concepts and recognising ourselves in role is arguably what makes an EP unique – in how they support people at their most vulnerable and create ways of thinking even where unconscious responses can be 'so powerful that it makes thinking impossible' (Bion, 1978, p. 45).

CHAPTER 5

The classroom-in-the-mind: psychoanalytic reflections on classroom practice

Dale Bartle and Xavier Eloquin

B y one reading, psychoanalysis is the study of emotion as it happens in the moment, arising as it does out of a relationship (Bion, 1962). Emotions are a central constituent of any form of human relating and yet in schools (indeed, in most organisations) the registering of them is curiously absent – or, rather, they are often bizarrely present, colour-coded and alphabetised, caricatured in emoji faces and stuck to a wall somewhere. They are presented as something to be known about in the abstract – out there. It is rare that emotions are recognised in the 'in here' of a direct relationship, and rarer still in the relationship between teacher and student. Instances of emotionality, when they do occur, are often 'problematised' as by-products of behaviour and seen as a disturbance or disruption of the typically expected order of the day. In our view (following Armstrong, 2005), this misses something vitally and essentially human.

This is both a loss and a concern. A loss because the threshing of emotion from the learning context denudes the inner worlds of both teachers and students, hollowing us out to be compliant paper cut-outs in place of humans to better suit the dictates of the school as 'conformatorium'. And it is a concern because emotions are in the context of something and are central to an experiential understanding of the situation. They are a source of information, and to dismiss them as an irrelevance or a burden is to dismiss the possibility of learning about oneself, the other and the link between the two.

In this chapter we want to consider how certain aspects of psycho-analytic theory can deepen the moment-by-moment experience of a teacher, and provide the possibility of greater insight into a pivotal and often neglected relationship: the emotional relating of student and teacher. In particular, we will explore the lived experiences of teachers as they are at work in school. This external world will be thought about in relation to the inner world or, as Armstrong notes, 'a world within a world'. We will introduce the concept of the classroom-in-the-mind and argue that this idea can be helpful in our work and our attempt to connect what is going on 'out there' with our internal experience.

Hatred

A teacher, Tom, working in a therapeutic school for adolescent registered sex offenders, became concerned about his thoughts and feelings when sitting next to a particular student, David, at lunch. In supervision, Tom described violent emotions and images arising in him, while outwardly he sat and ate his lunch. The intensity and repetition of these images led Tom to avoid the boy at all costs and he began to fear that he was a dangerous and violent man, unsuited to teaching.

In supervision, Tom eventually 'confessed' to images of beating the boy to a pulp. With the supervisor he explored his experiences. Did he feel like this at any other time, or with any other student? The answer was 'no', only David. If not originating from the teacher, then what might these experiences be communicating? Together they considered David's life: early rejection by his mother, and then moved from placement to care home and round again countless times. A boy bullied and teased for his physical disabilities, David was then vilified for his horrendous sexual offences. Even staff at the therapeutic unit used to 'target' him with almost invisible everyday cruelties.

A working hypothesis was developed: that David was splitting off and projecting out a high level of self-hatred, which was then picked up by Tom. The thought came: if he made Tom feel like this, what must it be like in his own skin? At this insight Tom experienced a wave of compassion for him. He resolved to seek

> David out at lunch, rather than avoid him, and engage with him in a
> more authentic manner. This he did, and, while difficult, the images
> ceased and a new way of relating – and teaching – developed.

It can be extremely hard to admit to strong negative feelings about
students – even to oneself. In our culture it often can seem that to have a
negative emotion about a child is equivalent to being a bad human being
or wanting to do bad things. Emotions, however, do not just go away,
and such suppression can be deleterious in many ways, from the risk of
burnout (suppression is expensive), to the loss of meaning that such a
denial entails. Emotions are a constituent of the inner world. They do not
manifest without cause, but are there to tell us something about what is
going on: they are a response to external or internal events.

In this example, Tom was able to explore these dark feelings. This
had the effect of offering vital psychological release; he was not a mon-
ster-in-denial, just a human being working with some very damaged and
challenging young people. It also radically altered Tom's view of David: in
supervision he was able to make links between his early years, his dismal
history of care and how, subjectively, the teacher was made to feel in his
compass. With his supervisor they developed a hypothesis that he was
conveying something of what it was like to be him, through a form of
shared emotion – projective identification. Happy people, after all, do not
make other people feel like this.

Typically, when we have an emotion, we tend to act on it. It is not a
'natural' act to interrogate and explore an emotion. It requires a degree of
effort and reflexivity, often working with others – in supervision or therapy – to get inside an emotion and become curious about just why one
is feeling about someone a certain way. So, what were the unconscious
processes at play here? While it is not possible to be sure, the recognition of a dynamic Unconscious, populated with partial representations
of primary caregivers and other authority figures, offers a compelling set
of hypotheses.

David's early experiences of neglect and abuse in the external world
provide an internalised template about how David relates to himself. He
takes in (introjects) his experience of key care figures in his life. They
become internal 'objects' and relate to his core self in a way that resonates with his experience of how they treated him externally. A lonely,
unloved, neglected boy will come to have internal objects that replicate

just those feelings, as if perpetually whispering, 'You are lonely, unloved, not worth caring for.' It is not hard to imagine the emotional toll such an inner world can exact on a person – not least a vulnerable, if dangerous, young man.

To manage this internal pressure, it can be hypothesised that David engaged in a related set of defensive manoeuvres in order to diminish that pressure. The first part is to split or separate that part of his psyche that is the cause of such distress – the internal objects that replicate the feelings of disdain and neglect. This is expelled, projected, out of him and located in others around him; they begin to feel, and sometimes even act, towards him as he feels and acts towards himself. They identify with the projected emotions and act on them, treating David as he has come to expect adults should treat him: with disdain, dislike, hatred. In David's case there is good evidence of this in reports of how other staff responded to him, often setting him up and then punishing him for minor rule infractions. With Tom the projective identification runs differently, thanks to his capacity to reflect on his feelings towards David. Through supervision he comes to see such feelings as an instance of David 'inducting' him into his own mind: how you feel about me is how I feel about myself.

This is the essential catalyst for change. Tom is able to hold these feelings in himself without reacting. This 'holding' allows the entire experience and relationship to be contemplated, as we have seen. And, from there, strong negative feelings undergo an almost alchemical transformation into something benign. He feels compassion and alters his behaviour towards him. We can only imagine what it must have been like for David, to have, for the first time, an adult seek him out at social times and signal interest in him and some level of enjoyment in his company. A positive and therapeutic relationship.

This is an extreme example. And yet children come to school with all manner of internal objects populating their inner worlds. Teaching staff, contending with a multitude of students each day, can be hard pressed to find the time and space to reflect on the reactions a child can call up in them. The nature and force of unconscious processes like projective identification means that they are difficult to spot in the moment. Opportunities for reflective discussions, such as individual or group consultation and supervision and work discussion groups (see Chapter 12), are becoming more common in schools and are, to our mind, necessary to help support schools and school staff to be able to reflect on some of the more extreme psychological processes that affect them.

Desire

A trainee teacher, Phil, was tasked to stay behind in the IT lab with some Year 9 students to finish their work, while the rest of the class returned to their class with the other teacher. Eventually only two girls remained, Laura and Kate. In the ensuing, relatively informal conversation, Laura asked a question, to which he replied somewhat flippantly. She then asked why men often joked about serious things, leading to another flippant response. At this point, Kate took Phil's hand and, staring at him, slapped his hand, saying in a rather adult and playful manner, 'Men!' In a rush of panic, Phil then finished the activity and they returned to the class. Fear, guilt, arousal, panic. These were the key emotions he described. A few days later, the class were tasked with putting posters up on school notice boards. Walking past Kate, Phil jokingly observed that she had not put any posters up high, to which she replied, again staring at him quite provocatively, 'I can't, sir.' When asked why, she replied 'If I raise up my arms, then my skirt will ride up above my knickers.' Phil had a similar emotional reaction to last time and from that day forward fanatically avoided any contact with Kate. He remained haunted and guilt-ridden until the end of his placement and he moved to his next training placement in relief.

This is a slightly extreme version of what is a rather commonplace situation in secondary schools, with genders of key players easily reversed. Indeed, some might even say that a major preoccupation in secondary schools is how to manage and keep at bay emerging adolescent sexuality. Adolescents need somewhere safe to explore strong, puzzling emotional imperatives such as desire and sexual attraction. Arguably, a key reason why teaching adolescents can be so challenging is that the civilising effect of education – effectively the passing on of culture – is in competition with the biological concerns we share with primates, not least of which are social status and mating. Often these tensions are poorly recognised or cast as misbehaviour, and the underlying emotional reality is ignored. In this example it is easy to see why.

So, what happened here? And what could have happened?

First, we want to state that, of all the unthinking reactions, this is the best. But it was not without cost. Kate, we can conjecture, entering adolescence, had found the trainee teacher an attractive alternative, somewhere between the age of a father and the boys she was at school with. Of all the people safe enough to have a crush on, he was it. Superficially her provocative comments did not lead anywhere. But internally two key emotions are likely: guilt and shame. Phil reported feelings of panic, paranoia and guilt. What had happened? Why had a part of him even enjoyed those interactions, even found them – exciting, erotic? It was not until much later that he was even able to think about, let alone talk about, what had happened, and for some time he was terrified that under it all he was a paedophile, who had 'accidentally' fallen into teaching. And for Kate? Well, we cannot know, but the abrupt change in emotional tone, the distancing and emotional closing, where there had once been a rapport, is likely to have had an effect.

And what of the alternatives? In psychoanalytic terms it can be argued that Kate was projecting an aspect of developmental desire into the teacher, something in need of containing. In the worst-case scenario, which is more common than we would like to think, such feeling states can come to be identified with – they are seen as 'my' feelings, which 'I' must act on. In younger teachers especially, they may still see themselves as somewhat adolescent, and psychologically and emotionally they may well be not much older than the children they teach. A psychological mirroring occurs, and the lively, sexual feelings projected into him or her can stir up similar feelings of adolescent desire only recently outgrown, if indeed they have been outgrown. The relationship, distorted by the secret bond of illicit attraction, can become manipulated by very primitive forces of sexual desire and the teacher, by dint of his or her role and power, is, with worrying ease, able to engineer school systems to his or her advantage: proximity, special tasks, extra detentions … A fiction emerges, 'we understand each other, we are the same … we are in love'.

We are all too aware of the damage that occurs next, with children's lives ruined, families destroyed, careers ended, and sometimes time spent in prison. Again, we want to reiterate we are not condoning such behaviour. And a distinction needs to be made between the types of example discussed here and the predatory behaviours of a paedophile or the impulsivity of a sex offender. In this case, a psychologically immature teacher may struggle to withstand very strong and primitive unconscious processes. Given that secondary teachers, especially, deal day in, day out with adolescent sexuality, we think this is an occupational hazard which is studiously avoided, to the detriment of all. It is one of the reasons we believe so strongly in the necessity of some form of reflective space for teachers to discuss such experiences, to make sense of them (Jackson, 2015).

How might Phil have responded in a more psychologically helpful way to Kate? We return to the premise that working with emotional experience leads to the growth of mind. The ability to 'think under fire' when presented with such strong affective material is the hallmark of a maturing capacity for thought. In such an instance as this, we are not advocating some sort of learning or pastoral plan, or any more formal approach, but rather, to register in the moment, 'Here is a young girl looking for a safe place to act out desire and I am it. Can I hold this in mind and bear all that such a realisation entails without moving into action – either fleeing or identifying with the projection?' To take such a stance is not easy. It requires, in the face of any strong emotion, a capacity for reflection, emotional steadfastness and equanimity. But responding in this way offers Kate a healthy experience of working through what could be her first 'crush' and a template for how to think in the face of strong emotion. The teacher could have become a thoughtful object in her internal world, a guide for how to approach and think about difficult material. He might have contributed to the growth of her mind. It might then have been a powerful instance of learning arising from experience.

Psychoanalytic theory holds that such strong emotional experiences are not just more frequent than we might think, but that they are developmentally necessary. How they are reacted to is the difference between ensuing feelings of guilt, shame and fear or maturity, confidence and growth. Pretending such forces do not occur, denying their existence, does not make one a better person.

Shame

Thus far, we have shared vignettes with a focus on themes of desire and hate. There is, however, a unifying, underlying theme – shame. This takes us further, and arguably deeper. The following experience was related to one of the authors by a newly qualified teacher:

The class were quietly working on a written task. One boy got up from his chair and danced across the classroom, arms aloft, twirling and singing.

The newly qualified teacher reported feeling an immediate surge of annoyance, sternly instructing the child to stand outside the classroom. He asked the class to continue working. The teacher then very firmly told the boy that his behaviour was unacceptable, before returning to the class and instructing the child to remain outside. He felt agitated before eventually inviting the boy back into the class.

The following day, the teacher apologised to the boy and attempted to repair the relationship.

On reflection, the teacher acknowledged that he had presented a sanitised version of the story. He 'confessed' that he had shouted as events unfolded. The teacher was also able to connect this experience with a sense of shame, of acting 'out of character' and of a previous experience in his teacher training, where he had felt out of control, and had feared that his struggle in responding to disruptive classroom behaviour had jeopardised his progress towards qualified teacher status.

This vignette may seem familiar to many teachers. What might we learn from the experience?

In an earlier vignette, we discussed the idea of an inner world, and of object relations. We considered how a young person might experience a persecutory state of mind, that he or she had internalised a cruel chorus creating an internal reality involving not being good enough. We suggested that this intolerable state can lead to projection of unwanted emotion.

These ideas of an inner world, object relations and projection may also help us when considering this teacher's experience. What evidence do we have? We know that the teacher held the memory of a persecutory experience during his training – where his struggle to manage disruptive behaviour had created a phantasy (or reality), where his hopes for gaining qualified teacher status were imperilled.

It is noted here that the actual experience of how minded the training providers were to supporting the teacher in training or to failing them is not important here. Rather, it is the experience that was taken in by the trainee teacher that is pertinent – a fear of failure related to managing children's behaviour. It is also noted that the teacher is unlikely perhaps to access this memory consciously, in-the-moment. This is an important point – that our memories are inscribed, that we carry our biographies within us.

We may hypothesise that the experience of a child dancing threw the teacher back into a persecutory state of mind, where he was at risk of losing control of the class, of being found out as 'not good enough' – a ghost of training past come to haunt the here-and-now. Again, it is noted that these thoughts may not have been consciously accessible in the moment. The reported sense of being 'out of control' offers us some evidence.

We may further hypothesise that this teacher (in-the-moment) was taken up in this interplay between a persecutory aspect of their inner world (and object relations – the harsh authority figure threatening catastrophe) and the unfolding events in the here-and-now. The psychic pain caused by this experience, it is hypothesised, led to the evacuation of the persecutory feeling – through shouting at the child (an enactment of the harsh internal authority figure), and literally placing him outside of the classroom.

We might see this as illustrative of a psychic process. The newly qualified teacher, with a fragile and developing identity, led to a defensive manoeuvre – where the disruptive behaviour is symbolically separated from the classroom (and the inner world?).

We may also consider a projective aspect of this experience. The teacher connected his recollection of the incident with shame. (At shouting? In relation to a harsh internal object? Of not being good enough?) We might suppose that the teacher projected an experience of shame into the child, thus (temporarily) relieving the teacher of this torment.

In summary, it is suggested that the concept of an inner world, of object relations, of states-of-mind and mechanisms such as projection can offer us insights into how unconscious collisions between the past and present may help us in making sense of confusion and disturbance experienced in teaching and learning relationships.

The classroom-in-the-mind

In this chapter, we have spoken of an 'inner world', which in the Kleinian sense might be viewed as a stage or theatre. We have also made reference to 'internal objects', which, to extend the metaphor, might be seen as the characters that are based on our experiences in the world. At times, these might be part-objects, bits of people (the breast or penis is often cited). We may also introject (take in) whole objects, the whole person (a mother or father). These objects and part-objects might be thought of as distorted versions and phantasies related to the external sources rather than exact replicas. It is also important to recognise that, in object relations theory, these objects are dynamic – they relate to one another and to the self in an endless play within the inner world.

In considering the teacher in context, we acknowledge the teacher as a person acting in role within an organisation. We recognise that a teacher has his or her own inner world. As do all those he or she comes into contact with. In drawing on psychoanalytic perspectives related to working in organisations, we refer to the seminal work of David Armstrong (2005), who offers the following definition of the organisation-in-the-mind (p. 6):

> *The 'organization-in-the-mind' has to be understood literally and not just metaphorically. It does not (only) refer to the client's conscious or unconscious mental constructs of the organization: the assumptions he or she makes about aim, task, authority, power, accountability, and so on. It refers also to the emotional resonances, registered and present in the mind of the client. This is the equivalent to Larry Hirschhorn's graphic phrase 'the workplace within'* (Hirschhorn, 1988).

This may be seen as a concept that could help the teacher in exploring his or her experience. In returning to the inner world, our rep theatre, and resident players, an ensemble, including the avant-garde 'part-objects' and the character actors or 'whole objects', we might add the 'meta-object' or the 'classroom-in-the-mind', involving a whole system that is internalised within the inner world (Armstrong, 2005, p. 4):

> *'organisation in the mind' is what the individual perceives in his or her head of how activities and relations are organised, structured and connected internally. It is a model internal to oneself, part of one's inner world, relying upon the inner experiences of my interactions, relations and the activities I engage in, which give rise to image, emotions, values and responses in me, which may*

consequently be influencing my own management and leadership, positively or adversely …

'Organization in the mind' helps me to look beyond the normative assessments of organisational issues and activity, to become alert to my inner experiences and give richer meaning to what is happening to me and around me. (Hutton, Bazalgette and Reed, 1997, p. 114)

In our iteration, the 'classroom-in-the-mind' might be explored through discussion and free association, in order to reveal some of the unconscious dynamics (or object relations) which are at play in our internal representation of our places of work. These can be very different from those held by colleagues, students and parents or carers, and can hold the potential for much misunderstanding and tension, which may be surfaced through psychoanalytically informed exploration. If we conceive of an internal classroom-in-the-mind, we might open the door to a multitude of possible points of reference and linkage.

The vignettes above might become illuminated:

- *Vignette 1 – Hate*: the class teacher seems to have a classroom-in-the-mind where aggressive thoughts and impulses were unacceptable to him – therefore, he had split off the young person in order to preserve the internal object.
- *Vignette 2 – Desire*: the class teacher seems to have a classroom-in-the-mind where sexualised behaviours are seen as fearful and dangerous – therefore, he split off the young person in order to preserve the internal object.
- *Vignette 3 – Shame*: the class teacher seems to have a classroom-in-the-mind where disruptive behaviour is seen as threatening and catastrophic – therefore, he split off the child in order to preserve the internal object.

These may be seen as simplified formulations, in the service of illustrating the idea of the classroom-in-the-mind. In practice, it would take time and commitment, with a practitioner trained in psychoanalytic approaches (and receiving supervision), to help elucidate the classroom-in-the-mind. We believe that this is a novel way of working and exploring the teacher experience, which may deepen and enrich understanding and experience in role.

In closing this section, we would like to share a final vignette:

In a mainstream secondary school, in a French lesson, a Year 9 student with a diagnosis of autism spectrum condition was asked by his teacher to move desks, as his teaching assistant was not with him that day. He refused. The teacher persisted, asking him again and reminding him of the sanctions policy as she escalated the consequences for non-compliance.

After a tense series of interactions, the student finally stood up and said angrily, 'You have not spoken to me once this year, so I am not going to listen to you now.' With that, he stormed out of the room.

We believe that this may be seen as further evidence of the classroom-in-the-mind, and the influence that this internal object might have in the real world. It is conceivable that the teacher had constructed a classroom-in-the-mind where the young person with complex needs (and a high level of support) was split off from the classroom and languished in isolation, beyond the thought and reverie of the teacher. We perhaps also gain a sense here of the possibility that the children and young people in our schools may also introject a 'classroom-in-the-mind'.

Conclusion

The school and the classroom are places where children and adults engage in a multitude of activities, different roles, tasks and interactions that are united by relational experiences. The full range of human emotions may be detected in organisations. We have argued that careful attention to emotional experiences can help us in our work and release us from unthinking activity.

We contend that a great deal of energy can be channelled into defending us from, and dismissing, disturbing emotional experiences. This line of argument, it is suggested, offers us a novel and perhaps counter-intuitive point. That moments of intense and raw emotion, such as anger, might be seen as genuine moments of connection, where – if we can tolerate the exploration, and resist the urge to dismiss, diminish, repress, reframe or revise – we might see these experiences as valuable forms of data, which have the potential to reveal something meaningful to us. This is something that may illuminate our understanding and awareness, and perhaps release us from emotional dragnets which impede and obfuscate our ability to act in role. By knowing and bringing together the good and the bad, the past and the present, in an integrated and embracing manner, we might free ourselves to access a more wholesome and lively engagement with ourselves and with others.

We have introduced the concept of the classroom-in-the-mind, which opens a multitude of possible lines of enquiry: how might our internal objects interact with the here-and-now of moment-to-moment learning and teaching, and the learning from teaching that may enrich our understanding and ability to access and use ourselves in an authentic and accepting way?

Psychoanalytic perspectives can enable us to learn from emotional experience, liberate us from shame and guilt, and provide a powerful source of knowledge, whereby the classroom can be seen as a place where the teacher and student meet in the service of meaningful growth and development.

PART III

ASSESSMENT

CHAPTER 6

Educational psychological assessment: a psychoanalytic approach

Liz Kennedy and Lee-Anne Eastwood

Introductory remarks

This chapter outlines the contribution that psychoanalytic ideas can make to educational psychology assessment. We want to examine some of the assumptions that underpin assessment practice more generally, before focusing more specifically upon psychoanalytic ideas. We particularly want to convey the interventive nature of assessment, and the possibilities for positive impact on participants that this implies.

Assessment has always been at the heart of the role of the educational psychologist (EP); it is our 'bread and butter'. For many of us it is the most engaging and fascinating aspect of a complex, demanding and diverse job. As David Satterly (1981) reminds us in his book, 'assessment' is derived from the Latin *assidere*, which means 'to sit beside'. This derivation points to assessment being a relational encounter with two (or more) active participants. It is a helpful reminder that, as psychologists, we need to get alongside our clients, suggesting an exchange of information and experience. Whether our clients are individual children, teachers, parents or groups and organisations, getting alongside implies being open to experiencing a process, being able to reflect on it, before being able to synthesise the information elicited to offer an explanatory formulation. We see assessment as a structured clinical intervention (see below) in and of itself. Psychoanalytic practice emphasises the mutually influencing nature of dialogue and of jointly generating meaning– this is a guiding principle for us in psychological assessment.

Current educational psychology assessment practice is dominated by legislative imperatives, in particular the demands of the Children and Families Act of 2014. The nature of assessment for the EP is contextually driven, as the definition of a special educational need and disability (SEND) is a *relative* not an *absolute* one (a non-ambulant child only has such a difficulty if the learning environment has steps). As Rachael Green (2019, personal communication) says, the focus can be 'on the generation of thinking around a presented situation, rather than guiding practice where in-depth individual assessment of learning [and we would also say other] needs may be required' (2019, personal communication). As Green quotes, the DECP (Division of Educational and Child Psychology) definition of educational psychology assessment speaks to 'a creative investigation' of a broad range of hypotheses that build on research from all areas of psychology (DECP, 2002, p. 24), and yet we feel that the legislative and systemic imperatives are likely to work in the opposite direction, to produce a more focused, more restricted (if only by time pressures if nothing else) approach to assessment where interventive opportunities can be missed or lost. Viewing assessment as therapeutically interventive can go some way towards addressing these 'overdetermining' system demands.

The dynamics of referrals

In practice the referral to an EP is already an intervention. A threshold has been reached and a position has changed, leading to an action that both signals and invites change. By definition, the school/parent has reached a point where they feel all has been done of which they are capable. New relationships are now aligned around the case, or existing relationships are understood differently as 'specialists/experts' become involved. For the EP, at this moment, there are important decisions to be made before they can become helpfully involved at a direct level. Three important questions need to be answered prior to taking any direct steps with the identified client (usually a child). Why is this referral being made *now*? Why is this referral being made to *me*? Why is *this* particular client being referred? In order to answer these questions, we need to do some investigative work, what Huffington, Cole and Brunning (1997) call 'scouting' and 'entry'. Most frequently, in our experience, the thoroughness of the scouting and entry stage will determine the nature and extent of the EP's involvement. Most frequently, EPs will have a planning/consultation meeting (see Chapter 9 in this volume), in order to establish a valid set of referral questions that are appropriate only for an EP to address at this moment. Sometimes such referral meetings are with the referrer, sometimes with both the family and the school, but they are a vital part of an exploratory process designed to open up dialogue with all involved parties. Such meetings, in our experience, are best not seen as 'problem solving', as no elegant solution to ongoing psychological problems is very likely; we feel they are constituted in order to generate hypotheses. Additionally, we would suggest that the EP does not approach scouting and entry activity hoping for greater clarity – other than how to take next steps – as our job is not to simplify/clarify, but to map out the complexity of all factors impinging on any given situation. Conducting/facilitating such meetings requires considerable skill, as those present are all dealing with issues of judgement, comparison, blame, worry and confusion; the task of the EP is to encourage, model and legitimise the open sharing of such feelings in a containing and thoughtful manner.

Assessments are not carried out in a 'neutral' context. By definition, someone, somewhere, has a difficulty or a concern. As Emilia Dowling (1990, p. 2) reminds us, if a child is described as 'disturbed', then someone is disturbed by that child (just as if a child is not learning, then those responsible for teaching that child will have feelings about the situation). Whatever the nature of the referral to the psychologist, somewhere in the system someone is failing to do something – make progress, behave consistently, develop skills, operate with greater social confidence and competence – and this failure comes with feelings attached, often of a challenging nature; 'a statement about someone's problem is a statement about someone else's difficulty to handle it' (Dowling, 1990). Shame can be a debilitating emotion, leading to a sense of frustration and inadequacy. Most of us would acknowledge that such feelings are likely to inhibit balanced, considered or measured thinking, but in our experience these feelings around referrals are not often explicitly addressed and yet they are likely to influence both the content of subsequent decisions and the process of making those decisions. Dowling also points out that how a problem is located will determine who is responsible for its origin, maintenance and resolution. At a point where the EP might want, in the service of creativity, to promote curiosity and to be 'playfully experimental' (Winnicott, 1989), feelings of embarrassment or shame are likely to work against such openness. Encouraging others to 'play' with ideas and experiences when they are feeling vulnerable and are being observed (and, we would suggest, assessed/judged) is likely to provoke discomfort. In turn, discomfort may lead to anxiety – in particular, 'performance anxiety', which can lead to defensiveness and attempts to negate, avoid or deny, such anxiety. Given that shame involves positioning (that is, a comparison with others) and is often hidden away or kept secret, then the process of referral will be fraught with hidden as well as surface dynamics *on all sides*.

Assessment, however, is integral to effective teaching and learning, but, as can be seen from the section above, all the 'players' have their own version of vulnerability and feeling vulnerable is rarely conducive to thoughtful practice/behaviour. As EPs we need to recognise, and work with, the dynamics of shame, to acknowledge that judgements and choices always involve a degree of anxiety but are a necessary part of the work. We need to find ways of working where the feelings of shame, guilt, anxiety and frustration can be turned into collaborative and constructive concern. Remember: we are part of the problem, we 'allow' access to resources or restrict access; we either share or withhold information/knowledge; we 'see' into people's heads or fail to 'see' anything that hasn't already been 'seen', etc.

Assessment as intervention

Assessment is a multi-purpose activity and should be formative, not just summative.

Statutory assessment, currently dominating a lot of educational psychology practice in local authorities, is frequently organised by questions of resourcing and placement. Being organised by such issues can lead, if we are not very careful, to a restricted focus; for example, exploring the nature and extent of learning difficulties with less emphasis on the emotional impact of these difficulties *on all parties*. As Jacobs (2012) reminds us, 'cognition is compromised by high levels of anxiety or emotional preoccupation, and ... learning problems create emotional distress' (p. 259). Perceiving assessment as an intervention implies a particular type of practice, a recognition that our involvement impacts on the system and that this can be actively and constructively exploited as a short piece of 'therapeutic' work. Much is written about the positive impact of active listening, of feeling heard; we also know that containment of (inevitable) anxieties creates the conditions for more constructive interaction and creative thinking. We need to take a comprehensive view of psychological assessment as being not just about the target child, but about the nature of involvement of all 'stakeholders'. Thus, we are trying to elicit information from parents, teachers and systems at the same time as intervening to support greater understanding both within and between everyone. Jacobs cites empirical research supporting better outcomes for children when parents are actively involved in the assessment process and when consistent views on the nature of the difficulties are held by all involved parties. Thus, when assessing we are actively trying to facilitate a shared understanding (knowing that this itself is interventive in shifting stuck or unhelpful positions), and giving time to this process is essential. One way in which the interventive nature of assessment can be enhanced is to see the child/parents/ teachers over time. As Sugarman and Kanner (2000) state,

> the [child's] personality is not static over the course of the testing. Psychological structures evolve temporally and situationally, and the ebb and flow of such structures during the hours and over the course of the sessions of the testing situation can be studies for insight into the [child's] personality processes. (p. 8)

A psychoanalytic approach particularly emphasises the dynamic nature of assessment and looks towards ideas such as establishing a therapeutic alliance, the transference and its manifestation(s), and the countertransference experience of the EP (see definitions below), the major implication being that the encounter is relational, and this element needs exploration and development. Hence, seeing a child more than once becomes an important element in the structuring of psychological assessments within this orientation. We are interested to know what sense the child made of the initial encounter and how he or she may have internalised elements of the experience. When using projective tests, we will also want to test out any hypotheses arising out of interpreting the material by discussing broad thematic observations with the child.

Psychoanalytic assessment explicitly places therapeutic change at its heart. Thus, the analytic EP is trying to effect therapeutic change in a short and focused exchange. This aim is present from the first point of contact and is therefore targeting all the 'players'. We are looking to contain inevitable anxieties, confusion, frustration, embarrassment/shame through modelling a thoughtful, receptive non-judgemental approach to the gathering, synthesising and sharing of information. We are working actively with the impact that these activities have on everyone involved (including ourselves) and attempting to manage these responses in a containing manner.

Psychoanalytic ideas

First, it is important to say that psychoanalytic theories are many and various. They all share attention to the operation of forces not available to consciousness, the unconscious. Psychoanalysis challenges our notions of being rational beings and is frequently unpopular as a result. Since Freud first proposed his early formulations, those ideas have been met with resistance, contempt and dismissal. The idea that we don't just deceive others but we continually deceive ourselves has not been received with warmth and acceptance. Despite Freud's scientific project, central tenets of psychoanalytic theory were difficult to establish empirically, but more recent developments in neuroscience have lent much weight to some of his original postulations. So why is there still so much suspicion and sometimes outright hostility to some of the ideas? As Jaffe (1990) says, 'careful observation and thoughtful analysis are hallmarks of psychoanalytic methods. In other words, psychoanalytic methods are soundly built on systematized knowledge that is based on observation and study, which is coincidentally Webster's [dictionary] definition of science' (p. 1). He goes on to remark that:

> when scientific investigation in ... psychology is limited to statistically analysed experimental data [P] psychoanalytic psychologists are mistakenly seen as employing a method that lacks precision. This bias can lead to the view that psychoanalytic psychologists use psychological tests like a horoscope, which is based on inner space rather than outer space. (p. 2)

We would want to echo Jaffe's remarks by seeing careful observation and thoughtful analysis as the hallmarks of a thorough assessment. We would also want to add that the observation and analysis are not just of the client but also of oneself when working psychoanalytically.

The fundamental tenets of psychoanalysis elaborate on unconscious intrapsychic functioning ('inner life') and unconscious transactions in the interpersonal. An appreciation of these ideas leads to big shifts in thinking about assessment, as we will be bringing not just our conscious beliefs, experience and values to the task, but also our unconscious versions. The client similarly will bring his or hers, and the two sets of feeling-full experience will interact at both conscious and unconscious levels. We will inevitably be treated as transference figures, as if we were people from past encounters; we will also have our own 'buried' past relationship feelings activated in ways that are not necessarily accessible to immediate conscious thought. Such interactions are dynamic and inevitable, and with skill we can make good use of them to enhance the information gained through tests and observations.

> Prior to an assessment, an EP was faced with a personal emergency that necessitated delaying the process and called the child's mother, Sophia, to explain that she would need to postpone. Sophia was very 'short' with the EP, agreeing to the postponement and trying to end the call quite abruptly. Sensing that Sophia was irritated, the EP asked her for a few more minutes acknowledging the frustration and expressing her concern and wish to understand. Initially Sophia denied any problem with the delay. The EP remained curious and persevered, feeling that Sophia was not comfortable with the delay. She spoke to the possible link between Sophia's response and what she knew about the history of the assessment. Sophia's son had been waiting for an assessment for more than five years, since the original application for an assessment was rejected. Her experience was one of a neglectful and withholding 'other'. On many occasions, her concerns were negated and she felt that her child was left without the support that she was so desperate for him to receive. Once this was opened up, Sophia was able to engage with the EP as a yet another 'neglectful other' and was able to talk about how she once again felt let down. With an understanding that Sophia was responding to her previous experiences, the EP was able to separate this from something that could have felt more personal. She was able to engage with how frustrating the process had been for Sophia and how let down she felt by the thought of another delay. In turn, this allowed a deeper connection and for a collaborative process to develop between the EP and Sophia.

The unconscious

The unconscious is seen as both a location and a dynamic system in which the ordinary expectations of rational thinking (a consciousness of sense impressions), perception, judgement, attention and memory do not pertain. Freud saw the unconscious as a repository of psychic material that has been repressed to reduce psychic tension/anxiety/pain. He described the unconscious as exerting a constant, but largely inaccessible, influence on conscious functioning; psychoanalytic treatment is seen as a means of identifying the operation of these forces on people's lives, giving them a greater degree of self-awareness and thereby self-regulation.

So how might unconscious dynamics enter the arena of assessment? We would start with considering the unconscious forces operating within the psychologist. Most of us are drawn to this helping profession to make a difference. What might be less obvious is that, for the vast majority of us, there is also a need to 'repair' aspects of ourselves through the work. Hawkins and Shohet (2000) remind us that we are 'wounded helpers' and that there is a danger in locating problems in the client and seeing the professional as problem-free. The desire to help, while benign in itself, can be unconsciously imbued with a 'fantasy of omnipotence and omniscience', that is, a somewhat seductive notion of being all-powerful and all-knowing. In this state of mind (very often unconscious), we may believe that *we* can offer up solutions/'diagnose' the problem. We need to remember that, although we can make an incredibly important contribution to the above, we are part of a system that is stuck with a particular viewpoint and position and that we alone are unlikely to prompt change. Thus, we need to be aware that we will be drawn into beliefs and expectations of others without necessarily being consciously aware, and that our own unconscious professional drivers might at times get in the way of staying with complexity and struggle.

The transference

In addition to these drivers, psychoanalytic theory reminds us that our, perhaps forgotten, past experiences impact on our interactions in the present, a phenomenon known as transference. We can, therefore, enact 'there-and-then' patterns of relating 'here-and-now' (a common example of which is the child calling the teacher 'Mummy'). Stephen Weiss writes about this as follows:

> *The classroom is a place where children experience satisfaction and frustration, pleasure and pain, love and anger-and may direct those feelings towards teachers and other children. However, many practitioners do not realize that their responses to children's struggles will be influenced by the ways in which they coped with their own developmental issues in the past.* (Weiss, 2000a, pp. 9–10)

> *Transference is the unconscious projection of attitudes and feelings from past relationships, particularly with family, onto other persons in the present.* (Weiss, 2002b, p. 109)

Freud described transference as a universal phenomenon and alongside it described the professional's own reaction to being the subject of a transferential encounter as countertransference – that is, our own relationship histories may be unconsciously stirred by an encounter, thus influencing our understanding of them.

> *The most problematic pupils are those whose negative transference triggers teachers' [and others] complementary negative countertransference. These children are often intensely hostile, fearful or pessimistic as an outgrowth of troubled interpersonal relationships within the family. Parents gradually and repeatedly convey to the children that they are worthless, ungratifying and an unpleasant responsibility. The children may have been physically and emotionally abused or seriously neglected ... A hurt and unhappy child, who often becomes labelled as emotionally disturbed, 'comes to believe that he is mean, bad anxious, or is a poor performer, and lives out these patterns with others outside the family' Paul and Epanchin (1991, p. 128).* (Weiss, 2002b, p. 116)

Because, as Freud observed, such very troubling passive experiences can later be enacted actively, such children can be hurtful and lacking in empathy. Attachment theory helps us understand how profound and damaging traumatic early experiences can be to psychological development, but these other psychoanalytic ideas enable us to see how attachment issues can be played out in classrooms and in assessments.

Isabelle was an 11-year-old girl brought by her foster mother for an assessment of her learning difficulties. In the initial consultation, the foster mother struggled to discuss her relationship with Isabelle and focused more on the school-related challenges. In the first session, Isabelle initially presented as sweet and compliant, the 'perfect' client. She was very focused on whether the EP was enjoying the assessment and declared that she loved her. As the session progressed, Isabelle became increasingly challenging while apparently trying to assess the EP's reaction to her behaviour. She became dismissive of the assessment tasks and openly critical of the EP. After some time of being more difficult, Isabelle's anxiety appeared to be increasing, as was that of the EP. Isabelle asked on a number of occasions if the EP loved her and if she wanted to see her again. The EP reported that she felt a huge pull to respond to Isabelle with rejection, by saying that she did not wish to work with her again. Fortunately, attachment theory brought an understanding of how Isabelle's traumatic attachment history led her to simultaneously fear rejection and to behaving in a way that provoked the very rejection that she feared. She was constantly testing the strength and reliability of all relationships. During the projective assessments, when asked to draw her family Isabelle drew a picture of a fridge and a dustbin, as if Isabelle's view of family providing life-sustaining sustenance contrasted with the constant threat of being discarded and rejected. The EP was able to both be aware of what was happening and reflect aloud on Isabelle's anxiety of being rejected. The EP was able to explore both ideas in a later session with Isabelle and in meeting with her foster mother. Isabelle's foster mother was so relieved by the thoughts brought by the EP that she was able to open up about the challenges that she was experiencing at home with Isabelle and her interactions with both herself and her other foster children. Together with her teacher, Isabelle's foster mother and the EP were now able to explore differently how Isabelle's behaviour was being experienced, promoting changes in the relationships at school as well as in her learning.

The countertransference

Although originally felt to be an unhelpful defensive response by the professional, countertransference now is seen as a potentially helpful tool in making sense of an encounter (Heimann, 1950; and, later, Bion, 1967). Feelings generated within the psychologist during an assessment need to be understood. Are the feelings only about the psychologist, or could they be to do with the child/family/system? Judicious and rigorous self-examination can identify those instances when an uncharacteristic set of responses or actions is in fact telling you something about the case.

Psychological defences

The idea that defences arise in all of us to protect from psychic pain is another crucial element to psychoanalytic theory. We have all developed response patterns or habits, some of which serve a defensive function. However, not all defences are helpful to the individual and, if maintained over time and across contexts, can actually impede development. A classic example of this is what we would call 'secondary learning difficulties', that is, the learned helplessness of the child in the face of sustained and enduring frustration and failure. A common defence is to unconsciously try to evacuate problematic feelings via 'projection' outside of the self. Projection and its opposite, 'introjection' (the taking in of experience), operate universally through unconscious attribution of negative (and positive) qualities to the other. Such unconscious exchanges can be powerful enough that the other is affected and may respond negatively (or positively) in ways not based on the reality of the relationship.

> Ahmed (8) was initially referred for an assessment due to his challenging behaviour at school and delays in his learning. He could be openly aggressive with his teachers and peers and refused to stay in the classroom. In the initial observation, it was immediately apparent that he was not engaging in any learning or, in fact, in any activity initiated by anyone in the school. When the EP was able to work with him individually, the extent of his 'psychic pain' around anything in any way linked to learning or assessment became obvious. The only cognitive assessment subtest administered revealed ability that was above average. Ahmed's

actual experiences in school, right from the start of his Reception year, were of ongoing struggles, frustration and failure. The anxiety that had developed due to his experiences seemed overwhelming and unbearable for Ahmed and had resulted in Ahmed protecting himself in the only way he knew. He had developed extremely defensive behaviour in the form of 'zoning out', distracting himself and others, leaving the classroom, becoming verbally aggressive and, on occasion, becoming physically aggressive. His 'fight, flight, freeze' behaviour had seemingly become the means he used to protect himself from the unbearable feelings generated by his learning struggles. Although he seemed to have above average learning potential, his behaviour resulted in significant 'secondary learning difficulties'. Subsequently, the teaching staff were able to reframe what they had initially viewed as aggressive and defiant behaviour. This shift in perspective helped them to address his difficulties and the resulting anxiety, rather than the behavioural manifestations. Ahmed was seen now as a child who was struggling both educationally and emotionally and needed help and nurturing, rather than a child who was difficult and badly behaved, needing discipline and a firm hand.

Containment

At this point it is important to explain Bion's (1967) contribution to this subject. He realised that there was a universal and unconscious communicative system inherent in all relationships through these unconscious exchanges. He describes how unconsciously the subject projects into the other who, if 'well balanced … can accept these and respond therapeutically: that is to say in a manner that makes the … [subject] … feel it is receiving its frightened … [feelings] … back again but in a form that it can tolerate' (Bion, 1967, pp. 114–15). This interpersonal process known as 'containment' has revolutionised our understanding of interpersonal interactions and their unconscious components.

In working with 6-year-old Freya, the EP knew of her history of abuse and neglect in her relationship with her mother that resulted in Freya being removed from her care at the age of 5. Freya presented in class with very challenging behaviour that was impacting her learning and her social interactions. Many of the adults involved with Freya perceived her as aggressive, uncaring and defiant. With this understanding, the EP was able to be thoughtful when Freya made very personal and insulting comments towards her during the assessment. The EP was able to see these in light of the underlying anxieties that Freya was experiencing and was able to reflect these back to Freya in a containing way. When she called the EP fat and stupid, the EP reflected on Freya's own anxieties that she may be perceived as not good enough, saying, 'I wonder if you're trying to help me to understand that sometimes you don't feel great about yourself?' Freya tested the EP's commitment to her through anxiously commenting on whether the EP wanted to see her again and querying if she saw other children. Instead of talking about other children, the EP was able to address Freya's underlying anxiety about being rejected. This also gave the EP an opportunity to talk about the limits of the interactions for an assessment and to pre-emptively engage with feelings that Freya might experience around not seeing the EP after the assessment. When Freya's behaviour became more aggressive, the EP was able to link this behaviour to Freya's need to test whether she would be rejected: 'I wonder if you're kicking the cupboard to check if I will keep working with you even if you don't behave. Maybe you're worried that I won't like you any more and I'll leave?' The EP's knowledge about Freya's attachment history enabled her to respond in this containing and empathic manner, giving Freya an experience of being understood, contained and accepted unconditionally.

We would say that the psychologist acting as a 'container' is an explicit therapeutic goal in assessment practice.

Hopefully, this section has illustrated how the active use of counter-transference feelings, a knowledge of how basic psychological defences can manifest and an appreciation of how the internal world might impact on external relationships has been exemplified. We will now turn to looking at the use of projective tests that specifically encourage these phenomena during an assessment.

Projective testing

Projective tests are ideographic tools used to explore how both adults and children make sense of themselves in the relational world. The term covers different types of stimulus material, but they all have in common a belief that the subject will produce responses that are determined in no small part by their 'inner world' perceptions and experiences. Most tests, therefore, are constructed using deliberately ambiguous stimuli onto which the subject will 'project' unconscious attributions, beliefs and values. Tests include drawings (such as Human Figure Drawings (DAP) and Kinetic Family Drawings), pictorial stimuli (such as the Children's Apperception Test (CAT), the Thematic Apperception Test (TAT) and the Object Relations Technique (ORT)), and written activities such as sentence completions.

Meersand (2011, p. 121) states that:

> contemporary child analytic literature emphasizes the following: the centrality of attachment relationships and their fundamental role in affect regulation, the child's emerging sense of self, and the crucial role of mentalization in social and emotional functioning. These qualitative capacities cannot be assessed via psychometrics alone, but can be discerned by examining parental attitudes and fantasies, the qualities of the children's narratives and play, their modes of relating to the examiner and their relation to projective tests.

The use of projective tests is contentious within the educational psychology profession, as their psychometric properties of validity, reliability and norms have been criticised. However, if treated with caution, material gathered using such techniques can prove very useful in broadening and deepening understanding of an individual's perceptions of him- or herself and others. They should be used, in our view, to generate hypotheses that can be subsequently tested, either directly with the child, the parents and teachers, or with both. They are best seen as bringing a qualitative dimension to the assessment and they rely on the psychologist developing experience and expertise in his or her administration and interpretation. While a psychometric orientation puts the test centre stage, projective testing puts the client centre stage. The aim of the use of projective testing is to understand the client in their complexity and uniqueness, with a view to making use of the understanding gained to make decisions about future interventions that could benefit them. Where in psychometric testing the psychologist can be seen as a source of possible bias and error, in projective testing the psychologist is part of the process and is a source of information.

The Human Figure Drawing/Draw-a-Person

By observing and analysing the drawings of children, an EP can gain insight into the social and emotional development of the child. Such material is not used in isolation but is combined with evidence from other types of assessment to broaden the final formulation.

> Martin was 10 when he was referred for an assessment due to difficulties concentrating in class and a request from his school for an 'ADHD referral'. A comprehensive assessment was done, but for the purposes of our discussion we will discuss his Draw-a-Person. He was asked to draw a person and told that he would have as much time as he needed (see Figure 6.1). Martin drew a marionette whom he called Pinocchio. The following questions were asked:
>
> 1.   What is Pinocchio doing? 'Acting like a puppet.'
>
> 2.   What makes Pinocchio happy? 'When he's with his friends.'
>
> 3.   What makes Pinocchio sad? 'When he lies that he's not a puppet to make it funny.'
>
> 4.   What makes Pinocchio cross? 'The same as what makes him sad, when he lies.'
>
> 5.   What makes Pinocchio scared? 'When it's dark.'
>
> 6.   Does Pinocchio ever dream? 'No.'
>
> 7.   If Pinocchio was an animal what would he like to be? 'A monkey.'
>
> 8.   Why would he like to be a monkey? 'He also has a long nose like a monkey.'
>
> 9.   What does Pinocchio do when he's being good? 'Saves the day.'
>
> 10.   What do Pinocchio's parents do when he's being good? 'Congratulate him.'
>
> 11.   What does Pinocchio do when he's being bad? 'Lies.'

12. What do Pinocchio's parents do when he's being bad? 'Shrink his nose.'

13. What would Pinocchio do if he was invisible? 'Scare people.'

14. If Pinocchio had three wishes, what would he wish for? 'To be taller, have superpowers and to be a superhero.'

The EP felt that, although he came across on the surface as a confident child, this was possibly a self-protective façade that he had developed, behind which Martin was actually feeling quite vulnerable (as possibly indicated by the small size of drawing and several erasures). The EP wondered aloud whether the drawing showed how some people have a self that they show to the world to protect themselves. Martin was then able to acknowledge how, at times, he was putting on a show and not being genuine to how he was feeling inside. He felt pressured by others to be funny and happy and, like a marionette, he was led by what others wanted from him. After his parents separated, there was a court battle that was difficult for everyone involved. No one apparently experienced concerns about Martin's emotional well-being because, on the surface, he was a happy child with good and close relationships with his family. Martin expressed that he felt ashamed that he was not happy all of the time and that he didn't want to worry his parents. Martin also seemed to be worried about his struggles at school; the 'ghost' of a very large hat suggests an unconscious focus on the cognitive (the head). Not being aware of these worries and not knowing what to do with them, it seemed as though he defended against his difficulties by acting as though he was happy and did not care about school or his schoolwork. By suggesting a different interpretation of Martin's difficulties in concentrating, his parents and school were more able to assist him emotionally.

The Kinetic Family Drawing

In 1970, Burns and Kaufman (1970) introduced the Kinetic Family Drawing (KFD) test. They saw children's emotional problems as frequently stemming from difficulties and disturbances within their family experiences and saw the test as a vehicle for examining the child's perceptions of those interpersonal dynamics.

Figure 6.1 **Evie's Kinetic Family Drawing**

Family drawings can also be used to gather more information and gain insight into how children perceive their families, as well as their place in the family unit. Often, the order and approach the child takes with the drawing, as well as their comments and self-talk, can provide important information.

Evie was a 12-year-old who had been adopted after spending the first five years of her life in an orphanage. Struggling in all areas, her parents brought her for an assessment hoping to find a way to help her. When Evie was asked to draw her family all doing something (see Figure 6.1), she commented, 'How can I fit them all onto this small page?' Initially, she drew her mother in the middle of the page, before commenting, 'She's floating in the air,' and erasing the image. Evie then drew a horizon line right at the bottom edge of the page. She redrew her mother at the bottom of the page. Next, Evie drew a figure that she also initially erased. While drawing she commented, 'Every time I draw my brother I forget to draw the other arm,' but still did not draw the arms. Evie then drew the third figure, her father, before drawing herself. After drawing all of the figures, Evie commented, 'Oh, they haven't got arms or faces.' She went back and added the mouths and eyes to the family members. She also added one arm to the picture of her mother and one arm to the picture of her father. The EP then chatted to Evie about her drawing, probing through the following questions, among others:

Question: 'What are they doing in the picture?'

Mum: 'Playing in the garden.'

Brother: 'Kicking a soccer ball.'

Daddy: 'Holding a book for me to read.'

Evie: 'Reading.'

Question: 'What kind of a person is X?'

Mum: 'Gentle, kind, loving, caring.'

Brother: 'Rough, likes to scold, like a 2-year-old.'

Daddy: 'Stern, loves us all, always caring.'

Evie: 'You already know.' The EP commented: 'Can you tell
            me what you think?' 'Sometimes rough. Sometimes
            not very nice to be with. Tired. Sometimes rough.'

Question: 'How does X feel in the picture?'

Mum: 'Happy to be in her garden'

Brother: 'Happy, he's having fun'

Daddy: 'Tired of holding the book, I guess. Wondering if he'll
            ever finish and wanting to relax.'

Evie: 'Happy. When I read, I'm always happy.'

Question: 'What is X thinking about in the picture?'

Mum: 'How her flowers won't survive the drought. I don't
            know; I can't see into her brain.'

Brother: 'That he will be a famous soccer player and also why
            isn't Daddy playing with him and only with me.'

Daddy: 'He's intrigued by the story.'

Evie: 'Hoping Daddy has enough strength to carry on
            holding the book.'

From the referral, the interactions in the assessment, as well
as the projective testing, it seemed that Evie was struggling
psychologically and in her family relationships.

Ideas generated by the EP from the KFD were raised with Evie's parents. The erased mother figure drawn initially might be seen as a representation of Evie's birth mother; she is there, but also not there, floating in Evie's thoughts and emotions rather than in her concrete reality. This enabled her parents to explore how it might be important to create the space for Evie's feelings about her family of origin. In drawing her adoptive mother, Evie drew her facing away from the family but tending to flowers that she was concerned may die due to a drought. Evie's mother shared that she was really struggling in her relationship with Evie and of finding any hope going forward. Her initial energy and passion for nurturing and loving Evie had been challenged by a very traumatic and turbulent seven-year relationship. She admitted that she had 'turned away' and that she was concerned that, in spite of all the love and care that she had given Evie, the current 'drought' of emotions that came from her turning away would not be something that Evie could survive. The complexity of these two maternal relationships seemed to be intermingled for Evie, the initial rejection by her birth mother creating a fertile soil for complexity in her relationship with her adoptive mother. Her adoptive mother's emotional withdrawal had caused more acting out from Evie due to her anxiety about a second maternal rejection.

Evie's father seemed to play a very supportive role for both Evie and his wife. As his wife struggled, Evie's father had taken on more of a role with Evie. In the picture, he was portrayed as being with Evie, while the other two family members were on their own. Evie's father was holding a book so that she could 'be happy' through reading. This could be seen as representing her father's ability to emotionally 'hold' Evie and provide containment and emotional safety for her. However, it was evident that Evie was feeling very anxious about this, as evidenced by her concern that he may not want to be 'holding' her emotionally or that he may not be strong enough to continue.

Although the KFD was not used in isolation, it was the most direct way that Evie was able to express her perspective on her family relationships.

The Child Apperception Test

Another verbal projective tool is the Children's Apperception Test (CAT) (Bellak, 1954). Ten picture cards are shown to the child who is invited to tell a story about each one. The cards depict common relational configurations and common emotional experiences. In an assessment where children can be preoccupied with getting items right or wrong, the emphasis that there are no right or wrong answers can 'free' the child to participate differently. In our experience, the stories are akin to 'free association' and can contain unconscious ideas, and preoccupations which are difficult to elicit directly as the child might be censoring themselves in conversation.

> Nathan (8) was struggling educationally. His teachers felt that he had potential that he was not reaching, in spite of learning support being put in place. The first picture (Figure 6.2) commonly elicits stories about nurturing. Nathan's story was as follows: 'The mother hen should have gived the babies food. They're very, very hungry so they're getting ready to eat. They like food … it's all they care about except their veggies. The mother must feed them or they will take their own.' The short story is suggestive of a need for more care and nurturance than was being received. Given a very difficult early period, during which he was quite neglected, Nathan and his mother moved to stay with his grandmother at the age of 2; after the assessment, she shared that Nathan was very focused on food, with a tendency to overeat, unless stopped by someone else. He also hoarded food in his bedroom. The CAT highlighted this physical need for food and might have been linked to these adverse early experiences. Sharing the material that came from the CAT, his grandmother was able to think about how to address the overeating in a way that wouldn't be interpreted by Nathan as a rejection.

> In another picture, two bears on one side are pulling a rope with a slightly larger bear on the opposite side. 'They're playing tug-of-war. The mum has one and the dad has two, so it's not equal really. The mum is sad because it isn't equal. The rope doesn't look right … it'll snap. The rope should be tighter and fatter. It's heavy on the baby's side and he can't hold it … it's too much. The mum is winning. She's happy but she might lose still.' In this card, feelings about the volatile relationship between his parents might be implicated. Nathan had been exposed to a lot of violence between them prior to a

very hostile separation. Additionally, his mother had experienced severe mental health difficulties. Nathan's comments on the lack of sturdiness of the rope may reflect his perceptions of the fragility of his parents and the fragile connections between himself and them, and his wish to be stronger and to stop them from 'falling'. His description of the rope being too 'heavy' and 'too much' is a good description of how his parents' 'tug-of-war' might have been for Nathan. As he had eventually left with his mother, he may have seen his mother as 'winning', but the rope snapping suggested he may have some anxiety that he could still be taken away from his mother and grandmother. In meeting with his grandmother, it was useful to think about how Nathan might have experienced his family and their fighting. It also showed how his feelings of being overwhelmed and 'not strong enough' might have made the vulnerable position of the learner quite intolerable for Nathan, possibly contributing to his learning difficulties.

Figure 6.2 Evie's KFD

Conclusions

In this chapter we have tried to argue that psychological assessment is a clinical activity taking place within a structured (and time-limited) relationship; it is a therapeutic intervention in its own right.

As Melanie Klein (1940) says, 'The fact that by being internalized, people, things, situations and happenings – the whole inner world which is being built up – becomes inaccessible to the child's [*and others'*] accurate observation and judgement, and cannot be verified by the means of perception which are available in connection with the tangible and palpable object-world' (p. 346, emphasis added). Our belief that these inner world drivers are unconsciously organising leads us to wonder openly about them in the service of generating new understanding in the child, parents and teaching staff. Our experiences of working within this modality suggest that opening up such avenues resonates with people's own life experiences and this can lead to greater empathy as well as understanding. We believe that not knowing generates anxiety, frustration and impatience and that offering different perceptions and descriptions can help to mitigate the worst effects such feelings can have on interpersonal relations. Being able to elicit areas of functioning not available to consciousness through attending to our own responses, and through using projective techniques, greatly enriches the assessment data.

Clearly these connections and insights can be achieved through many means, but an analytic stance is explicitly therapeutic in its aims, not just exploratory. Making active use of data from the process of assessment is quite different from trying to be 'neutral' or 'objective'. A psychoanalytic view embraces the verbal, non-verbal and the emotional (in both client and EP) exchanges and sees them as potentially rich sources of data enhancing other sources of information. As we consider a central tenet of psychological practice to be to introduce new ways of perceiving and understanding complex situations, then ideas about unconscious drivers and motivations are likely to contribute to this difference. Add to this the notion of containment, and the possibility of the assessment being experienced as therapeutic is much enhanced.

CHAPTER 7

The use of projective techniques in educational psychology assessments

Isabella Bernardo

This chapter introduces the use of projective techniques, initially developed within a psychodynamic frame, in the context of current assessment practice within educational psychology. It begins by providing background and context to the development of projective techniques and outlines some of the more common tools. A case study is presented to illustrate how projective techniques may be utilised as part of a broader educational psychology assessment and how they may contribute effectively to psychological formulation of a child or young person's strengths and needs. Benefits and limitations of using projective techniques from an educational psychology perspective are discussed with reference to how children and young people, as well as wider systems of concern, view these approaches. The chapter highlights their value in gaining further understanding of a child or young person's inner world, while recognising their limitations and the importance of caution when interpreting information gained. The importance of receiving training in using projective techniques, as well as access to ongoing supervision, is discussed. Finally, reference is also made to practitioner self-reflexivity as I explore how this plays an important role in the use of such techniques in practice.

A link to psychodynamic theory

Projective techniques are rooted largely in principles from psychodynamic theory; thus it is important to spend some time first revisiting key features of this model. Psychodynamic theory proposes that as individuals we each have conscious and unconscious thoughts, feelings, desires and worries, and that we interpret the world and other individuals based on previous experiences (Frosh, 2002). Psychodynamic psychology has traditionally focused on clinical aspects of work with clients, most traditionally in psychoanalytic therapy. A number of authors and practitioners over the years have highlighted the application of the theory in understanding the social and emotional world of a child, such as: Winnicott (1964) in identifying the 'good enough parent', Youell (2006) in identifying the emotional experience of learning and teaching, and perhaps the more recognised links with attachment theory (Bowlby, 1969). Within the educational psychology community, a small number of practitioners have supported the use of psychoanalytic principles in understanding complex casework (Pellegrini, 2010), in promoting effective multi-agency practice (Billington, 2006) and in working with schools as complex large systems using systems psychodynamics (Eloquin, 2016). More specifically, authors including Pellegrini and Billington have argued over the application of key psychodynamic principles such as splitting, projection and transference in the relationship aspect of educational psychology practice.

In a 2010 article, 'Pellegrini highlighted the limited research and publications within the educational psychology world with links to psychodynamic theory. More recently, King (2017) also found limited literature in this area. One can argue that there is some movement within the educational psychology community to raise the profile of psychodynamic principles, evident partly by the publication of this very book. However, there is little doubt this is a less discussed model.

It is beyond the scope of this chapter to comment on the possible reasons and hypotheses for the scarcity of the application of psychodynamic principles in educational psychology practice. However, the argument that psychodynamic theory lacks evidence and appears less clear (for example, by Brewin and Andrews, 2000) is still dominant and is likely to have contributed to this. Evidence-based practice is referred to as 'the integration of the best available research with clinical expertise in the context of patient characteristics, culture, and preferences' (American Psychological Association, 2006, p. 273). However, there is growing recognition of highlighting the practitioner–researcher role in psychology, recognising the importance of considering the real-life situations psychologists work in, which interact with and influence the application of practice. Kennedy and Monsen (2016) wrote a compelling article in this area, stipulating the importance of a broader meaning of 'evidence-based practice' in considering how applied psychologists effectively integrate research, clinical judgement and client choice in practice. The increasing scrutiny of evaluation of outcomes both in NHS and in local authority services and emphasis on the more 'traditionally' viewed evidence-based practice has led to the support of more cognitive and behaviour-based models. To counter this argument, some authors have argued the importance of considering the ideographic nature of educational psychology practice, considering the impact of individual casework on the practitioner and therefore embracing different models, including ideas from psychodynamic theory. As summarised by Pellegrini (2010), 'Dominant discourses of evidence-based practice and EPs as scientist-practitioners may be interpreted too rigidly, without the careful attention and evaluation that individual cases require' (p. 256).

This in part is the position I wish to take up in this chapter. I recognise the importance of the more 'traditionally' viewed evidence-based practice, but consider its wider definitions in working in applied practice.

Projective techniques

So what does 'projection' mean when we consider 'projective techniques'? Chandler (2003) refers to the dual meaning of projection and the importance of holding both in mind when using projective techniques in assessment. One meaning refers to projection being the externalisation of our traits and beliefs onto the world – that is, the tendency to view and interpret the world from our own unique experiences. However, in psychoanalytic principles, projection also serves as a defence mechanism, projecting intolerable thoughts or feelings onto another person (Frosh, 2002). Therefore, when considering this matter, the use of projective techniques in assessment may bring into question whether material generated reflects an individual's beliefs, thoughts and traits *and/or* aspects of an individual's inner world that may be denied (Chandler, 2003).

Psychodynamic theory proposes that unconscious thoughts and feelings impact on behaviour, and thus the focus on trying to understand the unconscious and inner world of a child helps us to understand their externalised behaviour (Frosh, 2002). Those practitioners who are influenced by psychoanalytic ideas are more likely to see the benefits of using projective techniques in assessment as a means of gathering this more subtle and nuanced information.

Projective techniques involve the sharing of ambiguous stimuli to a child or individual, who is then expected to respond either verbally or physically, such as by drawing. Unlike some other assessment tools, responses to projective techniques are not 'right' or 'wrong' in a traditional sense. Rather, responses to projective techniques are typically assumed to reflect the unconscious drives, wishes and/or feelings of a particular individual (Chandler, 2003). They are idiographic in nature – that is, they focus on seeking out the unique experience of the individual. Several projective techniques have been developed and used over the years with both adults and children. Projective techniques can be broadly categorised into four main areas: drawing approaches, such as the Draw-a-Person test (Goodenough, 1926), House–Tree–Person test (Buck, 1948) and Kinetic Family Drawing test (Burns and Kaufman, 1970); inkblot tests, such as the Rorschach test; sentence completion tasks, such as the Rotter Incomplete Sentence Blank (Rotter, Lah and Rafferty, 1950); and finally those that demand a story, such as the Thematic Apperception Test (Murray, 1943) and Children's Apperception Test (Bellak and Bellak, 1949).

Current climate of educational psychology assessment

Educational psychologists' (EPs') approaches to assessment have long been a point of discussion and debate within educational psychology literature. EPs continue to play a pivotal role in statutory assessments contributing to Education, Health and Care needs assessments. It is important to acknowledge that the use of projective assessments in assessment is likely to be influenced by the individual EP's position as well as, at a wider systemic level, the position of EP services.

The move towards traded services has, of course, placed pressure on services to market and deliver work in the community. However, as many colleagues have reflected, this has also supported the offer of more creative activities within EP services, broadening the scope of the

EP's role in what many would argue reflects the true skill and expertise of the role. MacKay (2007) argued that EPs are well positioned to offer therapeutic services to children and families, and thus this should be a core feature of EP services. It is interesting to note that in recent years educational psychology services and individual practitioners appear (from my observations) to be more involved in delivering therapeutic services such as offering cognitive–behavioural therapy (CBT) interventions, video interaction guidance and whole-school training on areas linked to well-being and mental health. At a systemic level some EP services are closely linked with the local Child and Adolescent Mental Health Service (CAMHS), including the local authority, in which I work, where a number of EPs are seconded to CAMHS. In addition, the government's Green Paper (DfE/DoH and SC, 2018) which highlighted the need to increase schools' access to mental health services, has led to some services being involved in local 'trailblazer' projects, supervising and developing Tier 2 brief CAMHS services in schools. Thus, it appears on the ground that educational psychology services do appear to be making a mark in delivering mental health services in the community, although of course it is acknowledged that across the country this may vary. It can be said that projective techniques can serve as useful tools when working in this area in assessing, and therefore supporting, the emotional well-being of children and young people.

King (2017) found from her research that projective techniques are not routinely used by EPs, perhaps influenced by inconsistent training received by colleagues but also by concerns regarding how they are viewed 'out there' by professionals. This appears to stand in contrast to the US context in which Miller and Nickerson (2006) reported that school psychologists use projective techniques frequently. Hojnoski, Morrison, Brown and Matthews (2006) found from their survey in the USA with school psychologists that projective techniques are positioned to be helpful and frequently used for a range of reasons, including special educational needs identification and identification of interventions.

Three projective techniques tests are described below: the Kinetic Family Drawing test (KFD), the House–Tree–Person test (HTP) and the Sentence Completion Tasks (SCTs). I regularly use these tools in my practice, and therefore they were chosen to be discussed in this chapter.

Kinetic Family Drawing test

Historically, drawings were first used by practitioners to assess a child's cognitive skills. For example, Goodenough (1926) developed the Draw-a-Person test, assessing a child's inclusion of key features and overall quality of the drawing by using a standardised scoring system. In the 1940s, interest in using drawing tools as a projective technique increased, as it was noted that more subtle factors such as 'personality' variables influenced drawings. The Draw a Family test (Hammer, 1958) involves asking a child to 'draw a picture of your whole family, you can do it anyway you want', allowing the child to depict who they want. This also allows the clinician to reflect on omissions or features of the drawing – for example, if a key member is not included, or body parts of particular people are omitted.

Burns and Kaufman (1972) added a 'kinetic' feature to the traditional 'Draw a Family' test with the instruction to 'draw everyone in your family, including you, doing something'. As Handler and Habenicht (1994) highlighted, the addition of the kinetic action 'doing something' allows the child to depict aspects of family dynamics or even communication styles existing in the family. Burns and Kaufman (1972) administered the KFD to nearly 10,000 children and identified four dimensions in analysing the drawings: qualities of each figure, composition of the figures on paper, symbols used, and movements. A scoring system was proposed, but has since been changed and modified in different ways by several researchers, meaning that it is hard to evaluate the test's validity. Although some studies have highlighted the validity of using the KFD (for example, Sobel and Sobel (1976) compared adolescents displaying 'antisocial behaviour' with a control group and found that the former did not use kinesis between family members, omitted family members and bodies of people), a number of studies have not been supportive of the use of KFD (for example, McCallister, 1983). Handler and Habenicht's article (1994) reviewed research on the use of the KFD, and called upon more research that assesses the holistic interpretation and analysis of the drawing rather than focusing on the validity of single variables, such as the size of figures measuring the importance of that figure in the child's life. They argued that assessing the validity of single variables deflects from the holistic and integrative nature that the KFD originally intended to have.

Sentence Completion Tasks

SCTs require the child or individual to complete an unfinished sentence by filling in the last part with whatever comes to mind. The beginning of the sentences, often referred to as stems, is designed to be as vague as possible to encourage projection. Overall the stems try to encourage answers that cannot be given in one or two words, to gain more insight into a child's internal world. Koppitz (1975) viewed the SCT as a useful 'icebreaker' when working with young people. Instructions for completing sentences usually require the child to 'complete each sentence by giving your real feelings' or simply to 'complete the sentences'. There is little research and literature available on the use of SCTs with children, particularly those carried out in the UK. Holaday, Smith and Sherry (2000) found, in their survey of 60 members of the Society for Personality Assessment in the USA, that the Rotter Incomplete Sentence Bank (RISB) (Rotter *et al.*, 1950) was the most commonly used SCT. These sentence stems include a variety of personally referenced topics, such as 'I like … ', 'People are … ' and 'My father … '. The standard way to deliver the RISB is to read the sentences aloud and for the child to respond verbally. Holaday *et al.* (2000) found most practitioners (80 per cent) did read out the sentences and record answers for their clients when working with children; 50 per cent said they did this with adolescents and one-third with adults. Holaday *et al.* (2000) argued that reading out the sentences allows more spontaneity and perhaps less worry regarding spelling and written performance. Clients are less likely to plan their responses or anticipate questions when presented with sentences orally. In addition, Holaday *et al.* (2000) found that most psychologists did not use a scoring system when using an SCT. Indeed, in my training, use of a scoring system was not taught; instead, teaching focused on using information gained in an integrative manner.

House–Tree–Person

Following Goodenough's Draw-a-Person projective test, Buck introduced the HTP in 1948. The testing had two stages: a pencil drawing of all the items on one piece of paper, and a post-drawing interview during which the client responded to specific questions posed by the practitioner. Buck selected these items to be drawn because they were thought to be familiar to children and therefore children would be more willing to draw and discuss these objects. Currently, the HTP is used frequently by clinicians, in many variations. In my own practice, the child is asked, 'I would like you to draw a house as best as you can.' Once completed, the child is then asked to draw a tree, followed by a person. Once all drawings are completed, questions that aim to elicit key features, as well the emotional aspect of the drawing, are asked. This may include questions such as the following:

House

Who lives here? What is the house like? Do other people visit the house? What goes on inside the house?

Tree

What type of tree is it? What season is it growing in? Has anyone tried to chop the tree down? Who waters the tree? Trees need sunshine to grow; does it get enough sunshine? Are there other trees nearby?

Person

Who is the person? How old is the person? What do they like doing/ not like doing? Who looks out for them? Has anyone tried to hurt them?

It is beyond the scope of this chapter to detail key HTP elements and possible symbolisations, and for more information on this the reader is directed to Groth-Marnat (1999). Examples include: house doors and windows may be associated with the outside world, and small bolted houses or/and barred windows may indicate some level of withdrawal from the outside world. With regard to trees, the trunk may symbolise an individual's self-esteem and inner strength, and branches may indicate reaching out to others and relationships. Indeed, trees have been used to symbolise an individual's internal states in other psychological tools, such as the narrative tool the 'Tree of Life' (Denborough, 2008). Finally, the size of the 'person' drawn may indicate the individual's self-esteem, mood and anxiety levels. Excessive shading may indicate some preoccupation or anxiety. As argued by Chandler (2003), projective drawing tests such as the HTP are thought to provide useful and hidden (both unintentionally and intentionally) information through a process that is non-threatening and familiar to the child.

In my own practice and assessment of children, I generally aim to include at least one projective technique in my work alongside standardised and/or non-standardised assessment. Material gained from the child is discussed with them to develop hypotheses around their presentation. Typically, I seek consent from the child to include their drawings or reference to SCTs in my reports. However, my clinical judgement is used on a case-by-case basis, to assess the appropriateness of this. For example, projective tools, as with other tools, can elicit sensitive information, which may not be appropriate to share with all readers of a report, but instead should be fed back to parents or appropriate professionals separately or in person. Indeed, the area of reporting information gathered from projective techniques has received very little discussion from the EP community. Post-EP qualification, as EPs gain more experience with casework, questions related to reporting and the skills needed to deliver and analyse projective techniques become more apparent. Peer supervision groups and support online (similar to online support offered for those practising dynamic assessment and video interaction guidance), as suggested by King (2017), would help to address this gap.

Below is a case study reflection on the use of projective techniques in assessment. All names and identifiable information have been changed for confidentiality reasons.

- Ana, a 12-year-old person, was identified for EP involvement from her teachers in regard to her social communication difficulties. Ana had recently received a diagnosis of autism spectrum disorder (ASD). She was a bright young person interested in learning, but her teachers were concerned about her apparent social isolation and their perceived belief that Ana's parents were struggling to understand their daughter's profile and diagnosis.
- Ana and her family had lived in the UK for little over a year following their move from a Spanish-speaking country. Spanish was Ana's first language and it could be said she was still struggling to adjust to living in London and attending a large inner London academy school.
- In working with this case, I was conscious of my own experiences and beliefs as a bilingual daughter of Portuguese immigrants educated in London. With personal experience of navigating different cultural contexts and beliefs, I was mindful of this

connection (although different) to Ana's experience.

- Ana's command of English was very good, thanks to her experience of learning English to date. However, when meeting Ana, she expressed that she could more easily express herself in Spanish; therefore Spanish was used in the assessment.
- A Talking Mats tool was used to gain Ana's views. Dynamic assessment was used to explore Ana's approaches to learning tasks and assess her cognitive skills. The HTP was used to gather further information regarding her views, as well as any possible preoccupations or worries.

Ana approached the HTP task with enthusiasm and interest, related perhaps to her love of drawing and art. She was noted to take her time in drawing and showed good focus, similar to what I observed during the dynamic assessment task. This was in line with information gathered from her teachers that Ana focuses well on tasks that she feels confident in.

Figure 7.1 **Picture of house**

Ana told me a girl lives on her own in this house (Figure 7.1); the girl is very happy living alone and she is comfortable in her home. The house is not near other houses and stands alone. The girl loves to write about animals when she is at home.

Figure 7.2 **Picture of tree**

Ana told me this is an apple tree (Figure 7.2); similar to the house, there are no other trees nearby. The girl (the owner of the house) waters the tree; it is well looked after and yields lots of fruit. Ana told me the girl is leaning by the tree; she likes to do this to feel calm. Ana was noted at this point to be in a relaxed state and her tone of voice softened.

Ana told me she wanted to draw the girl (Figure 7.3); in doing so, she commented, 'This girl is like me!' Ana told me the girl's parents died in a house fire so the girl grew up in the forest with animals. Ana shared that the girl is alone but one day she would like to marry and have a husband of her own.

Figure 7.3 **Picture of a girl**

There is a theme in Ana's pictures of 'being alone', indicated by the house and tree being separate from others. She informed me, using the Talking Mats activity, that she likes to be alone at school sometimes. Ana's pictures seemed to indicate a sense of being content in being alone, which was in line with her comments. I wondered whether her lived experience of being alone was related to both her experiences of having managed several transitions to date, as well as her social communication needs. Children with ASD can sometimes get caught between the adults' concern that they are socially isolated and the child's preference to be alone. Equally, children who have moved countries need to re-establish links and connections, which can take time and place demand on their social skills, and thus perhaps appear more isolated.

Ana's description of the girl's parents dying may be associated with her adolescent stage of development, wanting to separate more from her parents but still needing their love and care. Indeed, in consulting with Ana's mother, she reported that Ana had started to challenge family rules/boundaries and to seek greater independence from them. Ana's wish to marry one day perhaps indicates her developing sexuality and interest in romantic relationships. This view was not known to her parents or teachers, but the drawing and conversation about the girl somehow supported Ana in depicting her hopes for the future. Ana put herself in all three pictures, which may indicate her approaches in trying to find links between concepts/tasks. This was a view commented upon by her teachers, in that Ana showed good skills in making links with previous taught concepts. This skill was also noted from her responses in the dynamic assessment task.

A feedback meeting with Ana, her parents and teachers was held. Recommendations related to the use of projective techniques in this assessment included how to support Ana's understanding and learning of sex and relationships. In addition, the teachers' concern regarding Ana's apparent social isolation was reframed and more flexible perspectives on this view were discussed, including her resilience and preference to be alone given her experience of moving countries, as well as her autism profile.

Benefits from using projective techniques

Chandler (2003) stipulated that there are several advantages of using projective techniques with children. First, projective techniques can help gather information from a child in alternative ways that do not rely solely on language or interview. In addition, because of the subjective nature of the techniques rather than the activities being positioned as gaining a clear 'right' or 'wrong' answer or being a standardised activity, Chandler (2003) reported they allow for rapport building with the client. This may have supported Ana to voice her hopes for her future to me. In addition, King (2017) reported that projective techniques can contribute to gathering information about a child's views in line with the SEN Code of Practice. The free-drawing aspect of several projective techniques has been argued by some authors to be of value, helping to externalise perhaps complex inner experiences onto paper (Groth-Marnat, 1999). Finally, Knoff (2003) argued that projective techniques can help to generate hypotheses as opposed to confirming hypotheses.

Indeed, projective techniques can be positioned as a tool to gather helpful information about a child's inner world, such as their self-esteem, ability to express themselves (for example, by using the HTP) and how they position themselves in the family (by using the KFD, for instance).

Limitations of projective techniques

Projective techniques have been widely criticised for the lack of both their validity and reliability. Most of these tools were developed in the early to mid-twentieth century, so practitioners need to be assessing their appropriateness today. However, equally, just because a tool is not modern does not automatically make it redundant. Projective techniques have also been criticised for difficulties in defining what they report to assess and the lack of consideration of cultural influences. Standardised scoring systems such as with the KFD are very out of date and not applicable to current times.

It is important to note that there is limited research generally on the validity and reliability of using projective techniques with children. The studies that have been conducted appear to present conflicting views. Handler and Habenicht (1994) reported good reliability when using the KFD. Miller and Nickerson (2006), in their review, argued that projective techniques appear to lack incremental validity. Incremental validity is a type of validity that is used to determine whether assessments (typically psychometric) will increase the predictive ability beyond that provided by existing or more routine assessment tools (Miller and Nickerson, 2006). As acknowledged by Miller and Nickerson (2006), this is a very rigid and strict view on validity and no doubt there are several other educational psychology assessment tools that equally may lack incremental validity. Practitioners who use projective techniques, including myself, argue that they help to understand a child's inner world and/or help to gather additional information about their views on themselves or family. This is important when trying to assess presenting concerns around a child and develop hypotheses and formulations.

The limitations and benefits of projective assessments are influenced by the dilemmas facing the scientist–practitioner role and debate around what constitutes evidence-based practice. To bring some consensus to this issue, Miller and Nickerson (2006) reported that it is important to reflect on what the psychologist is hoping to gain from using projective techniques as part of an assessment. If projective techniques are being positioned as an assessment tool for gaining direct information about a child or for diagnostic purposes, then projective techniques lack validity and reliability. However, if they are being positioned as a tool to gather additional information about a child's presentation, and if that information is triangulated with other sources, projective techniques can be a helpful tool for gaining deeper insight and understanding about an individual, as acknowledged by many practitioners. As found by Piotrowski (2015) in his review of literature published between 1995 and 2015, at least one projective test was ranked among the top 5 psychological tests used in 14 of the 28 studies reviewed.

Self-reflexivity and supervision

I would like to argue that the use of projective techniques calls upon the psychologist's self-reflexivity skills, a principle rooted in systemic and family therapy models and practice. As discussed, projective techniques require the psychologist to make sense of a child's responses from the presentation of ambiguous stimuli, helping to further understand the child's internal states and current viewpoint on his or her reality. Thus it is important that the psychologist is mindful of his or her own biases, beliefs and internal states to ensure these are acknowledged and reflected upon when offering a hypothesis or reflection regarding information gained from using projective tests. Midgen and Theodoratou (2020), who have recently written about the value of self-reflexivity and reflexivity in EP practice, stipulated that self-reflexivity is about continually shedding a critical light on our interpretations of the world and our lived experience and 'examines the issues involved in acting responsibly and ethically' (Cunliffe, 2009, p. 93). It can be said that this links well with psychodynamic theory in reflecting upon the emotional experience of the relationships we encounter in our professional practice, be it with young people, parents or professionals.

'Second-order' systemic ideas argue that the reality practitioners operate in is subjective, and perceptions and hypotheses are shaped by the practitioner's own beliefs, thoughts and background. This stands in contrast to 'first-order' systemic ideas, which argue that there is an objective reality 'out there' and that practitioners are unaffected by the systems they operate in or are unaffected by the professional relationships they have, be it with clients or other professionals (Midgen and Theodoratou, 2020). The use of projective techniques, I would argue, calls upon 'second-order' systemic ideas as the psychologist is using his or her own self as a tool in making sense of the information gathered by projective techniques alongside other sources. For example, when gathering information from a KFD, themes potentially gained – such as separation, loss, sibling rivalry – may be influenced not only by the psychologist's psychological knowledge about these areas and professional experiences of working with clients affected by these issues, but also personal experiences and beliefs related to Burnham's (1992) SOCIAL GRACES (such as culture, religion), and therefore the importance of the psychologist practising self-reflexivity, understanding how his or her own beliefs and both professional and personal experiences to date may influence analysis of information and hypotheses generated about a child presentation. In the case study above, I used my own dual cultural background in helping Ana's teachers to be more curious about the impact of her move to the UK on her sense of self. In addition, I used self-reflexivity to connect with my own personal experiences of family migration, while ensuring this did not cloud my curiosity into Ana's unique and lived personal experience of this theme. The emphasis on the dialogue between the child and psychologist regarding information gathered is in line with the principle that reality is being co-constructed by both. The psychologist is open to the child's views and comments about his or her projected information, reassessing this as it is received to reformulate hypotheses.

King (2017) found from her research that access to supervision is a key contributing factor that supports EPs to continue to use projective techniques in practice. Undoubtedly, using projective techniques, as with other assessment tools, requires access to supervision that can help the practitioner to reflect on material gained, as well as develop the competencies and skills of delivering the tools. However, I would like to add that access to supervision that supports the psychologist to practise *self-reflexivity* is especially important when using projective techniques, supporting the psychologist to reflect upon how our core beliefs might 'helpfully or unhelpfully influence the professional task' (Mason, 2012, p. 177).

Training

Access to training in the use of projective techniques is important, as with other forms of assessment such as standardised assessments and non-standardised assessments. King (2017), unsurprisingly, found that EPs who did not receive training in projective techniques as part of their doctorate EP course were less likely to use them. King (2017) also found that training in projective techniques appears to be dominated by one training course in particular, and therefore suggested the importance of the profession reviewing the consistency and core offer of training courses. Access to projective techniques in assessment was also found to be dependent on their availability in EP services, and this again undoubtedly will impact on whether EPs can use projective techniques in their assessments. For example, I acknowledge that I do not use the CAT (Child Apperception Test) in my practice, as to date I have not worked in an EP service that has access to this tool. Building opportunities to connect with colleagues using projective techniques would be beneficial to increase access to resources and practice development.

Conclusion

Projective techniques provide another tool to gather information about a child's inner world, helping to formulate hypotheses regarding presenting concerns about a child's learning, development or behaviour. When using projective techniques, it is important to triangulate information with other sources to guard against overinterpretation or confusion with the psychologist's own feelings and beliefs. Training and ongoing supervision are important when using projective techniques, not only to develop the specific skills in using associated tests but also in reflecting on casework material. I have argued that the practice of self-reflexivity is particularly significant when using projective techniques, given the emphasis of the psychologist using him- or herself as a tool when making sense of children's projected responses.

PART IV

CONSULTATION AND SUPERVISION

CHAPTER 8

A distinctive helping relationship: historical and contemporary perspectives on psychodynamic thinking in consultation

Emma Kate Kennedy and Vikki Lee

Psychodynamic theory has long had much to offer those who work with children, young people and their families in schools and community contexts. One key contribution is the foregrounding of relationships, and the connectivity of emotion, thinking and learning. This moves beyond acknowledging that emotion affects thought, and towards appreciating that our very earliest experiences of containing relationships greatly affect our capacity for growth (Waddell, 2002). Eminent psychoanalysts such as Anna Freud and Erik Erikson were also teachers, and both broke new ground in applying psychodynamic thinking to learning and development. However, while the theory has continued to evolve from Sigmund Freud's original work, there has been a declining interest in its application in many human services professions. Indeed, some have argued that educational psychology itself has 'become almost entirely defined by psychometric and quasi administrative priorities that emphasize symptom management ... [M]issing ... is the unique perspective a psychodynamic model of thinking can contribute to understanding intrapsychic conflicts and interpersonal dynamics that interfere with a student's learning' (Sapountzis and Hyman, 2012, p. 172). Internationally, some school psychology training programmes influenced by psychodynamic thinking have closed (Warshaw, 2012); many teaching and psychological training programmes do not include it on their curricula, others provide only a cursory or even flippant introduction (Saltzman, 2006).

Consultation itself has its roots in psychodynamic theory, developed as it was in the late 1940s by the psychiatrist Gerald Caplan, who had had a psychoanalytic training. Consistent with wider trends, some approaches to consultation ignore or dismiss the potential value of psychodynamic thinking. This may in part be explained by the rise of the evidence-based practice movement, with an associated emphasis on 'the best available research' being used to inform the role and task of the educational psychologist (EP) (Fox, 2003; Burden, 2015; Kennedy and Monsen, 2016). The ubiquity of positivist paradigms in some school consultation research – which do not easily lend themselves as frames within which to explore the processes and impact of psychodynamically informed consultation – did not generate a sufficiently wide and robust evidence base upon which to draw (Sheridan, Welch and Orme, 1996; Gutkin and Curtis, 2009; Lopez and Nastasi, 2014). There are other reasons also: Knotek and Hylander (2014) noted that the psychoanalytic origins of the original Caplanian model were seen as too narrow and too abstract to be of practical use in schools, and it paid insufficient attention to the academic/learning issues that are often of concern to teacher–consultees.

This chapter challenges the presupposition that psychodynamic approaches have limited practical utility for the complexities faced by pre-service and qualified practitioners. It begins with defining consultation on the basis of common features across different models. It then makes the case for an appreciation of the historical context and evolution of consultation from a psychodynamic base and the place of frameworks and models within educational psychology more generally, with a particular focus on how well-explicated models aid the application of theory to practice. It argues for an enhanced awareness of the degree to which psychodynamic theory influences practice across consultation frameworks, emphasising as it does the central significance of relationships and the place of emotions in learning and teaching. The chapter then outlines the potential utility of a particular model – the Relational Model of Consultation (RMC) – for the application of contemporary psychodynamic thinking to consultation in schools. Limitations of the RMC, as well as some caveats for its introduction and use – specifically the place of professional development and ongoing supervision – are outlined. Finally, some suggestions for the development of the model are provided.

Consultation: consensus defining features

Although consultation has been defined in different ways, a consensus has emerged in the last decade regarding features that underpin a variety of approaches. Consultation is a professional helping relationship, triadic and indirect in nature, where a consultant (for example, an EP) works directly with a consultee (for example, a teacher) to support a client (for example, a child) (Erchul and Martens, 2012; Kratochwill, Altschaefl and Bice-Urbach, 2014; Newman, Hazel, Barrett, Chaudhuri and Fetterman, 2017; Wagner, 2017; Erchul and Fischer, 2018). There is, of course, direct contact between the client and consultant during consultation; indeed, influential figures such as Thomas Kratochwill argued for a more nuanced direct–indirect continuum as 'the consultant may, in fact, provide some direct services to the client at various stages during the consultation process' (Kratochwill and Pittman, 2002, p. 84). The goals of consultation are to: (i) enhance the functional improvement in and/or amelioration of the client's difficulty; and (ii) build the consultee's capacity to prevent similar difficulties arising for the same or another client in future. To achieve the latter preventative outcome, the consultant works with the consultee through a systematic problem-solving process, focusing on *professional* dimensions of the consultee's practice. As Newman and colleagues emphasised, 'consultation is not therapy' (Newman, Hazel *et al.*, 2017, p. 108).

Although empirical investigations have mainly focused on consultation at the level of psychologist–consultant and teacher–consultee, with the client most frequently a child or young person in the teacher's classroom, consensus approaches are broad enough to include parents/carers and other practitioner groups as consultees (Sheridan and Kratochwill, 2008; Sheridan, Bovird, Glover, Garbacz, Witte and Kwon, 2012; Kratochwill *et al.*, 2014). The client may also be a group (such as a group of students with whom the consultee is working to effect change in either learning and/or social–emotional outcomes); or be conducted with the intention of having 'an impact on large groups, targeted layers within a school, an entire school, or a school system (e.g., school district)' (Erchul and Fischer, 2018, p. 185) – so-called organisational development consultation. There is now a recognition of consultation's eco-systemic nature: problem solving that fails to attend to the nested systems within which children and young people are learning (and within which teachers are teaching and parents are parenting) is unlikely to be effective (Gutkin and

Curtis, 2009; Gutkin, 2012; Newman, Hazel *et al.*, 2017). Such a systemic focus on a fundamentally relational process has increasingly brought to the fore the cultural dimensions of consultation (Ingraham, 2000, 2014), and attendant notions of justice, power, privilege and oppression.

Consultation origins and models

Consultation and its origins in psychoanalysis

It is relatively rare for consultation's roots in psychodynamic thinking to be recognised in the UK educational psychology literature. There is admittedly some acknowledgement that consultation was developed by Gerald Caplan (for example, Wagner, 2017), but it is rarely much more than this. Caplan was a Liverpool-born psychiatrist, who worked in Israel after the Second World War. He and his colleagues were tasked with providing mental health services to more than 16,000 adolescent immigrants living in residential settings countrywide, many of whom were extremely traumatised (Rosenfeld and Caplan, 1954). Conventional psychological treatment could not address the sheer scale of need, and instead Caplan and his staff team travelled to the settings concerned – an approach referred to initially as counselling the counsellors (Caplan, Caplan and Erchul, 1994). As described by Erchul, 'the collegial dialogue with caregivers (i.e., consultees) frequently uncovered stereotyped, in-accurate perceptions of clients, which through sympathetic and objec-tive discussion gave rise to enhanced perspectives about how to better [work with them]' (2009, p. 96). This approach to professional helping was eventually renamed mental health consultation (MHC) and went on to influence any number of different consultation models (Knotek and Hylander, 2014; Erchul and Fischer, 2018).

Well before Caplan went to Israel, however, he was an adult psychi-atrist concerned about *preventing* psychological distress. Motivated by a desire to intervene earlier and more effectively, he was profoundly influ-enced by some of the most pre-eminent psychoanalysts working in the UK at the time. Recognising that his training with adults was insufficient for work with children, he undertook an individual analysis with Kate Friedlander (who herself was closely aligned with Anna Freud) and child psychiatry training with John Bowlby at the Tavistock Clinic. As part of an honorary appointment at the Clinic's Adult Department, Caplan worked alongside Wilfred Bion and John Rickman as they developed models of working therapeutically with groups (Caplan-Moskovitch, 1982). Michael Balint – the pioneer of small-group reflective practice for GPs – supervised some of Caplan's psychoanalytic treatment work. There is thus little doubt that psychodynamic thinking played a key role in the development of consultation in general and MHC in particular. Caplan *et al.* (1994) elucidated MHC principles that would be recognised as fundamental to many consultants working today. These include the following:

- the relationship between consultee and consultant is 'the cornerstone' (p. 3) of consultation
- contract clearly for consultation, including the 'sanction from the highest-level administrator' (p. 3), to ensure that the focus remains on meaningful interaction intended to facilitate change
- foster thoughtful reflection that acknowledges the emotional disequilibrium experienced by many consultees; through acknowledging and processing the emotional dimension of professional work, the consultant facilitates a wider cognitive bandwidth within which to explore the problem situation
- expand frames of reference when analysing the work problem 'within the interpenetrating contexts of intrapsychic, interpersonal, and institutional psychosocial systems of client, consultee and consultant' (pp. 4–5), always considering the wider systems context for consultation.

Practice frameworks in educational psychology

One of the challenges faced by Caplan and his colleagues all those years ago is somewhat recognisable today, in the sense that the demand for psychological services outstrips capacity to primarily deliver services directly to individual children and young people. A recent educational psychology workforce survey highlighted difficulties in recruitment, where more than half of respondents reported vacancies, and the overwhelming majority of principal EPs indicated that 'they were experiencing more demand for EP services that could currently be met' (Department for Education, 2019, p. 7). In the same survey, 78 per cent of qualified EPs reported increases in workload and that there was never enough time to get everything done. However, even if services were fully staffed and all practitioners had manageable workloads, ensuring that EPs work effectively at both a direct and an indirect level is essential. It is not an either/or dichotomy between direct and indirect work with clients, but rather ensuring that we take up the breadth and depth of the EP role across multiple levels (for example, individual-in-context, group and organisational). What is critical is the meaningful, purposeful and disciplined application of psychological theory and knowledge. This is the case whether one is providing a therapeutic intervention to a 16-year-old with mental health needs in a secondary school or working consultatively with an Early Years practitioner and a parent as their 3-year-old child with a visual impairment begins to transition from home to a community nursery.

Models and frameworks – explicit articulation of *how* an EP goes about applying psychological theory to practice – have long preoccupied the profession (Monsen, Graham, Frederickson and Cameron, 1998; Wicks, 2013; Kelly, 2017; Monsen and Fredrickson, 2017). This is particularly the case when the problems EPs are tasked with solving tend to be complex, ill defined and appear in the 'messy lowlands' of real-world contexts (Schön, 1991; Monsen *et al.*, 1998). Rittel and Webber (1973) introduced the term 'wicked problems' to describe those that do not have true solutions but rather 'many parties [who] are equally equipped, interested and/or entitled to judge the solutions … judgements are likely to differ widely to accord with their group or personal interests, their special value-sets, and their ideological predilections' (p. 163). Kelly (2017) convincingly outlined why we should be concerned with practice frameworks, given the role they can play in clarifying theory, methods and goals when we encounter wicked problems in schools and the community. Frameworks – of which consultation can be one – support practitioners to engage conceptually with bridging theory and practice, provide a psychologically informed rationale for their activities and better accounting for their distinctive contribution (Kelly, 2017; Eddleston and Atkinson, 2018). And, while there has been some critique of practice frameworks (for instance, whether they are too rigid and inflexible for real-world contexts), articulating the application of psychological theory through practice models has professional and pragmatic utility for trainees and qualified practitioners alike.

Psychological consultation models and the influence of psychodynamic theory

For EPs in the UK, there are models of consultation with which they will be more familiar, such as the staged systemic approach (e.g., Campbell, Draper and Huffington, 1991; Campbell and Huffington, 2008). At the individual-in-context level, a model many are conversant with is that elaborated by Patsy Wagner (Wagner, 1995, 2000, 2017). Developed at a time when preventative working was being advocated at a legislative/policy level but where referral-based systems led to long waiting lists for direct individual work, Wagner was keen to discard the language of consultant and consultee (driven by a desire to avoid connotations of consultant-as-expert and a desire for collaboration with teachers). A number of different theories underpin the model and its associated activity, including Kurt Lewin's social psychological work on conceptualising behaviour as a function of the person in their environment, Kelly's work on personal constructs, systems thinking and family therapy (Wagner, 2017). Wagner and her colleagues developed scripts to guide the consultation process, and the model as a whole has greatly influenced the practice of individual practitioners and whole EP services (MacHardy, Carmichael and Proctor, 1995; Larney, 2003; Dennis, 2004; Kennedy, Frederickson and Monsen, 2008). The other model with a long history in British and Irish schools is that of the consultation group (such as Hanko, 1999; Farouk, 2004; Hayes and Stringer, 2016; Davison and Duffy, 2017), where a consultant (for example, an EP) facilitates consultees (say, a group of teachers) to support one another in dealing with professional challenges in their work context.

This attention to group-based approaches is somewhat less apparent internationally. Individual-in-context models proliferate, and identifying these is easier to do chronologically. As noted above, the dominance of psychodynamic theory in the early part of the last century led to the development of MHC. With the rise of behaviourism, behavioural consultation (BC) models emerged (Bergan and Kratochwill, 1990; Kratchowill and Bergan, 1990) and emphasis was placed on functional behaviour analyses as part of the consultation process. As values regarding the involvement of parents/carers in their children's education changed, variants of BC emerged, e.g. conjoint behavioural consultation, where the parent/carer is a consultee partner with the teacher–consultee throughout the problem-solving process (Sheridan and Kratochwill, 2008). At the same time, the limitations of strict behavioural approaches that failed to attend to broader systemic factors led to further BC iterations, such as eco-behavioural and problem-solving consultation (Gutkin and Curtis, 2009; Kratochwill et al., 2014). Finally, consultee-centred consultation (CCC) expanded on one form of MHC, attempting to address some of its limitations. By drawing on a wider set of theoretical principles, broadening the focus from mental health specifically to work-related issues of concern to the consultee and prioritising the 'interaction and role-relation between consultee and client' (Knotek and Hylander, 2014, p. 157), CCC has gone on to have a significant impact on the work of psychologists in the USA, Israel and Sweden.

There are two key arguments to make about the influence of psychodynamic theory on consultation. One is that regardless of one's own personal perceptions of psychodynamic thinking, it has had a profound influence on all consultation models. The second is that there are models of consultation that explicitly acknowledge the contribution made by psychodynamic thinking and provide guidance for the consultant on how one may apply such thinking in practice. Elaborating on the first argument, it is important to initially acknowledge how fuzzy and ill-defined the concept of psychodynamic thinking may be. There is no single unified psychodynamic theory, and there is a rich diversity between various schools of thought. It is equally important to note that psychodynamic theory of any school sometimes appears misunderstood by a wider audience. While still recognising the salience and significance of much of his work, contemporary psychodynamic theory and practice have moved beyond much of Freud's original thinking. Indeed, psychologists such as Jonathan Shedler note how even those who would caricature psychodynamic practice as unscientific accept now empirically supported propositions that originated with psychoanalysis – for example, that a significant proportion of our cognitive and emotional processes are not accessible to our conscious awareness, that how we were treated in our earliest years influences our adult development, that talking can help alleviate emotional distress, and that people often have contradictory and conflictual feelings and motives (and that these can give rise to contradictory and conflictual behaviours) (Frosh, 2002; Davies, 2010; Shedler, 2010; Borden and Clark, 2012; Vaillant, 2012; Curtis, 2015).

Shedler wrote a seminal paper on the effectiveness of psychodynamic psychotherapy that began with a review of the core features of psychodynamic technique (Shedler, 2010). Two of these are also applicable to consultation: the focus on interpersonal relations; and the focus on the helping relationship itself. Put simply, relationships are what matter. With what has been referred to as psychoanalysis' 'relational turn', psychodynamically informed practitioners focus on 'the interface between individuals and their context ... psychoanalytic developmental theory has evolved, with research in neuroscience, infancy, and attachment theory supporting the importance of significant interpersonal relationships as pivotal to healthy development throughout the lifespan' (Warshaw, 2012, p. 170). We become who we are in relating to others, and problems often occur when things do not quite 'fit' between child and parent, between student and teacher. As such, *most* models of consultation are likely at some point to attend to the dynamic pattern of relating between client and consultee, in terms of it being both a key aspect of understanding the problem situation and a core change mechanism. Fraught relationships between children and their teachers are unlikely to facilitate sustained positive growth for either. Shedler also highlighted that helping relationships (such as therapy, supervision, consultation) themselves have significance and meaning. Attending to the experience of relating to one another in role is vital to understanding the patterns, themes and feelings that are of central significance to the consultee. Indeed, Frank and Kratochwill *et al.* highlighted the 'substantial amount of evidence spanning decades [that] has clearly demonstrated ... the quality of the relationship between the consultant and consultee is highly predictive of intervention adoption, implementation quality and ultimately student outcomes' (2014, p. 26).

Psychodynamic concepts also underpin specific models and approaches to consultation. Given the popularity of group consultation models in the UK, these are explored further here. Farouk (2004) noted that his process consultation groups fused Gerda Hanko's work on group problem solving with Edgar Schein's process consultation (PC) (Schein, 1999), and that this was a relatively straightforward adaptation given that both have roots in psychodynamic approaches. Indeed, Schein's work – so influential within organisational development and organisational culture/leadership fields – explicitly embraced psychodynamic thinking on relationships and unconscious processes. The text explicating PC includes chapters such as 'The psychodynamics of the helping relationship' and 'Intrapsychic processes: ORJI' (Schein, 1999).

Schein's PC model helpfully prioritised the emotional dimensions of the helping relationship, and how the one-up/one-down nature of such relating can have profound consequences for both the consultee and consultant. He outlined the O-R-J-I (Observation–Reaction–Judgement–Intervention), a simple outline of complex internal dynamics, drawing the consultant's attention to the feelings, biases, cognitive errors and motivations that distort effective analysis and judgement (Schein, 1999). Psychologists keen to make use of psychodynamic thinking in consultation could therefore benefit from reviewing PC and adapting it appropriately for the applied context of the school or other human service organisation.

The Relational Model of Consultation

Another consultation model that explicitly provides a framework for the application of psychodynamic concepts to educational psychology practice is the RMC. The RMC is an approach to professional helping, driven by the primacy of relationships between people across time and between, with and to systems. Developed over the last five years at the Tavistock and Portman NHS Foundation Trust, it privileges psychodynamic, attachment and systemic theories, which are apparent across different dimensions of the model (given the focus of this book, it is mainly the psychodynamic aspects of the RMC that are further explicated here). Privileging *any* psychological theory in applied practice, particularly those originating in clinical and therapeutic settings, is a complex endeavour. Key concepts need adjustment and adaptation, and it is preferable to frame the RMC as a consultation model informed by psychodynamic theory and one that is cognisant of the current professional practice context of educational psychology. It is also necessary to highlight from the outset that, in a multitude of ways, it is not new. It draws on a wealth of existing practice in other disciplines and from the wider consultation literature, synthesising different thinking into an approach to consultation in schools and other applied contexts. As such, the RMC is integrative in nature and has been designed for applied psychological practice, with all of the messiness and complexity that implies.

The RMC is bounded by a set of explicit values, principles and standards that acknowledge the wider systems and cultural contexts within which it is used. It includes an active multi-step approach to change and, similar to other consultation models, has two principal goals: to help the consultee help the client, and to enhance the capacity of the consultee to help others in future. It does, however, include an additional goal: by collaborating together on new ways of perceiving experiences and acting accordingly, it also is intended to enhance the consultant's learning about themselves-in-role. The RMC is especially concerned with the intrapsychic, interpersonal, group and broader contexts within which children, young people and adults grow and develop (Figure 8.1). It is worthwhile emphasising this point, in that a common misconception about psychodynamically informed approaches is that they are solely preoccupied by the internal world.

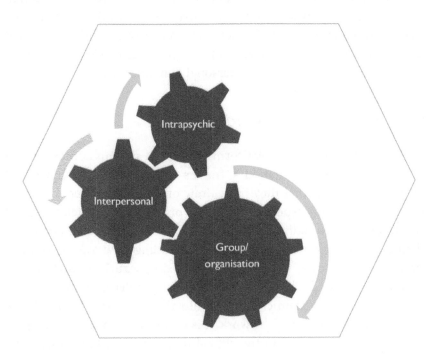

Figure 8.1 RMC frames of reference (after Caplan et al., 1994)

As noted previously, Caplan and his colleagues espoused as a guiding principle understanding consultation within its ecological context, as a networked field of forces that includes 'the organizations represented by the consultant and consultee, the consultant and consultee as individuals, the community, the client and the client's family, as well as the interplay of historical, sociocultural, and psychosocial forces' (Caplan *et al.*, 1994, p. 3). This is consistent with the systems–psychodynamics modality, where organisations are treated both as social systems and as work groupings that have dynamic influences acting beneath the surface (Armstrong and Huffington, 2004; Mosse, 2019; Obholzer and Roberts, 2019). Finally, and without claiming exact equivalence between distinct professions, Ruch's work on the nature of the social work task as defending and sustaining 'the complexity of human behaviour in the face of powerful pressures to oversimplify it' (2018, p. 23) has resonance for those applying the RMC. She highlighted that work with an emotional charge requires reflection on experience and on the emotional impact of the work, and that such reflection should inform any further work. A task of the RMC consultant is to be emotionally receptive and responsive to the consultee by paying close attention to intra- and interpersonal dynamics at work.

Values, principles and standards

The RMC values and principles form part of the systems context within which we practise consultation – frames within which the consultant acts and dimensions that they must draw on in practice (see Appendix to this chapter). This aspect of the RMC promotes the development of ethical sensitivities, adherence to robust professional standards and enhanced awareness of oneself-in-role (including how aspects of one's identities such as race, sex, gender, class, faith, sexual orientation and so on are contextually bound to positions of privilege, oppression and power). While the systemic lenses within the RMC greatly enrich the sociocultural dimension of the work, it is important to also note the psychodynamic contribution to the ethical dimensions of the RMC. Take, for example, the promotion of anti-discriminatory and anti-oppressive practice. It is impossible for consultants to adhere to this principle without first understanding themselves in relational context to others. The British Psychological Society (BPS) highlighted the sheer array of factors influencing decision making about clients (outside of relevant profession-al knowledge and skill), including the more than 150 cognitive biases that are inherent in thinking (BPS, 2017). Psychodynamic theory helps RMC consultants to develop and maintain ethical sensitivities by: (i) aiding us in understanding the power of more implicit thinking patterns over our behaviour, (ii) normalising less comfortable feelings that we may wish to avoid confronting and (iii) providing a psychological frame and process to develop our awareness and acknowledgement of bias.

Systematic problem-solving approach

The RMC has six stages (Figure 8.2), beginning with establishing the re-lational connection with the consultee.

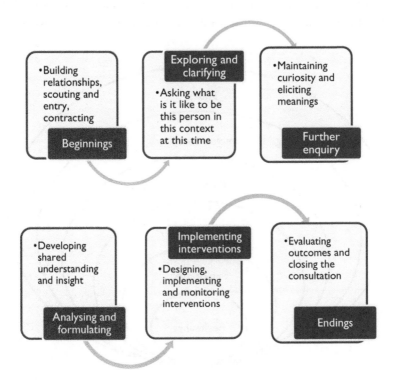

Figure 8.2 **RMC-staged problem-solving framework**

Having this clear and systematic process outline is helpful for consultants-in-training, and yet must always be partnered with the idea of concentric circles of containment (McLoughlin, 2010) (Figure 8.3). It is essential that the consultant does not move solely in a linear, sequential way, but rather appreciates that each stage is embedded in the experience of those before and after it, often illustrated with the image of the matryoshka doll.

The beginnings of the consultation relationship establish the secure and containing space where distress experienced by the consultee (for example, 'I don't know how to help this child; I should be much better at my work, I feel so frustrated by failure') is met by an empathically attuned consultant who acknowledges and helps process such experience. Relating in this way frees up space for thinking across stages, facilitating curiosity about the client and the context.

The first stage also includes determining whether it is appropriate to proceed with entry and contracting. This presents a critical opportunity to set out expectations, assumptions and roles (Newman and Rosenfield,

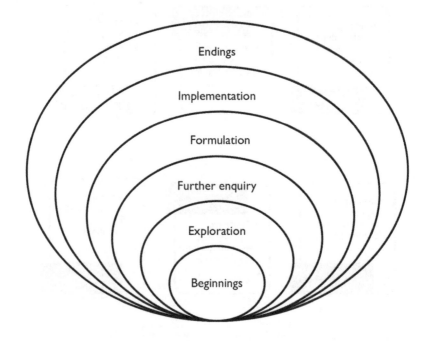

Figure 8.3 **Circles of containment in consultation (after McLoughlin, 2010)**

2019), establishing the boundaries within which the consultation takes place. Such boundary-setting further facilitates the consultee's experience of the RMC relationship as a space for thinking. In the second stage, the consultant explores with the consultee what it is like to be a person in the current situation, focusing on the meaning clients and consultees have made of their experiences thus far and generating questions and hypotheses for exploration. Activity traps are avoided by focusing on further enquiry in the third stage, trying as much as possible to stay in a not-knowing position, with a view to eventually arriving at a collaborative analysis and formulation at stage four. This understanding is 'good enough' to serve as a working model of the given situation that is open to further testing and change.

The formulation thus serves primarily as a punctuation point, and aids the system in designing an intervention at the fifth stage (and where the indirect nature of the consultation is particularly apparent, in that the consultant supports the consultee in intervention implementation rather than directly providing it themselves). Finally, the model separates evaluation from ending at the sixth stage and pays explicit attention to closing the consultation. The stages are dynamic and interactive, and at times recursive – for instance, what has been contracted for at the first stage may need recontracting following new information emerging at any of the other stages. Criticisms have been levelled at staged approaches to problem solving; for example, their suitability for applied contexts and, for some experienced practitioners, the 'difficulties generated by a somewhat positivist ideology which some find naïve if applied without recognition of … [their] limitations to real situations' (Kelly, 2006, p. 12). However, the pragmatic reality of work is that some conceptually sound structure that supports the application of psychology gives a sense of where one may enter and exit a consultation, even if the realities of practice mean that neat and logical progression from stage to stage is unlikely.

Relevant psychodynamic concepts influencing the RMC

Psychoanalysis has always foregrounded emotions and emotional development, and the connections of feelings, thinking and learning. Learning from a psychoanalytic perspective is not about mastery or knowledge *per se* but rather about a genuine desire to understand and to grow. Waddell movingly characterised this as learning that 'engages with life passionately and honestly, if painfully … [It] is a learning which encourages change, one which inspires growth and supports a person in thinking for himself and thereby becoming more genuinely himself' (2002, p. 122). A psychodynamically informed approach to consultation is therefore preoccupied with fostering this kind of learning, and thus with the concept of container/contained. Originally outlined by Wilfred Bion in the context of the infant–parent relationship, it pertains to an attuned and receptive adult taking in a baby's intense emotions and returning them in a more manageable and digestible form. In the context of applied work in schools with children and young people, containment has been likened to the experience of 'full empathic attention at every moment of the encounter' (McLoughlin, 2010, p. 235). The consultee and consultant come together to notice and attend to the complexity of feelings aroused by the situation, to process these so that they can be thought about in ways that aid a reflective response to the client. By adequately containing the consultee, the consultant facilitates the former's capacity to contain the client.

Ideas about boundary, task and authority are critical to a containing consultation relationship. The consultant establishes and maintains a robust enough space to enhance the consultee's psychological safety, but not a boundary so rigid it deadens the interaction and impedes any capacity for creativity or 'play'. Consultants take up their position at the boundary of the client–consultee system, not getting sucked too far in it or staying too far cut off from it that they inhibit their own empathy, curiosity and insight (Roberts, 2019). Emphasising both the beginning (especially the contracting component) and the inevitability of the ending further contributes to the containment necessary for the consultation to deliver what is needed. Another key psychodynamic concept that informs the RMC is the use of self. As Mosse (2019) described, it 'stands at the very heart of applied psychoanalytic work, the instrument … is oneself – one's own experience of and feelings about the shared situation' (2019, p. 6). As already noted, we are concerned with the place of feelings in professional life from the perspective of how acknowledging and processing the fullest range possible of emotion (both comfortable and uncomfortable) contains the consultee and thus frees him or her to *think* about the client. However, we cannot appropriately attend to the feelings of others without understanding what may belong to us and what to them. Developing one's self-awareness and ability to work with feelings in the context of relationships helps the consultant to more sensitively notice if certain feelings, themes and patterns repeat. This recurrence of interpersonal themes can get into any part of the consultation triad (that is, between the consultee and the consultee, or between the client and the consultee), thus providing an opportunity to explore and work with them.

Like all consultation models, the RMC is essentially triadic in nature with a consultee and consultant relating to one another about a concern the consultee has about a client (Figure 8.4).

Three-dimensional thinking is an important psychodynamic concept, attending to the adult interactions around a baby and how this fosters the infant's ability to see him- or herself in interaction with others (Kraemer, 2017). This nurtures the capacity 'for entertaining another point of view while retaining our own, for reflecting on ourselves while being ourselves' (Britton, 1989, p. 87). In the context of consultation, EPs relating to parents/carers, teachers, SENCos and so on may provide the required additional perspective about the client and thus facilitate this type of reflection. In the context of providing a good-enough containing

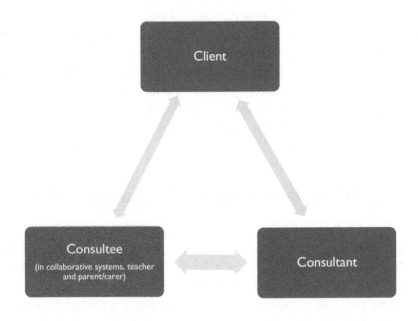

Figure 8.4 Triadic, indirect relating in consultation

experience for the consultee, this kind of three-dimensional thinking also contributes to the learning described previously.

Some models of consultation have explicit implementation procedures and some do not (Knotek and Sandoval, 2003; Newman, Hazel *et al.*, 2017); the RMC falls within the latter. There is a broad range of processes that an RMC consultant may use when working within the model, beginning with the use of self in service of the relationship. This includes, but is not limited to, the ways in which consultants develop their understanding of how their personal self and identities influence the ways in which they take up the consultant role, their self-awareness and presence of mind when relating with others and their complementary empathic and critically reflective stance. When faced with a consultee's question 'So what should I do?' 20 minutes into their first meeting, RMC consultants reflect inwards and are curious about their own feelings, what meaning they associate with these and how such feelings could be influencing their potential responses to the consultee. They also wonder about the impact of their responses on the consultee/their relationship, and attend to what kinds of thoughts, feelings and beliefs may be behind such a question. Such reflections are framed within the wider values, principles and standards (such as considering how one can act with integrity in response to this question) and with reference to the stage of relationship (in this example, at the beginning of the work together, where a consultant is in part concerned with system scouting, entry and contracting). Any number of potential responses are therefore possible, reflecting the dynamic nature of role and how each consultant is a self-in-role-in-relationship with another: what matters is what is psychologically helpful to this consultee in this context at this time.

RMC: limitations and areas for development

Caplan and colleagues (1994) described a range of caveats for MHC that are applicable to the RMC. One of these is the use of sophisticated and intellectually rigorous theoretical concepts by trained and experienced practitioners is not the same when 'given away' to consultees who lack the same training, experience and range of other associated aptitudes (such as skills in critically appraising the evidence base, including underpinning ontologies and epistemologies). A key theme throughout any

RMC training and application is therefore the need for caution, reflection and openness to changing one's mind/testing out one's thinking with others. To this end, supervision of one's consultation practice is essential. A second caveat they identified was the potential danger of consultees intervening without invitation into situations that they themselves define as 'need' – for example, where aspects of a child or young person's experience places them in an at-risk category. This may resonate somewhat for those EPs who have found themselves advocating watchful waiting following a critical incident when well-intentioned others immediately request counselling or therapy. The RMC orientation towards containment, towards surfacing distressing feelings that may be influencing behaviour, is intended to counteract consultee activity-without-mandate. If the adults in the system around the child or young person feel sufficiently well held to think about him or her, it reduces the likelihood of practice driven by factors other than professional knowledge and skill.

Caplan and colleagues referred to two further issues that are also potential limiting factors in RMC. One is the degree to which consultee skill, knowledge, self-efficacy/confidence and objectivity inhibit consultation effectiveness. While often these are the same factors that may have motivated the consultee to seek help in the first place (Hylander, 2014), EPs using the RMC have to weigh up some professional and even ethical tensions that may arise. For example, during the fourth and fifth stages of the consultation a teaching assistant (TA) may be enlisted to deliver aspects of the intervention collaboratively designed by the child, EP and SENCo. The TA may not have the confidence to deliver this intervention, may not be sufficiently well trained to do so, or be both confident and trained but their actual practice does not adhere to the intervention's content or process. The EP then needs to consider whether it is appropriate to continue or if a different course of action needs to be pursued. This links somewhat to concerns expressed about the practice of consultation in today's context, whether that pertains to the constraints on the time available to do so (Newman *et al.*, 2016) or a decreasing interest in a traded services environment to even commission consultation (Lee and Woods, 2017). The other issue – and perhaps the most important for the RMC – is the hazard posed by oversimplifying complex psychological theory and technique. The psychodynamic concepts underpinning the model are rich in depth, arrived at through experience and reflection on that experience. They are thus intended to be known, which as Lowe eloquently argued draws on Bion's distinction 'between knowing and knowing about, the latter of which can be a defence against *knowing a subject in a deeper and emotionally real way*' (Lowe, 2014, p. 11, emphasis added). This presents challenges in making use of the model, whether that is in training practitioners in its use, researching its impact or in the room with a client and a consultee.

There are a number of ways in which the RMC may be developed in future. Although various aspects of the model's conceptual base or practice components have an evidence base, it is vital that the myriad ways these are drawn together in the RMC and applied in school and community contexts are explored beyond the level of case or descriptive studies alone. Independent critical appraisal – non-partisan explorations of the experiences of those involved in both relational consultation and associated supervision – feels especially valuable at this time. The first and most urgent development is therefore research, informed by appropriate epistemological and ontological perspectives underpinning any further enquiry. For example, Daly and colleagues' evidence hierarchy for assessing qualitative research emphasises the potential benefits of studies that analyse data generated in a conceptually sound fashion that explicitly links to theory and related technique (Daly *et al.*, 2007). This is in keeping with the view that 'research on relational processes vital to consultation effectiveness is well suited to qualitative exploration ... on establishing in-depth understanding of dynamic processes and the complex relational context in which consultation takes place' (Newman *et al.*, 2016, p. 32). A second direction for future development is the ways in which the RMC is taught at a pre-service and in-service level and includes further exploration of the most effective pedagogies for novice consultants, as well as strategies to support interested and experienced consultants to incorporate the RMC into what they already know about consultation. Finally, relevant models of supervision for RMC practice is the third area for future development that may interest EPs. As noted, given the degree to which the use of self is a core process in the RMC, effective supervision is particularly critical as a mechanism to support the practitioner to reflect thoughtfully about consultation relational dynamics and feelings. To this end, alignment between the psychological theory informing supervisory practice and consultation practice makes some practical sense and the Relational Model of Supervision for Applied Psychological Practice (Kennedy, Keaney, Shaldon and Canagaratnam, 2018) undoubtedly complements the RMC.

Conclusions

Psychodynamic thinking has made a lasting contribution to psychological consultation, one that centres the primacy of feelings and relationships in professional helping. It continues to do so, especially for those consultants in community contexts because, in Caplan's own words, 'that's where the action is. That's where the decisions are taken in regard to the factors which may be reducing or exacerbating tension and stress and which may also raise the support for the other individuals exposed to these situations so they come out in a healthy way' (Caplan, quoted in Erchul, 1993, p. 71). As Erchul noticed, this is the reason why many of us became, and remain, committed to consultation in educational psychology practice. It gets us to where the action is and encourages us to use psychology to ensure clients and consultees 'come out healthy': surely a hugely worthwhile endeavour for us to not only protect but to extend and promote far more widely in the twenty-first century.

Appendix: RMC values, principles and standards

The RMC values and principles – which form part of the context within which any relational interaction takes place – include:

Beneficence (responsible caring): consultation makes a positive difference for clients, consultees and the wider system.

Respect: consultation maintains the dignity of all persons and recognises our common humanity; we respect both personal autonomy and our interdependence.

Equity: consultation promotes equality and addresses issues of privilege and oppression; as well as accommodating individual difference, we do different things for different people to achieve more equitable outcomes.

Integrity: we value honesty and accuracy in promoting trust in relationships.

Authenticity: consultation is firmly rooted in the real-life contexts within which children, young people, their families and those who work with them are operating.

Psychological: consultation is rooted in the application of robust psychological theory to practise, focusing on intrapsychic, interpersonal, group and wider systemic factors; our practice is evidence-informed and underpinned by critical and pragmatic appraisal of 'what works' for clients, consultees and the wider system.

Collaboration: consultation is a process of helping-in-relationship with others, and cannot be done without working together with clients, consultees and the wider system of concern

Humility: we recognise we do not 'know', value curiosity and openness to experience and appreciate the limitations of our own beliefs, values, and world view.

Acceptable: consultation is mutually agreed upon, and the approach must be considered worthwhile and acceptable to all.

Responsible: we have responsibilities to clients, consultees, the systems around them and to the professional discipline of psychology itself; we are accountable to our profession and act in ways to promote the advancement of psychology in community life.

Anti-oppressive: we have a moral, ethical and legal responsibility to actively challenge inequality and discrimination and to promote a more socially just world.

CHAPTER 9

The use of self in consultation: data from the 'total situation'

Xavier Eloquin

This chapter considers some of the unique contributions that psychoanalytic theory can offer to the act of consultation, as typically undertaken by educational psychologists (EPs). It is recognised that the word 'consultation' can represent any number of approaches, although it is essentially a problem-sharing conversation of some type occurring between two parties, typically a consultant (here the EP) and one or more consultees. This chapter will briefly explore consultation in the context of EP practice and then move on to consider relevant aspects of Kleinian and post-Kleinian psychoanalytic theory, culminating in the concept of the 'total situation' (Joseph, 1985), which proposes new channels of information or data that can be used in building rapport, in hypothesis development, and in the resultant action-planning.

Consultation and educational psychology

Consultation has been a central activity of EP practice for several decades now, recognised in two reviews of the EP's role and practice (Department for Education and Employment [DfEE], 2000; Farrell *et al.*, 2006). The Health and Care Professions Council (HCPC) recognises it as a core skill for practitioner psychologists (HCPC, 2012). It is often seen as a central, or at least an essential, component of an EPs' service delivery model (Leadbeater, 2000, 2006; Booker, 2005; Farrell *et al.*, 2006).

Although the term 'consultation' describes a variety of approaches, it can be seen, in its simplest form, as a 'helping relationship with a problem-solving focus' (Al-Khatib and Norris, 2015, p.7). Developing this further, Wagner describes consultation as a 'voluntary, collaborative, non-supervisory approach' the purpose of which is to ameliorate the functioning of 'a system and its interrelated systems' (Wagner, 2000, p. 11). What is important to emphasise here is that the act of consultation is one that has beneficial effects for the consultee – and for the system in which he or she operates, typically (but not exclusively) the school and the family. The outcome may ultimately be a series of actions, but the primary intention is to foster a change of perception in how the problem-holder construes the problem, and to do this the consultant draws on a range of psychological perspectives and skills that seek the 'difference that makes a difference' (Bateson, 1973, p. 459).

The incentive for EPs to take up a consultative approach is predicated on the assumption that it serves to build and strengthen capacity within schools to reflect on and own their problems, and the solving of them. Consultation, by involving problem-holders in the co-creation of hypotheses and solutions, limits the need for lengthier assessment sessions and even lengthier reports, freeing up time that can better serve the systems to which psychologists consult. By moving the focus away from within-child factors to the relations and interactions with the child, consultation works to test and challenge some of the assumptions role-holders in the system around the child may have, and which may serve to perpetuate the problem behaviour (Dowling and Osborne, 1994).

Drawing on existing forms of consultation, including mental health consultancy (Caplan, 1970; Caplan and Caplan, 1993) and process consultation (Schein, 1969, 1987), EPs adapted them to meet the specific demands of the discipline. Hanko (1985, 1999) promoted a form of psychodynamic group consultation in schools, which was later developed by Farouk (2004). The challenge for the EP is to engage simultaneously with a number of intersecting systems, chiefly the school and the family (Dowling and Osborne, 1994), and thus systems thinking, symbolic interactionism, personal construct psychology and social constructionism all played a part in developing a consultative perspective that the profession could use successfully (Wagner, 2000).

Psychoanalytic theory offers a further perspective on problem presentation: that the presenting problem is but a symptom of a deeper concern, one not easily articulated and that may or not be known to or recognised by the problem-holder. With its conception of an individual as comprised of conscious and unconscious aspects (more on this below), psychoanalytic theory holds that in any problem-presentation some aspect of the problem-presenter is present in the problem as it is perceived. In other words, we contribute something of ourselves to a problem, of which we are not aware.

The consultancy continuum

When taking up the consultant role, an EP can draw upon several psychological models and sources. In this regard, it can be said that they use their *expertise*, referencing a wide network of theoretical perspectives and practical approaches. But how this expertise manifests in the consultation itself can differ. Schein (1987) identified a continuum of styles along which a consultant may operate. At one end is that of the doctor, or expert, who draws on his or her authority in order to 'diagnose' the problem and impart the appropriate advice to fix this. At the other end of the scale is the process consultant, who is non-directive and operates under the assumption that the client is the expert in his or her field but, for whatever reason, is unable to discern at present the underlying gist of the problem. In process consultation listening, curiosity and reflection are the chief tools of the consultant that 'help the client to perceive, understand, and act upon events which occur in the client's environment' Schein (1969, p. 9). The skill and expertise of the consultant are here used to structure and frame a conversation in which the client can gain greater insight into the dynamics of the problem at hand. Psychoanalytically informed consultation tends towards this position where initial exploration seeks to gather as wide and deep an understanding of the presented problem as is possible, and to tease apart subjective sense from objective fact.

The process of consultation

The structure of a consultation session, informed by differing frameworks and perspectives, inevitably varies. In its simplest form it involves some degree of information gathering before a hypothesis is developed. This may be implicit in the consultant's own thinking, or more explicit, where hypotheses are shared with others. Action planning may simply be a result of greater insight or it may be a more procedural activity (see, for example, Monsen and Frederickson, 2008). Nolan and Moreland (2014) observe that there are few studies that explicitly describe the manner in which a consultation proceeds, but Farouk (2004) provides helpful steps for group process consultation, while Al-Khatib and Norris (2015) describe a one-session consultation approach for families.

Brunning, Cole and Huffington (1997) propose a staged model for consultation which places considerable emphasis on the preliminary stages of 'scouting' and 'entry' before one even moves to contracting. Only then does one move into 'data gathering' and 'diagnosis' (the interpretation and feedback of data) before considering further planning and intervention. The initial stages allow for curiosity and scrutiny of the problem situation, including consideration of how unconscious dynamics might shape the way the problem is presented

The next section explores some of the contributions psychoanalytic theory can make to the act of consultation, first looking at how certain ideas can facilitate a deeper sense of what is occurring in the consultation dynamic, as well as how new data sources can be used to develop greater insight, as a precursor to attitudinal, affective and behavioural change. It will then consider the theoretical implications of these features, working towards a more refined account of some of the unconscious dynamics at play in a consultation and how these can be helpfully incorporated into the consultation itself.

Theoretical exposition

It begins with the unconscious and the recognition that in an individual, alone, in pairs or groups, there are in operation conscious processes – of which we are by definition aware (in the consultation process, for example, thinking what type of question we might ask next to elucidate the problem) – and there are unconscious processes – of which we have no, or limited, awareness. Ferenczi spoke of a 'dialogue of unconsciouses' (cited in Haynal, 2002, p. 57) and, when engaged in psychoanalytically informed consultation, the recognition of a dynamic unconscious that influences and informs intrapsychic and interpersonal relating is fundamental to the conception of what happens when two individuals meet.

It provides an explanation, rooted in the idea of an unconscious which meets, shapes and responds to the current moment through the lens of previous experiences. This explains, to give a brief example, why one can have such markedly different experiences consulting to one teacher – feeling intense dislike – and something very different when consulting to someone else.

The unconscious is dynamic and, descending to ever greater depths (see, for example, Matte-Blanco, 1975), holds within it emotional and biographical data from infancy onwards. Importantly, this data is not stored in temporally linear form but is associative and symmetrical, in that one thing can stand in for another. For example, a teacher can represent in the child's mind a version of a parent. These internal representations shape an individual's emotional and perceptual worlds. It is this latter point that highlights the relevance of a psychoanalytic approach to consultation: the past influences the present in ways that are not immediately obvious. Sometimes such recollection or association is accompanied by emotions that are too unbearable for the conscious mind to manage. It is then that defence mechanisms are deployed to bring about a degree of psychic equilibrium. Defences themselves are developmental, starting with more primitive and extreme defences which grow into more mature defences over time, with the move from the paranoid–schizoid to the depressive position (discussed next).

Seeing the whole

Kleinian theory (Klein, 1935; 1946) provides a model of mental states or positions, charting a bidirectional growth from infancy into maturity, each with a set of preoccupations and defences specific to that position. These positions, in a very real sense, perceive the world in qualitatively different ways. In its simplest form, Klein's theory of objects and part-objects suggest a relational inner world modelled on experiences of the outer world, where perceptions of key figures are internalised or intro-jected. In the earliest days of infancy, a baby does not have the necessary perceptual or cognitive capacity to conceive of the mother as a whole person, or object, but sees her through the experiencing of how various somatic and psychological needs are met, or not. She is reduced to her functions: nappy, breast, bottle, comfort and so on.

How these inner and outer objects are perceived and related to depends on one's state of mind, as one inhabits one of two 'positions'. The first is the paranoid–schizoid position, which refers to the primitive and binary state of mind encountered in infancy. This is a position of absolutes (characterised by all-or-nothing, right-and-wrong thinking) and threats, where frustration, tension and uncertainty cannot be borne, and are experienced as persecutory entities, to be attacked, evacuated or avoided. It is a state of action or reaction that cannot conceive of tolerating discomfort and conflicting emotions. Indeed, this capacity to tolerate uncertainty and discomfort is the province of the second mind-state, the depressive position. Here, as the mind develops, it can learn to withstand uncertainty without being driven to action. It can also entertain complexity and bear emotional discomfort, including the discomfort of hating and loving the same person. This recognition leads to a desire for making amends, for reparations, further developing a capacity for perspective taking, empathy and frustration tolerance.

Although these states are observed in infancy and early childhood, with the depressive position developing after the paranoid–schizoid, they are observable in adulthood. Importantly, Kleinian theory holds that they are psychological 'positions' situated at opposing poles along a continuum, along which we move back and forth, with more or less frequency. The symbol PS↔D represents this bidirectional movement along this continuum. Where we are on this continuum shapes how we perceive the world, others and ourselves at any given moment. A key feature of each position is how it causes us to perceive others: as a part-object, serving some function that is intended, successfully or not to satisfy a need or diminish a frustration; or as a whole object – a complete and whole person in their own right.

> A psychologist was offering consultation to two teachers, who shared teaching of a class. The subject was an 8-year-old girl and the concern was a lack of progress in her literacy. The reason was not clear, much to their consternation. She had, the teachers explained, been assessed for reading difficulties, processing difficulties, hearing and so on, and there were no organic concerns. She just was not progressing, and they were exasperated by this, worried about her performance in the imminent end-of-year tests.

Listening to them, the psychologist was struck by how the little girl was presented – as if she was a problem to be unpicked and restored to order – and how hard it was to see her as a person. He asked about her home life and there was a pause before one of the teachers reported that her mother had been diagnosed with cancer and had only months to live. In itself, this fact was enough to explain her situation, but the consultation was able to go further into the case and the way it was presented. What was the meaning of her lack of progress? As the three reflected, they began to have a sense of what it might say about her mind, and what a little girl whose mother was dying would want to do to time – namely, freeze it. Her sudden arrest in learning began to make more sense as the teachers considered just what it was like for this little girl. As one said, 'I must have known that this was going on, but I just didn't know how to think about it.'

One feature of the paranoid–schizoid position is the tendency to reduce objects to their primary function. For the infant this might be splitting the mother into various part-objects, such as 'breast' or 'warmth' or 'comforter' or 'cleaner' (Hinshelwood, 1994). In this instance, teachers, pressured to ensure children achieve the best possible grades, had lost sight of the whole child and (in this case) her tragic home life. It was as if, until having a chance to reflect, they could not connect to the 'unthought known' (Bollas, 1987) and needed a time and space in which they could pause and step outside the everyday pressures of school. In such an environment, they were able to consider the problem in a new, calmer light, and they began to see the whole 'object', not just a student failing to make progress in literacy. Importantly, out of this arose a recognition that the main error lay with their expectations, not with the little girl. This case highlights why it is called the depressive position: it describes the rather muted affect people drop into when they realise that their earlier perspective had missed seeing the whole and, by doing so, had caused some harm or damage.

What is less well elaborated in this case is how the emotional 'flavour' of the consultation – a sort of arid, emotion-free 'stuckness' – was used by the psychologist to inform his questioning. This will be discussed next.

Emotional 'intelligence'

Psychoanalytic theory invites us to be curious about our emotional states and what they might tell us about what is going on in the 'below the surface'. Transference and countertransference are phenomena that describe the emotional residue inherent in the encounter between the analyst and the analysand (the one being analysed), specifically feelings the client transfers on to the analyst from his or her past and the latter's own emotional response to this (de Rementeria, 2011). These technical terms refer to phenomena specific to the therapeutic encounter, entailing, as they do, many hours of analysis on the part of the analyst in order to have a clearer sense of his or her own emotional baseline. And yet, by dint of the process of projection and projective identification, something similar occurs in the act of consultation (Gilmore and Krantz, 1985), where non-verbal material is conveyed to the consultant – provided he or she is open to it.

The mechanism of projection deserves further elaboration, as it provides a valuable source of information to the consultant, potentially inducting them into the consultee's way of experiencing the problem-situation. Projection is a paranoid-schizoid defence that was first hypothesised in infants as a way of managing intolerable sensations and feelings (hunger, for example). By separating and locating these feelings and the objects associated with them elsewhere, internal distress is outsourced and made, by degree, more tolerable. But to secure them 'out there', such projections must be located and fixed in the other, lest they 'ping' back: the projection must be identified as part of the other, hence projective identification, where the other is viewed as the originator of the difficult feeling projected. A relatable example is when a young child stumbles into a piece of furniture then blames the chair/table for hurting *him or her*. Over time theorists and practitioners have come to identify projection and projective identification as a more or less universal phenomenon operating anywhere human beings exist and relate. This includes children, adults, parents and teachers, and groups and teams within schools (Emmanuel, 1997; Pellegrini, 2010 Eloquin, 2016). What makes projection and projective identification useful for therapists and consultants is that it is more than a defensive evacuation of difficult feeling. It is also a form of communication about how one is feeling and the foundation of empathy, where one can try to sense how the other is feeling (Moustaki-Smilalensky, 1994). It is in this manner that it can be used to inform what is taking place at an unconscious level, as is demonstrated in the next vignette.

> An EP was offering fortnightly consultation to the principal of a residential school for students with social, emotional and mental health difficulties. This had arisen out of discussion between the pair of them about the challenges the principal faced in managing education, care and therapy teams while his background was solely in care. Once the consultations began, however, the EP was struck by the lack of progression; the principal flitted from one topic to the next, seizing on an idea and implementing it, only to forget about it completely by the next consultation. When this tendency was raised in the consultation, the principal dismissed the problem as being 'out there' in the school and nothing to do with him.
>
> After several sessions, the EP was questioning the purpose and utility of the endeavour: what had started so promisingly seemed to have culminated in a series of superficial, circular conversations. Throughout this period, he had experienced, but disregarded, a terror that he was not quite up to the task and that at any minute he would be fired. Initially he had assumed it was just part of his own set of insecurities, but as he reflected on it he noted that in different settings, doing similar work, no such terror arose.
>
> In the next session, he recounted his experience, wondering aloud if the principal ever felt like this. The principal sagged with relief and remarked that he lived in perpetual fear of others (many of whom had degrees, while he did not) discovering that he was out of his depth and, as a result, he lived in fear of being fired. He found himself in a state of perpetual agitation, which he managed, or avoided, by coming up with on-the-spur initiatives. These provided fleeting respite, but because they were never followed through with appropriate political attention and authority they were, in reality, fleeting will-o'-the-wisps. This further heightened his sense of impotence, increasing his agitation, until the next event. This fear, and the wider systemic effects of it in terms of his decision making as principal, then became the focus of more productive work – for the principal and the school as a whole.

Armstrong (2005) writes of seeking to use emotions as 'intelligence', in consultancy, presenting it as a form of information or data that can be incorporated into one's hypothesising about the issues presented in a consultation. If we can be mindful of projective and other defensive processes at play in individuals who themselves hold roles in organisations, then this intelligence can inform hypotheses about what is going on at an unconscious level. In the above example, it took some time for the EP to recognise how his felt experience might be a fractal of a wider experiential field. In other words, the feeling state into which he was inducted during this consultation refers not just to the principal's unconscious patterning, but was intrinsic to the organisational context of which he was a part: his fear of being out of depth was both his own and also something fixed in the culture of the school (indeed, the school was eventually shut down and all were made redundant). By noticing and attending to this emotional 'intelligence', it was possible to introduce it into the consultation, which served to advance thinking about the principal's fears along more productive lines: rather than reacting to each organisational 'crisis', he began to use the consultations to think about what the present situation actually required. The next vignette gives a clear example about how projected emotional states can inform hypotheses, which guide further questions and comments from the consultant.

Emotional data in hypothesis development

An EP was asked to consult to a group of ten teaching assistants (TAs) working in a special support centre (SSC) for children with social communication difficulties. The focus was the dismal morale within the team, manifesting as infighting, absenteeism and inadequately responding to the complex needs of the students they worked with. As the session progressed, there arose an apparent consensus within the group that the cause of the problem was the teacher in charge (TiC) of the SSC. Several people spoke in turn cataloguing her faults. It seemed a done deal.

The EP, however, became aware of a rising urge within himself to spring to the TiC's defence. For several minutes he stayed with this urge, observing and processing it – incubating it until it took a more coherent form. After a lengthy silence following these complaints, he commented on his feeling a desire to stand up for the TiC and wondered if this might be a view held by some of those who had not spoken in the session. More silence followed and little else was said until the end of the session. Afterwards, however, a letter was delivered to him, signed by several TAs. They disagreed strongly with the colleagues who had spoken. They believed the TiC to be reasonable and not the cause of the problems, providing examples to support their beliefs. They had not felt confident to talk in the group this time, fearful of the strength of feeling held by their vociferous colleagues. In the next group, however, members were able to articulate different points of view about why morale and practice were so poor, and the group began to focus on things that they could improve themselves.

In this vignette we see how projective identification can be used in a more methodical fashion. The EP was actively engaged in a form of dual attention: outwardly, he was tracking the behaviour of the group, glances, silences, who spoke to or after whom, and so forth. Internally, he was monitoring his own mental and physiological state and, as a result, was sensitive to a developing impulse – somatic and emotional – to defend the TiC. Note that he does not act on it, and in time this urge develops into a thought about why he might be feeling this. The EP was able to recognise a disturbance in his body (muscle tension) and emotions (a strong wish to protect) and entertained the idea that this was projected material from within the group. Externally, it was observed that a number of the group had not spoken, nor had they indicated agreement with the views previously expressed. The combined data sources were used to develop a hypothesis that not everyone in the group thought and felt the same way about the TiC, which he shared with the group. The subsequent actions of group members suggest that this hypothesis had some validity.

This vignette demonstrates a concept essential to psychoanalytically informed consultation: containment, or rather the concept of container/ contained (Bion, 1963). This describes the dynamic relationship between a container (that which holds) and the contained (that which needs holding). Drawing on analyst/patient and mother/infant dyads, the container/contained presents a model of how thought and meaning emerge – or not (Symington and Symington, 1996). In both instances, the infant/patient seeks to rid him- or herself of discomfort or pain, manifested initially in violent projections. Through the containing presence of the analyst/mother's mind, these unprocessed sensory experiences can be made sense of, thought about and given meaning.

Crucial to the development of thought is the capacity, on the part of the container, to withstand and tolerate discomforting emotions, including uncertainty, as it is this capacity that allows for the growth of thought,* by not capitulating to action as a way of avoiding thought. This has relevance for EPs engaged in consultation, for we are frequently encountering difficult emotions in our work. Indeed, the work is as much emotional as it is cognitive! Psychoanalytic theory provides a framework for recognising and using emotion. In the example above, the EP was able to remain with the strong urge to defend or rescue and not act on it. By staying with this urge to act, it was possible to refine it and link its meaning to what was occurring in the group, culminating in the formulation of a hypothesis. In practical terms, the psychoanalytically informed consultant is required to resist foreclosing on an idea: to remain, instead, open to uncertainty until a clarified thought percolates into conscious awareness. This can then be worked into a hypothesis to share with consultees.

The conception of container/contained provides a model of how one person can contain the somatic/emotional/psychic distress of another, allowing for thought and meaning to develop, which they do in iterative fashion, moving rightwards along the continuum PS←→D. Here we have considered how this can be used in hypothesis development. The next section builds on this, exploring how the registering of certain emotional or psychological experiences within the consultation itself can serve as a form of intervention.

The total situation of the consultation experience

It is now possible to consider how the above processes contribute to action-planning. Psychoanalytic theory and practice hold that, in parallel with conscious and ratiocinative communications, there exists an unconscious communication between the two parties, where information of a different order passes between the two at a more emotional and less conscious level.

In psychoanalytic practice, a great deal of training is required to enable the analyst to parse his or her idiosyncratic responses from what might be, through the transference/countertransference experience, something evoked by the client about his or her internal experience. And yet, when it is possible to make use of one's experiences in this way, it can contribute to the development of some searching hypotheses regarding the client's inner world. We want to stress here that this use of one's own subjective state as a form of data is something that requires learning, practice and supervision, and yet to ignore sources of data in a consultation for this reason would be regrettable, and even unscientific.

As discussed in Chapter 1, transference can be described as past, emotionally patterned forms of relating that the patient brings to the present relationship with the therapist. Originally transference was viewed as a new version of an old impulse, which, not having been articulated in verbal form, lent itself more immediately to re-enactment through the relationship. As conceptions of transference developed through clinical experience and theorising, a refined version of it emerged. Joseph (1985), building on Klein and Heimann's accounts of how analysts responded to the transference, the countertransference, wrote of a 'total transference', where the analyst took into account the total situation of the analytic experience as a means of revealing the lattice of unconscious defences, anxieties and preoccupations within the client.

Thus, alongside observation and verbal data, psychoanalysis suggests, with caveats, that one's own emotional responses and general psychic state provide insight about what is occurring in the client. This requires very close, fine-grain attention to the moment-by-moment relating between the analyst and the client. In such a state the analyst's mind is more open and available to the projections of the client. The task is to take in (introject) those projections and, through a process analogous to that of food, to metabolise them; to sift unprocessed emotional experience through the act of thinking so that it can be made sense of. This is a powerful action it itself, and in time the client can re-introject (take back) psychological material in a modified form and think about it rather than (re)act on it.

There are, with caveats, practical applications of countertransference to the act of consultation. In both therapy and consultation – to simplify – a problem is brought, often with an emotional component. The problem-holder's current frame is constricted and he or she therefore sees the situation as – a problem. It could be hypothesised that there is an 'unmetabolised' aspect of the frame, something that cannot be thought about, and which lies outside of conscious awareness. It might be said that some part of the experience could not be mentally digested. The act of consultation, like psychoanalytic therapy, is to mentally work on their experience to provide a metabolised conception of the situation, something that can then be re-introjected and made sense of. The following vignette describes just such a situation: initially, on one level, all was going well, and yet little headway was made. By attending to his total experience of the consultation, including a distinct feeling of losing control and lack of connection, the EP was able to approach the material in a different, ultimately more fruitful, manner.

> An EP met with a tutor – Sam – of a Year 9 group in a school for children with ASC (autistic spectrum condition) and SEMH (social, emotional and mental health) difficulties. Sam had 'inherited' the group halfway through the academic year. The group had already had two other tutors that year, with both tutors departing unexpectedly. Sam was concerned about the behaviour of the group in general. She had tried numerous approaches but with minimal success and her experience was that of losing control more and more each day. Stressed and demoralised, she was beginning to question her ability to manage a class or a tutor group.

> On the surface, the consultation appeared to progress well. Establishing good rapport, the EP listened actively and through regular summarising established they were understanding each other well. Sam was able to identify a preferred outcome and said she was keen to receive guidance and advice. And yet, as they progressed, the EP sensed a level of disconnect between them as they started to explore possible actions. Ideas were discussed but never seemed to take hold. Sam would listen appreciatively, but responded in a tepid and unmotivated manner when it came to think about how an intervention might be developed.

> The EP experienced a rising sense of anxiety and there was a growing realisation that, while he was doing his best, it was not going to be good enough. He paused and slowed the pace and focus of the consultation, focusing on the interrelational aspects and the felt experience of feeling increasingly disconnected from Sam, as well as the sense of losing control of the consultation. As they explored these phenomena, the issue of her taking on the tutor group halfway through the year returned. What was that like?

It was at this point that the consultation dropped into a deeper register of feeling as they noted similarities between her experience of the tutor group and the EP's experience of the consultation, with a parallel sense of distance, loss of skill and feeling out of control. Try as she might, Sam just could not relate to the class, just as the EP was struggling to relate to her. Together, they explored her thoughts and feelings about the tutor group: there were surface feelings of care and concern, yes, but also indifference and dislike. She felt she had been 'dropped' into the group halfway through the year and did not really know them. Their behaviour to her, now seen as a response to the third tutor they had had in a year, had prevented her developing any real affection for them. Indeed, she felt deskilled and rejected: whatever she tried was rendered ineffective. She feared the loss of control, something that was alien to her. This in turn led her to become more of a disciplinarian than she felt comfortable with, further perpetuating the lack of warmth and care she wished she felt for them.

The consultation began to consider how she might build a more genuine relationship with her class, one that required an attitudinal shift in herself. Having been able to articulate her ambivalence and the reasons for it, Sam did alter her attitude to one that was congruent with her aims. The more action-orientated interventions were left alone.

In this example we see that use was made of the experience of the consultation in its totality. It was not just the manifest content of the consultation that gave a link to the underlying issue of poor relations and a lack of bonding. Indeed, this was missed at first, as both consultant and consultee focused in on more behaviour management strategies. It was only at the point of rising anxiety and a sense of losing control that the EP was able to pause and reflect on the disconnect he experienced with Sam. Slowly it came to be seen that the situation arising in the consultation was similar to her experiences with her class. This was the nub of her concern, but it took a while for an understanding of this to emerge, for it to come into focus.

Using one's own psychological experiences as data is not in itself sufficient as a form of information, but it can point to a deeper register of meaning, which, if attended to, accesses a qualitatively different form of insight. A psychoanalytic approach can engage with the 'total situation' of the consultation: what is said, what is observed and what is experienced. And, in this case, it was insight arising from a reflection of the experience of the consultant–consultee relationship that led, when it was reflected upon by both, to a shift in Sam's perspective and attitude. The intervention was this very attitudinal shift.

We can now turn to how the discussed aspects of psychoanalytic practice can be incorporated into a more structured approach to consultation.

The consultation process

It is now possible to review the process of a psychoanalytically informed consultation. It is important to state here that this approach does not obviate fact finding, questioning and so on. And, second, to emphasise that this is the briefest of models, the ideas discussed here can be worked into various models. Nevertheless, it can be said that – after introductions, rapport building and (in some cases) an initial hypothesis – there are three main steps:

1. *Data gathering.* Information is derived from three main sources:
    i.   Verbal information, primarily obtained through questions and previous reading of paperwork, etc.
    ii. Observation of non-verbal behaviour, including silence, tension, and other indications of possible defences.
    iii. Registering one's own associative, emotional and physiological responses and shifts – what is occurring in me and how might it be related to the consultation?

2. *Sense making and hypothesis development.* The above data are gathered into a hypothesis. This need not be a formally presented one, but rather can be offered tentatively and with the intention of inviting further reflection and questioning. If accepted, one can move to action planning. If it is rejected, its rejection becomes data for a further round of hypothesising. Note that this can be done alone or with the consultee: 'We have been talking about X and, as we spoke, I have been feeling Y … I wonder if this might be because … What do you think?'

3. *Action planning.* A move to practical planning based on a shared agreement of what the issue might be. It is often

remarked by EPs that they feel they have done 'nothing' in a consultation. In fact, by containing anxieties they allow for mental processing of the issue and this constitutes a form of intervention that, while not explicit, does serve the same end: a new attitude and/or action is considered.

Caveats

Psychoanalytically orientated consultation offers a new perspective on what is at play when individuals meet. Beneath the surface of our quotidian awareness, another channel of communication exists: a world of emotions and associative logic. This requires an openness on the part of the consultant towards discomfort and uncertainty, the very things we tend to defend against. It can be mentally and emotionally fatiguing to consult in this manner, and it is important to recognise the need to rest and reflect on how one is mobilised by the projections of another. Without such pauses, it is all too likely that one shuts down to the emotional undertow of the consultation and, as a result, a more mechanical, inauthentic connection occurs. Over time this can lead to burnout.

Self-knowledge is a prerequisite, though this does not necessarily entail analysis. Psychoanalytically informed supervision is recommended, for it is hard to recognise such intrapsychic processes at play on one's own. Some work on oneself and an awareness of what type of issues, emotions and situations can trigger or mobilise us is important. Indeed, one less than helpful way of defending against some of the more challenging psychic realities arising in a consultation can be a move to arid or overly complex hypotheses. Similarly, the rush to come up with a solution as a way of escape is understandable, but ultimately avoids the underlying problem.

Conclusion

This chapter has sought to make links between psychoanalytic theory and the practice of consultation, arguing that the former has much that it can offer. By considering the cognitive, the emotional and the somatic, we become alive to the situation and present to ourselves and others. It is in such a moment that true creativity arises, whether this be in the development of new attitudes or practical, reality-based interventions that have been more deeply considered, processed and therefore owned by those who seek out consultation.

Note

*A recent study by (Wilson, Reinhard, Westgate, Gilbert and Ellerbeck 2014) shows just how hard it can be to bear even an empty room, let alone a difficult thought! Participants preferred mild electric shocks to doing nothing.

CHAPTER 10

Feelings, relationships and 'being held': the experience of psychodynamically informed supervision

Chris Shaldon, Caoimhe McBay, Caroline Keaney,
Emma Kate Kennedy, Sara Reid, Nicole Schnackenberg
and Sinead Walker

Ten years ago, the British Psychological Society (BPS) Division of Educational and Child Psychology (DECP) issued professional guidelines underscoring the centrality of supervision to the 'delivery of high-quality psychological services' (Dunsmuir and Leadbetter, 2010, p. 2). Supervision has also been promoted by the Health and Care Professions Council (HCPC) in terms of their statutory standards for (i) conduct, performance and ethics and (ii) proficiency for initial and continuing registration. These latter standards for all practitioner psychologists emphasise both the importance of understanding supervisory models and of participating in supervision that facilitates autonomous and reflective practice. More recently, however, it has been argued that supervision models originating in therapeutic practice may confuse supervisory task, boundary and role. Others have argued that the distinctive breadth and depth of the educational psychologist (EP) role requires supervision models developed specifically within an EP frame.

This chapter begins by exploring the professional context of supervision in educational psychology. Highlighting the primacy accorded to the supervisory relationship, we outline a supervision model developed specifically within the educational psychology and related school and community setting context – the Relational Model of Supervision for

Applied Psychology Practice (RMSAPP). The RMSAPP is explicitly informed by psychological theory from the psychodynamic, systemic and attachment traditions, adapted for the real world of applied practice. In the chapter, we attend particularly to the psychodynamic components of the RMSAPP. We examine how it places emotion, relational dynamics and containment at the centre of the process, enabling practitioners to engage in thinking and learning about themselves-in-role-in-relationship across the course of their career.

Because the model privileges the bidirectional nature of the supervisory relationship, we illustrate the application of key psychodynamic concepts to supervisory practice through foregrounding a reflective dialogue between supervisees and supervisors who use the model.

Such dialogue sustains the relational and reflexive cycle inherent in the model itself and illustrates important implications for educational psychology supervisory practice. Some cautions as regards use of the model in practice are offered, as well as a rationale for appropriate professional development and ongoing supervision on supervision. Finally, some suggestions for future developments of the RMSAPP – including practice-based research enquiry – are explored.

Educational psychology supervision: past and present context

Historical context

The practice of supervision originated from psychodynamic therapeutic training in the early part of the last century and was subsequently developed within a variety of therapy-bound frameworks (Carroll, 2007). From the 1970s onwards, supervision emerged as an independent process for a range of different professions (for example, social work) with an emphasis on tasks, roles and learning development. So-called generic models of supervision grew and supervisory practice for psychologists widened in the UK (Creaner, 2014; Page and Wosket, 2015), particularly in the fields of clinical and counselling psychology. Hawkins and Shohet's *Supervision in the Helping Professions* was first published in 1989 and Scaife's *General Supervision Framework* in 1993. At the same time, and influenced by these developments, there was what could be described as the first wave of educational psychology interest in supervision. One of the themes that emerged from early research into supervision within the profession was uncertainty as to the purpose and understanding of supervision (Pomerantz, 1990, 1993; Lunt, 1993; Pomerantz and Lunt, 1993; Lunt and Sayeed, 1995).

Pomerantz (1990) speculated that a confusion and misunderstanding of the influence of psychotherapy may also have acted as a source of resistance to the profession's realisation of supervisory possibilities:

> There is a ... point of resistance that may well account for our not changing with the times as other professional groups have chosen to do. It is about confusing supervision with psychotherapy or psychoanalysis. The latter approaches actually have a great potential in influencing training in supervision. They inform us as to where to go looking for some of the basic material to be discussed in a supervisory session. One must be quite clear about what one is doing or offering. However, there are many good lessons to learn from therapists in order to bring life to supervision and rescue it from just being a 'reporting back' session on Friday afternoon. (p. 57)

It could be argued that wariness of engaging with this basic material and the relational complexity of the process are factors that have influenced and limited the construction of supervision within educational psychology as a profession. Lunt and Sayeed (1995) summarised their research on newly qualified entrants with the comment: 'The idea of supervision as an administrative rather than a clinical activity and process must be of concern to a profession concerned with the mental health and psychological wellbeing of young people and parents, many of whom are experiencing considerable distress' (p. 30).

The need for a model

Developing a model of supervision that can address both the complex and wide context in which EPs operate and also access the basic material of the dyadic supervisory encounter has become an ever more pressing requirement. The urgency of this need has been evident from recent resurgence in research on supervision carried out with trainee educational psychologists (TEPs) (Hill et al., 2015; Woods et al., 2015; Gibbs et al.,

2016). Until very recently, EPs in search of supervision models have been reliant on borrowing and adapting from other psychological disciplines to make sense of and develop their understanding of supervision (Simon, Cruise, Huber, Swerdik and Newman, 2014; Hill *et al.*, 2015). Some have questioned whether such models are fully fit for purpose within the EP context; writing of school psychologists in the US, Simon and colleagues argued that these models 'fail to address the multifaceted practice roles that school psychology embraces' (2014, p. 637). Indeed, Hill and colleagues explored how useful how one such model – the Developmental/ Ecological/Problem-solving Model (DEP) – might be for understanding the supervisory experiences of TEPs in the UK. Based on their in-depth analysis of focus group data, they proposed that the DEP captured 'additional dimensions of the EP role that are absent in the supervision models currently in use that have their origins in counselling psychology' (Hill *et al.*, 2015, p. 129).

Gibbs and colleagues (2016) used data generated from an earlier study (Woods *et al.*, 2015) as the basis for a questionnaire survey to explore the extent to which different supervisory factors were valued by EPs at different stages of training. Their research identified three core factors that were incorporated into a theoretical framework: safe space for authentic learning, instructional support and reference points for professional learning. They concluded that their study added validity to the emphasis placed on both the emotionally supportive function of supervision found across different theoretical models and on models that fully acknowledge the significance of the supervisory context. As such, these emergent frameworks for EP supervision acknowledge the importance of the supportive relationship between supervisor and supervisee while holding in mind the wider system. The RMSAPP offers a distinct contribution to this ongoing movement of understanding and developing EP practice around supervision by privileging and exploring in depth the relational dynamics and interaction that takes place between supervisor and supervisee. The model also holds the context of the supervision at its core and provides a theoretical underpinning that is fundamental to understanding this complexity. It has been developed by EPs for EPs (Kennedy, Keaney, Shaldon and Canagaratnam, 2018) and has proved applicable to others within the helping professions (Kennedy and Laverick, 2019).

Relational Model of Supervision for Applied Psychology Practice

The RMSAPP defines supervision as a work-based learning relationship, characterised by relating and reflecting (Figure 10.1).

Drawing on the evidence base as regards the significance of relationship in supervision, the most fundamental orientation of the supervisor is towards establishing, maintaining and ending this learning relationship with their supervisee. Various aspects of the model are outlined below.

Ecologies of applied practice

All supervision relationships take place within a context, referred to in the RMSAPP as 'the ecologies of applied practice'. This encompasses the broad national, legal, ethical and policy dimensions relevant to both supervisee and supervisor as well as any specific local constraints that must be accounted for (management structures, team and service culture and ethos, etc.). For example, the HCPC *Standards of Conduct, Performance and Ethics* and the BPS *Professional Practice Guidelines* are influencing factors on the supervisory relationship. Educational Psychology Services and other work settings may also have supervision policies outlining various aspects of process such as frequency, location, length, recording and the purpose of supervisory sessions. The RMSAPP explicitly draws both parties' attention to all relevant aspects of the ecologies of practice, including where there are potential tensions between them. One such tension could be between the BPS *Professional Practice Guidelines* highlighting the ways in which supervision offers a space 'where it is possible to open up thinking to the mind of another with a view to extending knowledge about the self' (2017, p. 12) and a local understanding of supervision as a primarily managerial function. In the RMSAPP, it is crucial that both parties (i) bear in mind the context, (ii) contract for the supervisory space and (iii) strive to be self-aware and attuned to the impact of ecologies of practice.

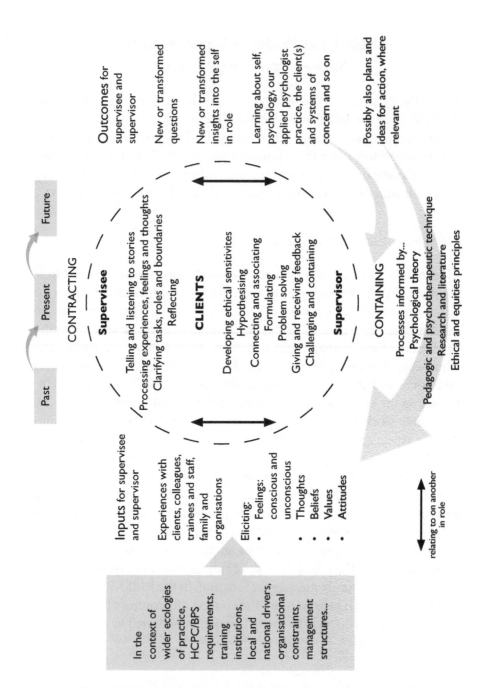

Figure 10.1 A visual representation of the inputs, processes and
outcomes in the Relational Model of Supervision for
Applied Psychology Practice (RMSAPP)

Inputs, processes and outcomes

Inputs refer to experiences that both the supervisee and supervisor may have had with clients, families, colleagues and/or aspects of systems and organisations. These may be quite proximate to the supervision session itself (for example, a young person with whom the supervisee worked the previous week) or somewhat distal (such as their previous experiences of working with young people of a similar background and need in their previous work setting). The model is predicated on the fact that all inputs elicit feelings, thoughts, beliefs, values, attitudes, some of which may be at the level of conscious awareness and some of which are far more implicit. A supervisee may bring his or her feelings of frustration and worry about the young person as the work he or she had done did not seem to have gone well and the young person failed to respond to the supervisee's approach. Less explicit – but nonetheless important – is the supervisee's belief that he or she should be able to work effectively with *all* young people and that anything that does not go as expected is a failure on his or her part. Through the interpersonal connection established with a supervisor, the supervisee feels contained enough during the supervision session(s) to reflect on what might have been going on during the work with the young person. This reflection is facilitated through the supervisor's use of technique/process, and ultimately leads to supervisory 'outcome' – new or transformed questions, new or transformed insights into the self-in-role, learning about applied psychological practice, the client, the system(s) of concern, and perhaps also plans and ideas for action where relevant.

Outcomes are also for both supervisee and supervisor, and the RMSAPP attends to the cyclical nature of the past influencing the present with implications for the future. Repeated themes and patterns may emerge over time, providing the supervisor with a different and richer sense of what may be going on for the supervisee. Critically, this sense making is always ultimately oriented towards the client: if the supervisor can work together with the supervisee to understand what may be influencing and shaping the supervisee's feelings, thoughts and behaviours, he or she will be enabled to better help the client from a psychologically informed position. Developing a sense of comfort with uncertainty – that not every session will conclude with a neat 'outcome' or action – is part of the RMSAPP, acknowledging that learning takes time and patience.

Enabling comfort with 'not knowing' (even in the face of at times quite powerful demands to 'know') is curiosity and one's ability to remain open to receiving the experiences of the supervisee. Such curiosity and openness is modelled through the use of genuine enquiry, where the supervisor is driven by his or her own authentic desire to learn and not by the need to put across his or her own point of view (Le Fevre, Robinson and Sinnema, 2015). RMSAPP-informed supervisors recognise that important outcomes for them include learning about themselves-in-role as supervisor, thus enhancing their professional supervisory practice in the future.

Between the inputs and the outcomes is the process of supervision. This is represented in Figure 10.1 as the circle with a perforated edge, highlighting how the supervisory space is an open system. It is a system influenced by, and in turn acts upon, the surrounding context. This is a circular rather than linear influence. It is in the supervisory space that the work of supervision takes place within a contracted and containing frame. Here the model locates the exchanges between supervisor and supervisee, such as questioning, thinking, reflecting, telling, listening, challenging, sharing, hypothesising, directing and so on. The third party in this space is always the client. Underpinning this working space is the understanding and application of theory – and in particular psychodynamic thinking. To illustrate the model in practice, in the following section we present short accounts from three newly qualified EPs who experienced the RMSAPP model in their supervision while training. Each account is followed by reflections that link to psychodynamic thinking.

Psychodynamic thinking in relational supervision: theory in practice

The inputs that supervisee and supervisor bring to supervision often come in as unprocessed, unconscious feeling-states that both parties might struggle to notice and make sense of. If they create a lot of anxiety and are experienced as overwhelming, there might be resistance to and avoidance of exploration at the expense of practitioner well-being, professional growth and client outcome. Psychodynamic ideas can offer ways of facilitating the dyad's receptiveness to and containment of powerful and confusing feeling-states until they can be processed and better understood. In the examples that follow, the voices of the supervisees within the dyads gives a sense of how psychodynamic ideas provide a framework to contain uncertainty and anxiety to enable exploration, reflection and professional development. Each supervisee reflection is followed by a supervisory practice-to-theory link.

Supervisee 1

The experience of a non-judgemental, containing space felt really alien to me at first. Coming from a teaching background, my only experience of thinking about work came from line management meetings or informal chats in the staff room. It took a while for me to get to the point where I realised that it was safe to share my experience (I was a bit suspicious at first!). It was early in my training, so as well as being new to the practice of genuinely reflecting on my experience I was also quite 'full up' from the early days of being a trainee and working with young people in a therapeutic way. I found that I was often entering the supervision space feeling like I had no idea what I was going to talk about, but feeling physically full – a sense of heaviness across my chest. It was often within the containing space of the supervision that I was helped to surface what I was feeling in my body and be able to put the emotional aspect of my experience into words. Thus, one of the things that supervision helped me to realise was that I was often not fully in touch with how I was feeling emotionally, that I was quite good at intellectualising my experiences.

Another key realisation for me came when my supervisor gently pointed out that I was often berating myself for doing the 'wrong' thing – did I believe that there really was a 'wrong' and a 'right' way to be? She helped me to reflect on my inner critic. This was a light bulb moment for me because I realised that I had been experiencing my supervisor and other tutors as somewhat persecutory figures, as part of me was always somehow dreading that I would be found out as having done the 'wrong' thing. As such, I was not fully able to be genuine and open, because on some level I was always trying to be 'right'.

Supervisee 1 spoke to their feelings on entering into a new professional relationship, a new role in a new context. They talked about how emotions can be experienced as physical sensations which may not be fully understood or processed. Their words highlight the importance of the supervisor providing a containing space in which feelings can be surfaced and in which understanding of oneself can be realised. Such relational supervisory processes are located at the core of the RSMAPP model. Supervisee 1 described how their supervisor was able to attend to and sensitively surface aspects of the relational patterns occurring between them. In turn, this provided the supervisee with an understanding of how they experienced authority figures (such as members of the course team) to be somewhat judging and looking for evidence of their shortcomings. They became aware of psychological defences that could be deployed to manage the feelings experienced when their inner critic is activated and they begin to feel persecutory anxiety.

Applying psychodynamic theory: reflections on reflections I

Defences and learning

Psychological defence mechanisms are unconsciously used by all of us and many are essential to manage the tasks and challenges of everyday life without becoming overwhelmed. Donald Meltzer (1978) eloquently described such defences as lies we tell ourselves to evade pain. This evasion can be helpful in the short term, such as when facing the truth would render the reality of life intolerable. When rigidly adopted, however, and excessively used in the long term, they can come at a cost. The supervisee described adopting the defence of intellectualisation and 'always trying to be right' as a way to avoid experiencing uncertainty and, as they perceived, to avoid the risk of being found to have 'done the wrong thing'. This defence may have been helpful to them in the early days of training while adapting to new experiences and relationships, when understandably we may seek to avoid feeling overexposed or simply not yet ready to reveal more vulnerable aspects of ourselves. However, if the supervisee had continued to use this defence further into their training and remained unable to show or think about what they did not know and needed support with, a large part of themselves may have remained hidden and not known to them or to others. This could have then adversely affected their enjoyment of the training journey, professional growth and efficacy in role.

Bion (1984) recognised the importance of the relationship between learning and emotions and understood that all thinking and knowing has its origins in unknown, unprocessed feeling-states. The supervisee conveyed this when they described how the supervisory relationship helped them to put the emotional aspects of their experience into words. Bion made the distinction between intellectual knowledge (sometimes referred to as knowing *about* something) and the type of knowing that leads to growth and change. This latter knowing requires being able to tolerate the uncertainty and anxiety that the learning process brings with it. As the supervisor noticed, responded to and tolerated this uncertainty, Supervisee 1 was able to explore what they had come to understand about themselves and to manage the process of 'not knowing', thus learning and coming to the deeper knowing that Bion described.

Transference and countertransference

The experience of important past and present relationships often influence the thoughts and feelings that enter the supervisory space and how it is experienced. In psychodynamic terms, this is known as transference and countertransference. Transference permeates all relationships as we bring aspects of our experiences with caregivers and significant others into our personal and professional relationships throughout our lives (Freud, 1905; Klein, 1952; Sandler and Davidson, 1973; Spillius, Milton, Garvey, Couve and Steiner, 2011). The power differential between supervisor and supervisee and the relationship with and to an authority figure can often evoke thoughts and feelings that are revivals of the past (Sandler and Davidson, 1973). If not attended to, such feelings can create challenges that make the supervisory space difficult to use as a learning opportunity. By attending to the countertransference (that is, how the supervisor finds him- or herself thinking, feeling and responding to what is transferred from the supervisee (Benjamin, 2004; Freud, 1962; Spillius *et al.*, 2011)], the supervisor is better able to support the supervisee to explore and understand his or her relationship to aspects of power and authority and how this might impact him or her in role.

Supervisee 2

To place relationality at the heart of the supervisory process perhaps seems obvious. Yet, having engaged in supervision across varied roles and institutions, my experience of the RMSAPP is that it is revolutionary in its lens and approach. Its process, in part, is served through vigilance and curiosity towards the affect arising in the supervisory space. I recall a pervasive sense of fear being a characteristic of my first term as a trainee EP. I had a notion that relationships across time, which I had so much valued as a teacher in a single school community, would no longer be possible. I brought this dilemma to supervision as my input, fearful my concerns would be brushed aside as inconsequential or judged as evidence of a lack of emotional capacity and robustness for the EP profession.

Within the RMSAPP process, not only were my verbalisations contained, digested and offered back for processing, but my projective identifications also in the form of unspoken emotions and related psychobiological transferences. I remember a supervision session in which my supervisor shared, 'I feel my heart skip a beat when you talk about leaving the teaching profession behind. Is this how it feels for you?' Supporting me to surface and verbalise unconscious affect allowed me to acknowledge and attend to it. This facilitated an appreciation of the depth of what I gradually understood to be grief, accompanied by a desire to allow myself the space for the grieving process. With gentle guidance from my supervisor, I was also able to reframe my struggle as a testimony to my belief in the power of relationships. I was left with the sense that my valences would be transformed and not lost. The output was therefore a renewed commitment to, and passion for, the EP profession alongside a heightened sense of my place within it. This, I believe, would have been far less possible without a containing supervisory space focused on the illuminating messages my emotions offered.

Supervisee 2 described the experience of ending a familiar role and beginning a new journey as they entered EP training and the fears and anxieties that came with them early on in the supervisory relationship. Again, as with Supervisee 1's account, there was an appreciation of how attending to emotional processes enabled them to make sense of the powerful affect they were experiencing. Conveying that this allowed her to understand her grief and mourn the loss of her previous role and identity was coupled with the sense of then beginning the training journey in a state of mind available for learning. This was made possible by their supervisor attending to the dialogue of the unconscious (Ferenczi, 1994), where their unconscious communications were received and treated as 'data' that held important information to be surfaced and explored.

Applying psychodynamic theory: reflections on reflections II

Projection

Psychoanalytic theorists and practitioners conceive that no person knows him- or herself fully, as part of the mind is unconscious, containing thoughts and behaviours not known to the self and aspects one is resistant to finding out about (Freud, 1915, 1917, 1923). Projection is a psychological defence used very early in life by the infant, who gets rid of intolerable and overwhelming feelings into the caregiver to hold on to the good aspects of his or her experience (Segal, 1973; Klein, 1975). It is an unconscious process that can be adopted at other times in life when a person is feeling anxious and uncertain, when he or she might disown (or project) aspects of him- or herself and attribute these aspects to another to assuage difficult-to-hold feelings. There are inevitably times when EPs might feel they are not doing a good-enough job and are feeling pressured to solve complex, ill-defined problems within challenging time constraints. In supervision, emotionally attuned supervisors may find themselves feeling excessively and unusually critical of their supervisees. This could in fact be supervisees unconsciously ridding themselves of feelings of self-criticism and self-judgement and projecting them into their supervisor. This could be a way in which supervisees are trying to hang on to currently fragile feelings of competency and efficacy in role. Receiving projections as a communication can help to surface thoughts and feelings that otherwise remain unspoken but which can hinder supervisees in their work, as well as their capacity to use supervision as a space for learning and growth.

Supervisee 2 gave a sense of how projection can be a helpful communication in supervision when their supervisor shared with them that they themselves were experiencing such powerful affect, that it felt as if the supervisor's own heart skipped a beat. Through being open to receiving emotions as meaningful and useful data, the supervisor was aware of feelings that did not seem to belong to them and demonstrated curiosity in checking out with Supervisee 2 whether they could be a communication from them. This describes the process of the supervisor receiving the supervisee's projected, unconscious feeling-states that felt too much for the supervisee to hold on to at the time. Through 'digesting' and thinking about this communication, the supervisor provided the mental space and containment the supervisee needed to come to know, explore and process their own experience. One can see from the account how it may have been difficult for a supervisee to be available for learning and to move with commitment into the EP role if their emotional experiences and anxiety remain free-floating and unprocessed.

Supervisee 3

The experience of containment in supervision particularly facilitated my professional growth and role identity development. There were many times throughout my training where uncomfortable feelings were stirred, such as when struggling to find my voice in complex systems, when engaging with challenging cases, and when striving to find the mental space to think about my practice while being new to a professional role. I was permitted to explore how I wanted to practise as an EP; my supervisor was dynamic, curious and respectful of my interests and preoccupations; they purposefully enquired how I might approach a situation, and at the same time shared some of their own experiences and values.

During the three years of training, more personal vulnerabilities such as feelings of self-doubt and confusion were held and tolerated by my supervisor, who facilitated exploration through reflexive questioning, purposeful intention – demonstrated simply by the way they held themselves, and responded to what was being communicated – and through paying attention to their own emotional responses to the conscious/unconscious feelings transferred within the space between us, and then naming those feelings. My supervisor responded to the emotional undercurrents present within the space and surfaced some of the emotions felt. This process permitted us to find meaning and, at times, reframe the emotional experiences. By providing this feedback, I was helped to discover some of my 'blind spots' and consider how my own thoughts, feelings and values might affect how I relate to others in role. This experience of containment enabled me to disclose my vulnerabilities and preoccupations, and process the feelings that might otherwise prove to be a distraction within my practice.

This supervisory space that enabled openness, vulnerability and growth is fundamentally held by the quality of the relationship that I had with my supervisor, characterised by trust, commitment and containment.

Supervisee 3's account highlighted the central importance of the supervisee having the experience of supervision as a containing space to hold vulnerabilities, self-doubt and confusion. The reference to the space between resonates with Donald Winnicott's notion of an 'in-between space' or transitional area, where intimate relationships and creativity occur to facilitate the emergence of the true self (Winnicott, 1953). Being able to bring one's real and authentic self into supervision enabled Supervisee 3 to take risks to explore their emotional responses to a new role and the challenges faced in some of the work to understand and learn from their experiences.

Applying psychodynamic theory: reflections on reflections III

Containment and splitting

Bion's concept of containment conveys an experience of being understood and having one's feelings attended to (Bion, 1963), linking somewhat to Winnicott's 'holding environment' (Winnicott, 1971, p. 150). Bion described a containing state of mind as having the quality of reverie, which is present in supervision when the supervisor maintains an open, curious and exploratory stance to receive and digest what is being brought by the supervisee. This sense of containment and subsequent reflection on patterns and themes that presented repeatedly was powerfully conveyed in Supervisee 3's account. If containment of projections goes well in the supervisory dyad, then over time the supervisee can develop the capacity to better tolerate and contain the inevitable anxieties of their work. This can help them to become less reliant on adopting what can be unhelpful psychological defences, such as having a somewhat 'split' view of themselves and/or the EP role as being 'all good' or 'all bad' (Klein, 1940, 1975) or taking an omnipotent stance of being the all-knowing expert or, conversely, feeling ineffectual and projecting a sense of efficacy and competency into others.

Concluding reflections and links with the RMSAPP

One of the significant challenges within the supervisory relationship is to provide help to someone without simultaneously causing the other person to feel diminished or ashamed, sometimes referred to as the learning paradox (Sanford, 1999). The RMSAPP considers a number of helpful approaches for practitioners to develop growth-fostering relationships that are supervisee-centred and feel safe enough to increase the agency, empowerment and relational connections within supervisees. The containment provided by the supervisory relationship enables supervisees to become more open and sufficiently comfortable to disclose dilemmas and struggles, as illustrated in the reflective dialogue between supervisees and supervisors who use the model. The supervisory relationship within the RMSAPP therefore functions as the mediating variable that facilitates psychological entry into the learning process (Mangione, Mears, Vincent and Hawes, 2011).

Learning to think in service of professional learning

Thinking in service of professional learning requires learning mindfully from experience. The supervisory dyad reflections and reflections on reflections illustrate multiple examples of supervisory processes that are further explored and understood through the application of the psychodynamic lens. Talking about thinking involves talking about knowing and 'not knowing', and includes how one comes to know. Thinking and knowing have their origin in emotional responses, and thinking is therefore an active process of tolerating anxieties and enabling links to be formed. In addition, if we can think about our own feelings with curiosity, then we can possibly think about the feelings of others with curiosity, most importantly our clients (Curtis, 2015). RMSAPP-informed supervision provides containment, offers a space to experience the interest and concern of another and to think with another, fulfilling the supervisory function to extend knowledge about the self (BPS, 2017). Waddell (2002) proposed that each of us holds a desire to understand the self and the other and to explore the self through the help of another's mind. Within the RMSAPP, bidirectional learning occurs, as both parties occupy teaching and learning positions. Supervisees need to help supervisors understand their learning and supervisors need to learn how supervisees make connections with and from their experiences. The supervisory relationship offers an invitation to think and make sense of being in the professional world together with an acceptance of imperfection (Bibby, 2011).

Cautions when using the RMSAPP in practice

There are important practice considerations to be accounted for when making use of the RMSAPP, especially in terms of quality assurance (QA). QA within the RMSAPP is concerned with the skills of the supervisor in terms of their personal reflexivity and ethical sensitivities so that the supervisory process prioritises learning about the work in service of the client. Supervision literature emphasises the importance of QA, particularly for supervisors, given the power differential and responsibility they hold for setting the tone and conditions for discussing the supervisory relationship (Hawkins and Shohet, 2006). Training and supervision on supervision are two critical components of QA. Within the professions of educational and school psychology, the impact of training on supervision for the supervisory relationship has received little attention in the research literature (Kaufman, Hughes and Riccio, 2010). The importance of training for supervisors has, however, been addressed within the broader literature on psychological supervision (Constantine and Sue, 2007; Dickson, Moberly, Marshall and Reilly, 2011). The metaperspective is also considered significant for the supervisory relationship and this requires talking about the supervisory relationship itself within supervision sessions (Dunsmuir and Leadbetter, 2010; Mangione *et al.*, 2011).

Cautions when using the RMSAPP are especially significant, given that the model requires the supervisor to have meaningful levels of self-awareness and insight into their own internal processes and patterns of interpersonal relating. Mangione and colleagues (2011) discussed the importance of protecting space for reflecting upon how supervisors and supervisees perceive both themselves and each other within the supervisory space. The supervisor has an important role setting time aside for both parties to attempt to try to understand what is happening between them, thus adopting an intentionally reflexive position. In doing so, reflexivity is encouraged and opportunities are created for enhanced learning for both parties within the dyad (Lizzio, Wilson and Que, 2009). In terms of the supervisor's role, such intentional reflexivity is best achieved through supervision on supervision, where supervisors have the opportunity to learn from one another. By providing a space for attending to the impact of feelings within the supervisory process, supervision on supervision allows for the careful unpicking of potential challenges arising from reflective relating. It has the potential to increase the supervisor's awareness of self-in-role and maintain a professional, reflective space, rather than responding via reactivity or countertransference (Grant, Schofield and Crawford, 2012). More widely, thinking on the quality of the supervisory relationship could be helpfully included in local supervision policy and more explicitly inform professional guidance on supervision.

Limitations and future research directions

Although there are a number of theories and approaches to supervision, there are few evidence-informed models to support supervisory enterprise. A constraint for the RMSAPP is the current limited evidence on the impact of implementation and its effect on the quality of the supervisory relationship as experienced by both supervisor and supervisee. However, we believe this chapter is the beginning of exploring and evidencing the workings of the RMSAPP. It qualitatively explores psychodynamically informed mechanisms within the RMSAPP for effectiveness within the supervisory process from the perspectives of three unique supervisory dyads. Building on this, future research could analyse in greater depth the supervisor perspective within the supervisory relationship, particularly the supervisor's experience of applying psychodynamically informed thinking and how to develop interventions to improve the experiences of supervisees. It would be interesting to explore how such enhancing features develop within the supervisory relationship (for example, contracting, giving feedback, managing difficulties and reviewing over time) and at different phases across the career span.

The relationship between effective models of supervision and the impact on work with clients has yet to be explored. In relation to the RMSAPP, it would be important to understand the processes by which the quality of the supervisory relationship impacts on outcomes for children, families, schools and wider systems. For example, how can psychodynamically informed supervision shape practice with clients through greater reflection and understanding of the relational dynamics within the triad of supervisee, supervisor and client? There are many further rich areas of potential exploration within the supervisory relationship, such as the impact of attachment and relating styles, ways of managing conflict or other challenges within the supervisory dyad and how the sociocultural context in which the RMSAPP is practised shapes its workings – for example, in schools, local services, multi-agency teams or training institutions.

More broadly, the role of RMSAPP could be researched in terms of its wider impact, such as supporting the development of professional identity through explorations of self-in-role and its function in promoting professional well-being given its focus on restorative interactions and containment.

Conclusions

If what influences how we work with clients is left unsurfaced, never attended to and never spoken about, it is then presumably never questioned. It is therefore inherently worthwhile to bring to conscious awareness the feelings, thoughts, beliefs and attitudes we hold and to think about them in service of learning and development. Applying the RMSAPP in supervision is one mechanism to facilitate this kind of reflective and reflexive practice, through its emphasis on (i) making connections between supervisee and supervisor, (ii) containing the often distressing and overwhelming experiences evoked by the work and (iii) critically challenging ourselves in our professional roles. The voices of the supervisory dyads and reflections in this chapter illustrate how a psychodynamic lens can shape understandings about professional growth. What has been illuminating, and at times challenging, is the degree to which supervisors have been enabled to learn about themselves-in-role in relationship with supervisees. The RMSAPP offers an ongoing framework for relational and dynamic growth of the supervisee and supervisor, with the ultimate aim of achieving better outcomes for clients. To this end, we endeavour to continue to explore and understand relational supervision through capturing and analysing the experience and quality of the supervisory relationship for the learning and development of EPs.

PART V

WORKING WITH GROUPS

CHAPTER 11

Reverie groups:
space, free association and the
recovery of thought

Dale Bartle

Early reflections

The process has allowed me to think about a situation or case in so much more detail. Hearing others talk about and question a case from a different perspective allowed me to generate hypotheses and thoughts that I hadn't considered before.

And:

The process of being the person who wonders aloud has also been of great benefit. By talking about a case and exploring my thoughts and ideas with another person (without feeling that I have to come up with a solution) has resulted in me just focusing on discussing and questioning the case. This has been so helpful and thought provoking.

These reflections were offered by a group member, following involvement in a sequence of group supervision sessions, the nature of which will be discussed in this chapter. These quotes suggest that, through talking and hearing others talk, something new can be found. How insight can be generated in the interactional, in the spaces between people. These ideas will be considered in relation to psychoanalytic concepts, and how they may help us in our work in groups.

An attitudinal stance

This way of working links with a suggestion (Bartle, 2015) that greater emphasis on the relational aspect of supervision is merited in guidelines to the profession (Dunsmuir and Leadbetter, 2010). I maintain this view, and believe that this account of working in groups connects with this ongoing commitment. Other writers have also been developing thought and practice in this regard. Kennedy, Keaney, Shaldon and Canagaratnam (2018) describe 'A relational model of supervision for applied psychology practice: professional growth through relating and reflecting', which suggests that 'The core task of supervision is to engage in a relational process that provides containing and security, thus facilitating professional growth through reflection on experience' (p. 282).

This expression of the core task of supervision is aligned with the fundamental task as discussed in this chapter – of enabling reverie (Bion, 1962). Further reflections on those influencing this way of working will follow. The aim of this chapter is to offer an account of an evolving way of working in groups. The account is psychoanalytically informed and prizes the relational as a space, where there is opportunity for exploration, discovery and transformation.

Defensive grasping

In a paper describing the implementation of four models of group supervision in a specialist setting (Bartle and Trevis, 2015), different ways of working with groups were discussed and included the use of a solution-focused approach. The decision to embed a solution-focused approach was in some ways a vestige of my initial training (and socialisation into a system). I wonder now if this approach may tell us something of the lived experience of working with children and young people with complex needs. In short, I believe that the general popularity of solution-focused approaches within this context can be seen as a clue. The approach may be seen as a manifestation of what goes on within the system – grasping for solutions. The solution circle approach, which we embedded, is broken down into six minutes of problem presentation, before the group immediately offers a storm of solutions. Focus is then put on operationalising change. I believe that this model in some way symbolises the fear and defence that is inherent in the work.

Social defences, which may be mobilised through working with children and young people with complex needs, will be explored in greater depth in subsequent chapters. These ideas have relevance to the thinking being presented here, and will be briefly considered.

Through my experience of working for children and young people with complex needs, I suspect that this task generates a range of unspoken anxieties. In essence, there seems an inherent tension. In order to strive to promote equal opportunities, those involved are faced with a reality of unequal opportunities. Children and young people referred for consultation commonly have experienced adversity and disadvantage. These disadvantages can be hard to tolerate. The avoidance of this conflict manifests in a multitude of ways within individuals and within the system. The system appears to generate behaviours, which include busyness and grasping for solutions. These behaviours appear functional and task orientated – rational. It is, however, possible that these behaviours serve a protective function. They may enable us to avoid facing the painful reality of meeting a child who has profound and multiple difficulties, experience of abuse or the many other experiences that bring children to our attention. Furthermore, it is possible that the lived experience of engaging with disadvantaged children generates complex and at times uncomfortable feelings. If we consider the educational system as a whole, there may be something painful involving failure – failure to promote progress. The very task that the educational system embodies. It follows that a conceivable, and often unspoken, response to working with (and failing with) this diverse group elicits shame and guilt. Shame and guilt in the inadequacy of the systems and the people within the system to make all children equal enough. These unbearable experiences, unacknowledged feelings and unthinkable thoughts have force and energy, which mobilise defensive behaviours. Ways of working evolve to protect those involved from facing these painful realties.

Regaining the capacity for thought

Bion's (1962) idea of the container–contained has relevance. In essence, the argument follows that persecutory, unbearable thoughts and experiences can be mediated by another, who – through demonstrating their capacity to digest, tolerate and survive the pain – can provide the other with the opportunity to take those difficult thoughts back, in a way that makes them more bearable, and less likely to be pushed away.

Experiences in groups

These ideas have relevance to the experience of working in groups. Throughout the development of this chapter, I have experienced uncertainty as to how to describe my attempts to develop a way of working in groups. What to call it? There are certainly debts to various traditions, including the Balint group and work discussion groups. There are, however, also differences. It seems to me, on reflection, that 'reverie groups', might well be an apposite term.

I will begin by offering some personal reflections on my attempts to facilitate thinking in groups. In advance of group sessions, I have often found myself moving furniture in various rooms. To clear a space, where a circle of chairs creates the technology for change.* I have worked with many different groups, sometimes constituting school staff, sometimes educational psychologists (EPs), trainee EPs or leaders of psychology services. I have noticed a common experience when taking up a facilitator role. As the discussion unfolds, I have often found myself in a state of confusion. Uncertain as to what is happening, and what ought to be attended to. Often the pace of interactions and the shifts in focus are disconcerting. Contributions can feel distracting and disturbing. I experience a sense of things flickering before disappearing – a sense of disconnection between ideas. Interruption to thought. Interference and invasion. This disorienting experience is compounded by attempts to acknowledge and engage all group members. To keep them safe and satisfied. My frequent experience of confusion has been a source of tension. If the facilitator feels lost, what hope is there?

More recently, I have begun to wonder if this confusion might be seen as a resource rather than a deficit. By attempting to stay with the confusion and to maintain curiosity, something valuable may be found.

This idea is present in the literature, and is often referred to as negative capability. From a range of possible sources, I have selected Mary Oliver's (1998) discussion of negative capability. Who better to consider the concept, proposed by a poet, than a fellow poet? Oliver writes:

> *Negative capability is not a contemporary concept, but a phrase originating with Keats. His idea was, simply but momentously, that the poet should be a kind of negative force – that only by remaining himself negative, or in some way empty, is the poet able to fill himself with an understanding of, or sympathy for, or empathy with, the subject of his poem.* (1998, pp. 81–84)

Oliver quotes Keats (letter to his brothers) as follows: 'it struck me, what quality went to form a Man of Achievement especially in Literature & which Shakespeare possessed so enormously – I mean *Negative Capability*, that is when a man is capable of being in uncertainties, Mysteries, doubts, without any irritable reaching after fact & reason.' The reader will make their own interpretation of Oliver's reflections. It is pertinent, perhaps, to note that Oliver goes on to comment: 'Now, as then, the concept of negative capability goes to the heart of the matter', and considers this 'an absolutely essential quality of real feeling' (1998, p. 84).

I once had the opportunity to spend five days working in a small group with David Armstrong, who consulted to our training group. He writes about his experiences of working in a group with Wilfred Bion, and of how Bion embodied a culture of pure enquiry. This was my experience of working with David Armstrong. A powerful sense of concerted curiosity. Of being open to what is happening in the here-and-now. In what follows, my aim is to explore my own experience of what can be distinctive and at times enlightening when working with a group of people sitting in a circle, talking, thinking together.

Holding structures

I have facilitated groups of people using a range of structures and processes. Commonly, group members (including the facilitator) benefit from these holding structures. The holding function that boundaries provide, in knowing how long is dedicated to a part of the process and in having a clear enough description of the task, serves as a containing function for the group. Without these structures, there is good evidence to suggest that anxieties within the group can rapidly manifest in various ways.

Reverie groups

As my work with groups has evolved, I have found various iterations of the following approach to have been helpful. The process seems characteristic of a way of working that has been developed at the Tavistock, and which in turn draws on a founder member's association with Quaker groups and meetings. Andrew Cooper (2018) rather elegantly captures the essence of this process as involving the invitation to 'sit back and listen'.

In short, this seemingly simple mechanism involves a presenter describing a stuck situation for around ten minutes. They are then asked to sit away from the group (sometimes by turning their back) and to listen to the group discussion. They may, perhaps, take notes or they may prefer to listen and notice what they notice. The group is then asked to talk about any thoughts that have come to mind, any associations, feelings, images. The group members are encouraged to resist the temptation to solve the problem, or to give advice. After 30 minutes or so of group discussion, the presenter is then invited to re-join the group and offer any reflections, should they wish, about what they have heard. They are not required to plan any next steps. They are able to take any consequent course of action they so choose.

Why ask the group to resist giving advice?

This, in my experience, brings us to the seminal difference between this way of working and other models. Reverie (Bion, 1962). I do not aim to give a definitive explanation of what this might involve. This seems to miss the point. It is manifest in the act, not the telling. It is relational, not theoretical. As Cooper (2018) comments, it is about attunement.

In my experience, there is a possibility that making reference to theory in a group session can be used as a way of defending against engagement with the experiential learning that could be accessed. I will, however, briefly offer some connections here between my experience of learning with groups and the literature.

Waddell (2002) offers a description of reverie when discussing a 'mother's capacity to hold her baby's anxiety and her own, to go on thinking in the face of puzzling and increasingly intense protest and distress, drawing on and offering her inner resources' (p. 33). Ogden (1999) discusses reverie in one-to-one therapeutic work, and describes a 'psychic field' where conscious and unconscious material can interact and generate new insights and possibilities.

These ideas also seem to have relevance to working with groups.

Foulkes (1948), offered the idea of the group matrix, which is discussed by Nitsun (1996):

> *At the centre of his vision was the group matrix, which Foulkes saw as the 'hypothetical web of communication' that draws on the past, present, and future lives of the individual members, conscious and unconscious, verbal and non-verbal, to become the dynamic core of group development.* (pp. 21–22)

Nitsun further elaborates :

> *The matrix has the properties of a container, symbolically linked to the mother … It provides a context for transformation of both the individual and the group (Roberts, 1983). This aspect has been associated with Winnicott's notion of the transitional space (Winnicott, 1953), in which the space within the group circle becomes a projective screen, a practicing ground for early interactions, an immediate area of play and discovery, and a place for everyday creativity (Anthony, 1983; Garland, 1982; Schlachet, 1986).* (Nitsun, 1996, p. 22)

The key point here is the notion of reverie – of a meaningful attunement, where difficulties can be expressed, explored and thought about, within dyads and within groups. This may be seen as the fundamental task of the group.

We might make a distinction next between the task and the tools. As described, the structures and boundaries may be seen as tools used to enable reverie within a group. A question remains, in terms of how the group might access their shared resources, in the service of the presenter. In my experience, the fundamental tool that can help here is the use of free association. To summarise, we may think of the fundamental task of the group as reverie, and the fundamental tool as free association. Additional supporting mechanisms can help – including structures and consistency in time, place, regularity, membership. The fundamental task and tool, however, may be seen as primary.

Free association in groups

This practice may be seen as associated with Foulkes' (1948) description of a free-floating discussion, described by Nitsun (1996) as 'the equivalent of free association in psychoanalysis. Since various members of the group contribute spontaneously to this process, the associative pattern in a group can build up in particularly rich, imaginative ways, releasing unconscious imagery and emotional expressiveness that lead to insight and understanding (Schlapobersky, 1994).' I commonly encourage group members to try to work loosely. To try to notice, to put words to any images, feelings, stray thoughts or faint recollections, which come to mind when hearing the problem presentation or subsequent discussion. In my experience, there is a dream-like quality in attempting to observe these (often fleeting) associations.

Adamo, Serieri, Gusti and Contarini (2008) describe how the group can act as a containing 'cradle' (p. 243): 'Paraphrasing Bion, we could say that what was produced in the group frequently bore resemblance to doodles in sound (Bion, 1963, p. 52).'

Andrew Cooper describes this approach as 'the means of revealing the unexpected but meaningful series of connections' (2018, p. 86). He goes on to argue that, through free association, thoughts can deepen, thicken and become more textured. There is also the possibility of a discovery. The following vignette is offered as an illustration:

> I was recently working with a small group, when one trainee psychologist offered a moving account of a child who had been adopted, and who was experiencing difficulty at school. It seems that the staff had received training in attachment theory, and had developed a provision where some children worked in a designated room with a small number of peers and a relatively high staffing ratio. It was reported that this child was observed clinging to a key adult, wrapping their legs around them tightly. Staff suggested that this was a familiar behaviour, which was given priority over any other activity and was reported to occupy the child and adult for prolonged periods of the day. As the group discussed their ideas about the presentation, this image was returned to. The group empathised and struggled with a sense of the pain expressed through the image. Then, a jarring association was made. Perhaps, the staff had become the parent? Had the educational task been lost? As the conversation proceeded, there was a sense of a shift. A provisional understanding had emerged. The presenter seemed to find this connection new and helpful, offering a possibility for exploration in their future involvement.

Readers will make their own interpretation of this vignette. It seems important to note that any understanding emerging from the discussion is provisional. It is not claimed as a truth. Rather, as a possibility, which may be helpful to explore further. It is not the correctness of a hypothesis that is being claimed here. All hypotheses are provisional, and complex human systems are not reducible to singular interpretations. The point here that is perhaps worth noticing relates to how the image of a child clinging to an adult was held in mind by a group member and fed into the discussion, which seemed to act as a catalyst for further connections.

These moments seem characteristic of discussions where free association is encouraged. It is the unexpected but meaningful series of connections – a child clinging to an adult – an association with parenting – the role of school staff – which opened up new possibilities. It is suggested here that this loose, free associative approach may be seen as a radical alternative to other consultation and problem-solving approaches.

It is perhaps worth noting that the encouragement to use free association within groups is often unfamiliar, and may be disconcerting. In my experience, groups often become more accustomed to this way of working over time, and can benefit from hearing facilitators explain why this might be helpful, while also modelling this approach when working with the group. The facilitator may also be accustomed to more traditional problem-solving approaches and need to resist his or her inclination to offer solutions. It is likely that a psychoanalytically informed facilitator may be helpful.

I am grateful to the presenter for consenting for the following vignette to be included.

> In a group of organisational leaders, the presenter spoke of a difficult relationship with their manager. The presenter led an educational psychology service, and spoke of the abrupt and at times hostile nature of communication during one-to-one discussions with this colleague. As the discussion followed, one group member made a gesture – moving their hands together and apart repeatedly. Another group member stated that this gesture had made them think about magnets repelling one another when pushed together. The group became interested in what repulsion might be present within the dynamic. It was suggested that the leader of the educational psychology service may represent a dangerous force to their colleague. Local authorities are under

financial strain, in part through the expenditure on children with complex needs, and the educational psychology service leader might represent this threat.

There are, of course, many reasons and possible explanations for the tense communications described in this illustration. It is not the correctness of the hypothesis that is being claimed here. As previously noted, all hypotheses are provisional, and complex human systems are not reducible to singular interpretations. There was, however, a moment where the analogy of magnets and repulsion was expressed. Offering the possibility of an unexpected but meaningful series of connections: magnetic repulsion – financial strain – leaders as symbolic – threat and conflict.

It may be noted that the group engaged in the task – floating in the reverie, noticing and commenting on associations. In my experience, this way of working can be liberating. Groups can gain a sense of creativity and insight. There is often a liveliness experienced in the work. Making and experiencing new connections is stimulating, and an indication that the group have, perhaps, regained a capacity for thought. The familiar pattern recognition that many professionals rely on (Dutton, 1995) can be interrupted. The possibility of glimpsing unspoken, part-noticed but influential forces becomes available.

Winnicott (1953, 1971) offers the thought that the boundary between the internal world and the external is where life is lived. Winnicott refers to this as an 'intermediate area', a 'third area' or 'transitional space'. It is possible that the group provides an intermediate area between the individual and the organisation, and that it is within groups that the organisation lives.

We may also wonder about the experience of the presenter. Often his or her feedback after listening to the discussion involves an expression of gratitude. This links, perhaps, with the notion of the container–contained. To reiterate, the argument follows that the group acts as a maternal container, able to receive, tolerate, and think about a difficult experience, and to offer it back in a more digestible form. Through being heard and through listening to the responses, the presenter may become more able to take his or her thoughts back. It is then likely that he or she will be more able to think the situation through.

A broader systemic reflection returns us to the possibility that the nature of the work – in this case, working with children with complex needs – is likely to evoke particular social defences. A focus on activity and generation of solutions, rather than thinking (which may involve facing stuckness, misery and uncertainty), has been suggested as a protective behaviour. Defending the adults from the pain of some children's experience of the world. The group process described here is seen as a way in which thinking may be reclaimed by the group. This offers the potential for more meaningful engagement in the work.

Free associations on working in groups

In this final part, I will attempt to share some associations that have emerged during the writing of this chapter. This is not intended to be a theoretical account of working in groups, rather a free-floating reverie. This approach seems aligned with the attitudinal stance described throughout. The reader is invited to freely associate and to make any connections he or she chooses. To notice what lands, what links he or she may make, develop and explore.

In preparing to write this chapter, I enjoyed a pleasant sojourn in beloved literature. Long train rides provided opportunity to float in a daydream. Social defences, my experience in role, my past experiences, my current struggles. Groups. Confusion. Bion, Armstrong and Cooper.

During this period a news item emerged, reporting that David Hockney had become stuck in a lift. He was in Amsterdam, trapped for hours, while attempting to leave the building to smoke a cigarette. He was involved in an exhibition, placing his art alongside Van Gogh. A *Guardian* article (Brown, 2019) quotes Hockney at the time, speaking of Van Gogh:

He could see space very clearly. He hated photography. I'm a bit similar actually – you must look at the world. Van Gogh is telling us that there is a marvellous world in your own back garden, you've just got to look at it, really look, I think that's his message. It's thrilling if you really look, the world is beautiful actually, it is, but you have to really look at it.

Hockney encourages us to 'really look', which in some ways connects with the experience of free association in groups – to attempt to find something, to make a discovery, through the commitment and attempt to see differently. The opening line of this quotation stayed with me. The idea of space became a point of departure, where unexpected connections emerged.

Negative space (Ma)

The Japanese concept of 'Ma' is described by Fox (in Harding, 2019) as follows:

> *Ma is of fundamental importance to Japanese aesthetics, and it's way of life. It refers to the negative spaces between things. The most obvious example of Ma is silence … in Japanese thought, that gap, that interval is just as full, and just as full of meaning as the words that surround it. Ma appears in many Japanese art forms, it appears in painting and calligraphy, in drama and in martial arts, but it's also present in Japanese homes. Just look around and you'll find negative space everywhere.*

Nitschke (1993) gives the following description of this concept:

> 間, *which in Japanese is pronounced chiefly as* ma. *Originally, this character consisted of the pictorial sign for 'moon' (*月*) – not the present-day 'sun' (*日*) – under the sign for 'gate' (*門*). For a Chinese or Japanese person using language consciously, this ideogram, depicts a delicate moment of moonlight streaming through a chink in the entranceway.*

This notion of Ma relates to my experience of learning in groups. The structures described earlier of place, time and task may be seen as the gates. I believe that the group can then, through free association and reverie, create the conditions in which something new can emerge. A glimpse of light. The negative space between the people and between thoughts may be seen as one way of expressing what is of interest in psychoanalytic terms. From the void, or the group matrix (the unknown nexus of combined experience within the group), an element, a flicker, may be noticed. This may fade away, or this may provide opportunities for a chain of connections to emerge. To illuminate.

I associate the concept of Ma with a line from Bion's private correspondence and translation of a letter by Freud (1966), cited in

Grotstein (2018, p. 133): 'The analyst must cast a beam of intense darkness into the interior of the patient's associations so that some object that has hitherto been obscured in the light can now glow in the darkness.'

Earlier in this chapter, it was noted that a 'technology', of creating a circle of people, brought together to think, draws on a founder member's experience of Quaker meetings. I would like to suggest that a further connection may be seen with the notion of Ma. Something, perhaps similar, may be seen within Japanese culture, Quakerism and the Tavistock project. It is argued that the concepts of negative space (or Ma), and negative capability, may be seen as connected. By attending to negative space, and utilising negative capability, these cultures and institutions provide members with the opportunity to develop understanding and to find meaning. One way of conceptualising the reverie group is to think of a circle of people looking together into the void, striving to see what might be noticed. A conjunction between negative space and negative capability. A curious double negative.

At the time of writing, I had also been running psychosocial research supervision groups, which involves a number of researchers sharing an aspect or extract of their data-gathering experience and using the group to help them explore connections, through free association. Andrew Cooper describes the process thus (2018, p. 252):

> *The model is indebted to Bion's thinking about the process of reverie and role of containment in enabling thoughts that take shape as 'beta elements' become transformed with the aid of what he termed 'alpha function', as they are 'won from the formless void and infinite', which is the realm of the unconscious.*

The technical ideas expressed here are explored more fully in other chapters. In brief, Bion argued that we are bombarded with persecutory stimuli (beta elements), which remain in a persecutory form, unless processed through the experience of containment (alpha function), which involves having our disturbing experiences thought about and handed back in a more tolerable form.

As Andrew Cooper explains, the use of reverie within groups can enable the possibility of transformation. Partially known, or unacknowledged, thoughts can become available for consideration. This shift – from a disconnected, fragmented state to a more connected and integrated state – is what underpins the notion of individuals and groups regaining their capacity for thought.

The mobilisation of reverie when working with groups operational-ises this process. It seems to me that alternative methods, such as solution-focused approaches, tend to step over this critical phase of reverie, which might enable an unanticipated discovery, the possibility of making a connection.

Why might reverie be less commonly embedded in working with groups?

It is likely that the attempt to look into painful experiences will be anxiety provoking. Who knows what might be found? Perhaps it seems safer to hold on to linear, rational models, which defend us against this threat?

The argument, however, may be more nuanced. I am indebted to Xavier Eloquin for the following reflection. In discussing a draft of this chapter, it was suggested that there seems a critical tone when a solution-focused approach enters the discussion. Xavier spoke of the possi-bility of a more inclusive attitude. This feedback enabled me to identify something that I have been dimly aware of. I believe that, over time, I have been influenced by what we may see as a 'split'. Klein (1961) offered the concept of splitting – a process involving the splitting or separation of things into 'good' and 'bad'. This process is seen to distort objects and a sense of reality. The theory follows that it is possible to identify ex-periences of splitting and that there is the potential to move to a more integrated position, which may be more attuned to reality. A position that acknowledges the potential for both 'good' and 'bad' to coexist.

In relation to my own understanding of a solution-focused approach, I now accept that I have in recent years constructed this approach as 'bad'. I have perhaps been seduced by my constructions of a psychoan-alytic perspective, and framed a solution-focused approach as its foil. A counterpoint which, through the distorting process of splitting, serves to elevate a psychoanalytic perspective and in turn denigrate a self-sculpted 'opposite'. As I write this, I am beginning to acknowledge that a solu-tion-focused approach does indeed have a contribution to make. I re-cently spoke with a principal EP who described our work as a helping profession. It follows that, if we are there to help and to enable change, that perhaps there may be a more integrated perspective that views a solution-focused approach as one among many, which have a meaningful contribution to make in working with people to help in bringing about change. The reader will, of course, have his or her own perspective.

In closing, I will offer a final association. A recollection, which when examined again offers a further connection. Approximately two years ago I was involved in welcoming a new cohort onto a training programme in educational psychology. We had arranged various activities in the induction week, which took place after a walking tour of the city. We ended at a museum and gallery. The group was asked to form pairs and to then explore the museum and gallery independently. All were asked to walk around and notice any piece of art or artefact that stood out to them, and then asked to meet with their partner, take them to the piece and to have a conversation about the art and their experience of taking up their role on the course. I recall inviting my colleague to look at a sculpture by Anish Kapoor. It was a large stone, cut cross-section, revealing a smooth black interior, with a rectangular space within, that shone brightly in the gallery.

I struggled to express to my colleague what had drawn me to this artwork. I recall saying something about the difference between the exterior and interior. The connection I now make with this sculpture (and what, perhaps, drew me to it) relates to the essence of this chapter – the attempt to utilise the group to discover something: 'So you read the volume as being fully present; in fact of course it's not, and I wondered if, if emptiness might be the content, or if, if a new content might arise out of the empty. Out of the so called void' (Kapoor, in Wason, 1999).

Note

*A child psychiatrist and family therapist who worked at the Tavistock Clinic for over thirty years was fond of saying, 'You can observe the Tavistock's core technology anytime you want to. Just walk down Fitzjohn's Avenue and look through the windows of the seminar rooms. What do you see? You see groups of people sitting in a circle, talking, thinking together.' Cooper, 2018, p81.

CHAPTER 12

Providing 'good-enough care': work discussion groups as a reflective space for designated safeguarding leads

Katharine Ellis

This chapter looks at an attempt to introduce psychoanalytically in-formed group supervision to support the well-being of designated safeguarding leads (DSLs) in schools. A project was designed to offer a pilot to all DSLs before offering a traded supervision package.

The role of DSLs

Every school in the UK is required by law to have a DSL (HM Government, 2004). DSLs are responsible for ensuring that children and young people are kept safe. Government legislation places huge responsibilities and expectations on DSLs in schools to ensure that children in their care are protected (Department for Education, 2019). DSLs are expected to: make sure all school staff are trained in safeguarding; refer concerns to social care and other appropriate bodies; monitor children and maintain ac-curate and secure records (Department for Education, 2019). In recent case reviews, DSLs working in schools have been open to criticism, with staff even losing their jobs (Connor, 2019). Psychoanalytic theory would indicate that any individual under such high pressure would experience anxiety and seek to protect themselves from such overwhelming feelings by adopting social defences (Armstrong and Rustin, 2015).

The manner in which concerns about child abuse and neglect are reported varies from country to country, though most will have a mandatory requirement of some sort to inform the appropriate authorities. In the USA, for example, key professionals, including teachers, are 'mandated reporters' (Child Welfare Information Gateway, 2019) and are required to report by law any suspicion of child abuse or neglect to the appropriate government agency, determined by the state or residence of the child. School counsellors often take up the role of co-ordinating the response, but in a similar way to the UK this role can be taken up by other administrators. Regardless of the outward form of the role, or how it is operationalised, the stresses and strains of listening to children report abuse and then formally hold the responsibility of ensuring their well-being while the necessary social services support is engaged are universal. It is this emotional load that is discussed in this chapter.

The role of EPs

Educational psychologists (EPs) have a role to support schools and their staff to ensure positive outcomes for the most vulnerable children within schools. The role of the DSL is to try to provide the best outcomes for a subset of those children and they can often act as an attachment figure for them. An attachment figure can provide the support needed to ensure that children and young people can benefit from the shielding effect of qualifications and access to education and employment (Bedford, 2015). EPs are experienced not only in bringing research and evidence-based interventions into schools but also in providing confidential and supportive spaces for adults in which they have time and space to reflect. Support for such key adults has been shown to reduce staff absence and help professionals feel more well equipped to manage their roles (Jackson, 2008). When the adults are supported through such work, they can then be helped to understand how to support children and young people to ensure that placements can continue and staff can maintain well-being.

EPs working to support DSLs to manage their anxiety and stay thinking and focused on the child would appear to be an important task to take up. This chapter looks at one project using psychoanalytic thinking to try to hold, handle and hand back the very complex and often emotionally overwhelming cases being managed by staff in schools in order to maximise outcomes for the children and young people involved.

Anxiety and defences

Freud hypothesised that anxiety is triggered when the individual feels helpless in the face of a traumatic situation or the perception of an imminent trauma (Bibby, 2011). The role of the DSL involves regularly encountering work in which the child they are working with has either experienced trauma or could potentially be at risk of imminent trauma. For Freud, anxiety was experienced whenever a person experienced the feeling of being overwhelmed (Armstrong and Rustin, 2015). Freud differentiated between fear, which was in response to a known object, and anxiety, which was to a situation or threat in the mind. Psychoanalytic theory suggests that in response to anxiety individuals will take up some form of defence.

Defence mechanisms are hypothesised to be a mechanism by which an individual is safeguarded unconsciously from such overwhelming feelings. Tucker (2015) has suggested that schools are under unique pressure to solve the problems of society, and the health and well-being of staff are under threat if we cannot support those individuals then we risk staff becoming alienated, stressed and mentally unwell. Given the additional stress faced by DSLs and the lack of support given to them, it felt important to develop an intervention to support individuals to become more aware of the psychodynamic processes at work. It could be hypothesised that DSLs faced with such difficult and overwhelming feelings may have unconsciously built up defences to safeguard themselves from being overwhelmed.

Some individuals may transfer their difficult feelings onto other agencies. Other individuals might fall into a form of narcissism in which the individual feels only they can be the saviour and others or the victim is incapable. Defences such as this can have many positive effects, such as the DSL taking up responsibility for protecting the child and liaising with other agencies, but the impact on the individual can be huge and the ability to work in collaboration with others can be limited, as the narcissistic defence causes the individual to devalue or depreciate other input and take up too much responsibility themselves, slipping into other professionals' roles (Rosenfeld, 2008).

Esther Bick (Lucey, 2015) identified the desire to take on a 'second skin' to prevent oneself 'falling apart' as another form of defence. In taking on a 'second skin' the individual may focus on a rigidity of process and beliefs to prevent being overwhelmed by the perceived or impending trauma (Bick, 1968). School staff with the pressures of outside judgements and pressures may feel they are encouraged to present a confident presence to pupils and outsiders, and DSLs may fall into a pattern of appearing strong and impermeable. Often following an admission of vulnerability or having shed a tear, an individual DSL snaps involuntarily back into this defence. Common phrases included 'I'm tough', 'It's OK because I'm strong' or 'That's why I can't share it with others.'

Jacques identified organisational defences in which the organisation becomes suspicious of outsiders and focuses on internal systems and policies (De Board, 2006). Many of the DSLs would begin by listing the procedures they had followed and want some sort of flow diagram that they could follow so that they wouldn't make mistakes. At these times the strength of following procedures and ensuring that they had done the right thing was strong, but with the possible cost of failing to hold in mind the child and his or her family as human beings.

Containment and 'good-enough' care

Containment builds on Klein's theory of projective identification (Segal, 1988). In Klein's theory a baby projects its needs onto a carer through its emotions and, when its needs are met, the baby and carer are held in a feeling of 'reverie'. Bion hypothesised that adults had the same need for their needs to be met by another who could manage their feelings and hand them back so that they were more manageable. Bion saw containment as a symbiotic process in which the container and the contained would listen and modify each other (in Bibby, 2011). To try to emulate this, a therapist attempts to hold the boundary of time and space so that the clients' thoughts and fears can be discussed and returned in a digestible way so that the client can hold in mind different, often conflicting, feelings and emotions and reflect on a way forward (Riesenberg-Malcolm, 2009). One model for containment in groups is to use a work discussion model that provides a structured and predictable format and in a way that feels safe and meaningful to all the members (Rustin, 2008).

Winnicott (in Kahr, 2016) saw this symbiotic relationship as the key to a person feeling contained. In Winnicott's thinking, a mother 'holds' her baby not only physically but also psychologically. The mother can physically protect the child but also psychologically protect the child by 'holding in mind' through her thoughts and level of attentiveness. The mother, then, has a role in 'handling' the baby's emotions and soothing him or her when he or she is overwhelmed. Last, the mother has a role in preparing the child to know that the world outside the family is safe. The mother does this by introducing the baby to the world and enabling the child to know that he or she can return to a parent who is holding the child in mind and can manage any emotions he or she encounters (Kahr, 2016). The aim of such interaction is to move towards independence. Winnicott hypothesised that if the therapist provided 'good-enough' care within a holding and facilitating environment, then the client would have the capacity to think and develop away from the therapist. The aim of the work discussion is that the group itself would aim to hold each other in mind and attend to each other's needs.

Using work discussion groups to support the practitioner

Why work discussion?

The assumption that DSLs needed space and time to think using a psychoanalytic model was developed after reading work by Isabel Menzies Lyth (Menzies, 1959). Menzies wrote about the group defences taken up by nurses in response to huge pressures and anxiety (Menzies, 1959). It felt possible that this would be similar for DSLs in schools. In addition, my own experiences of taking part in a non-judgemental listening group which focused on attending to the presenter led me to believe that it could create an atmosphere that would support DSLs to feel contained (Rustin, 2008).

A work discussion group format seemed an appropriate format to offer to DSLs, allowing DSLs to present their cases and work together to avoid falling into the 'basic assumptions' of dependence, pairing and fight/flight (Bibby, 2011). Bion suggested that the first aim of a group is to manage individual members' anxiety and as such take on various emotional states to try to manage this. Some groups may manage by looking to a leader to save them and provide security. Others will focus on two individuals to pair up, removing the focus from individuals. Alternatively, the group may choose to attack those outside of their group or avoid the task of the group completely (Bibby, 2011).

The aim was to have a non-judgemental atmosphere and space to sustain an atmosphere of enquiry alongside a space where the painful narratives of safeguarding could be relayed in a safe and containing space. The purpose of supervision was to offer individuals the opportunity to have a space to reflect on the cases they were dealing with. In addition, there was a role for the group members to offer alternative feedback on cases and offer up different narratives for the case holder to consider. By staying in touch with possible 'basic assumptions' and defences, the facilitator would support the group to be able to focus on the work task of ensuring the best possible outcomes for young people.

Work discussion groups are a well-established practice in terms of their format and use in clinical practice. Emil Jackson has developed their use among school settings (Jackson, 2008, 2015). Each meeting involves a group coming together, facilitated by an external consultant who supports the group to focus on the psychodynamic aspects rather than solely searching for a solution (Hulusi and Maggs, 2015). One or two members present a case, which is then thought about in conversation with the other members as a way of opening up thoughts and considering alternative perspectives. Unseen processes or alternative viewpoints on systems provide the presenters with a new way to consider their case and move forward as they feel appropriate. Hulusi and Maggs (2015) have argued that this type of supervision for school staff, run by EPs, is a useful way to support staff to make sense of the complex issues they face and bear the feelings they encounter.

DSLs in schools often have little, if any, experience of supervision and it was therefore a risk to try such a format. I initially encountered similar barriers to those outlined by Hulusi and Maggs (2015), with school staff believing they needed more clarity over systems or more access to decision makers rather than time to talk. My initial discussion with safeguarding professionals in the local authority led me to identify that supervision was offered to designated leads in hospitals and in social care, and I gained support in attempting to see if it was also possible in schools.

A Work Discussion Group (WDG) model was therefore initially taken forward as a pilot and had to be financed by the schools if they were willing to place value on it.

The pilot

Initially all DSLs in the local authority were invited to a free taster session in which they could experience the work discussion model. This allowed DSLs to experience a type of supervision that they may not have previously experienced or engaged with before having to commit financially. This was essential given that many school staff have no experience of supervision and many felt guarded about an outsider witnessing the challenges they faced. The taster sessions were run in a number of locations and at different times of day, including before and after school to allow as many DSLs as possible to have an opportunity to take part. At the end of each taster session those present were asked to think about how and if they would like to take the model on. There was an opportunity to discuss proposals around the timings of meetings, membership, confidentiality and location before an offer for schools was finalised.

Membership

Discussions led to a number of different groups being developed. The initial members requested groups with a similar focus, and so one group was for special school DSLs, one for primary, and another for secondary schools. Jackson has spoken of the need for members to be different, but not too different, so that they feel safe enough to take the risk of sharing, and this resonated with this group (Jackson, 2008).

It was agreed that DSLs would initially sign up for a year of supervision so that membership would be consistent and the group could develop and relationships of trust could be established.

Membership was voluntary and schools paid directly for staff to join the relevant group. Not everyone who wanted to join was given permission by their schools. Throughout the work, the cost of the discussion groups proved to be a significant barrier. Some schools were taken over by different trusts, and so priorities changed, bringing different individuals into the groups, meaning that some left.

A number of schools, having paid for a place, requested the opportunity to alternate their attendance between the DSL and a deputy. Jackson has suggested that membership should be consistent and, given the need for confidentiality and trust within the group, this was a difficult negotiation. It was agreed within the groups that a maximum of two people could alternate but everyone must attend the initial contracting meeting so that trust and confidentiality could be established.

Group size

Membership was limited to a maximum of six members in negotiation with those who signed up. This was agreed so that each person would be able to present cases regularly and everyone's voice would be heard and valued. A minimum number for each group was set at four DSLs. This was a useful minimum number, as outside pressures sometimes meant that on occasions the numbers became a more intimate two, due to staff commitments. The structure meant that, even when the size was smaller, the group remained focused and did not drift. The yearly commitment meant that, although attendance fluctuated, all of the DSLs attended 80 per cent of the sessions.

Timing and duration

Each session was designed to last for 90 minutes, with the opportunity for two members to present a case each lasting 30 minutes.

It was agreed that the groups would meet each half-term, so that they were frequent enough to begin to develop relationships and trust between members, and thus more in-depth reflections could happen. This felt like a comfortable frequency that DSLs agreed they could commit to, as more frequent meetings would be difficult within their schedules.

Location

For each group the location negotiated was different. One group chose to meet in a neutral location so that all members were free of distractions and felt they were in a safe space. Another group chose to meet regularly in one school that could facilitate parking, refreshments and a room that was free of distractions. Alternatively, one group wanted to move around schools and take turns to host and provide a space and refreshments.

There were benefits and downsides to each of the arrangements. The neutral space was always safe and free of distractions, but felt like an additional responsibility in terms of hosting and providing refreshments for the facilitator. The group that stayed in one school eventually chose to move around, as members felt they also wanted to host. The group that always moved required frequent emails to remind them when and where the meeting was going to be on each occasion. While the locations changed, the members felt happy to take ownership of the refreshments in turn and a secure space free of distractions was maintained.

The session structure

The sessions each followed a tight structure and participants were provided with a written reminder of how each session would run. This provided a concrete framework that was beneficial for all. At the start and end of each session, all the members had a chance to check in. Following the initial check-in at the start of each session, the group decided who would present. At the end, after the two 30-minute case presentations, there was a final check with all members.

The members did not have to bring any prepared notes, although on occasion some had noted down important things they wanted to say. After an initial five-minute presentation of the problem, other members were able to ask any clarifying questions, before the group moved into a reflection about the case or issue. This was followed by the case presenter being invited to comment on what he or she had heard. Case presenters regularly commented that they found it beneficial to have space to have their cases heard and discussed so that they could listen and reflect. In their reflections at the end, case presenters often referred to the benefit of being able to hear such a variety of ideas and thoughts about what they had brought to the session.

Process notes

Following each session, I wrote up my notes from each session. The aim of these process notes is so that the facilitator can begin to see patterns or issues that may need to be returned to at a later date. They also serve to provide opportunities for the facilitator to reflect more deeply on what might be going on for both individuals and the group, so that containment and development of psychodynamic ideas can be provided.

Benefits of work discussion for this group

This chapter gives a small opportunity to reflect on the opportunities a work discussion group gave DSLs to share their thoughts and feelings and have them held and handled by a group before taking them back and returning again to their work.

The blame game

Many of the DSLs were very experienced and well aware of which social workers they perceived as 'good'. The DSLs often felt that they were alone in a system that was not able to think about children; I was aware that, with the stories that they brought, they often needed to project their anxieties into other organisations and onto other professional groups. Early on, the groups often focused their stories around a failure by social care to take up their referrals. Later on, groups became better at holding the individual in mind and handling the projections that were being displaced onto other institutions.

> One case example was brought by Mary, a DSL in a secondary school. She explained that a child in her care called Angel had been raped by a brother of a peer. Since this episode Angel had engaged in more risk-taking behaviour and her behaviour in school had become increasingly challenging. Angel had also befriended a younger girl in school, whom she was involving in her activities. The most recent events that Mary wanted to discuss involved Angel being brought back after being missing for two weeks. Angel had been found in a squat far away from home in a different county. Mary was angry that the social worker had just returned her back home with no support. Mary appeared frustrated that the school had not been offered support and guidance about how to help Angel, and Mary felt angry with other staff within the school who were reacting to Angel's challenging behaviour with

detentions and sanctions. Mary seemed angry with Angel, who appeared not to want to accept any help offered.

The group hypothesised that Mary may feel responsible for Angel and had no idea how to save her from the continuing downward spiral. The group was able to comment on the overwhelming feeling of being out of control explicit in her account and implicit in her presentation of the case and what it evoked in the group. The work discussion group commented on the role of different professionals and tried to keep thinking about how Angel might feel and what was possible. As a group, we tried to help Mary hold Angel in mind and to consider what she thought might help.

When we returned to hear from Mary again, she was able to think about the network and why it was difficult for anyone to do more. She was also able to think about Angel and what might help to support staff in school to help her. It was noticeable to me that I experienced Mary as no longer so angry. It felt that, having named her biggest fears for Angel, Mary recognised her own, as well as the networks' limitations in the face of Angel experiencing such significant trauma. Mary seemed to recognise that no agency or individual might have the 'answer' or a magic wand, and we were all able to sit with a feeling of sadness that maybe we had to think what 'good enough' care would look like for Angel, given her current reluctance to accept support and when she may be able to accept support in the future.

Everyone needs a hero

One aspect of the DSL role that arose was the huge responsibility placed on DSLs. *Keeping Children Safe in Education* sets out that the role of the DSL is to 'take lead responsibility for safeguarding and child protection (including online safety)'. DSLs need to advise others in school, contribute to multi-agency meetings and ensure up-to-date files are kept (Department for Education, 2019). The DSL is expected to be available out of hours and term time or to arrange appropriate and adequate cover. This is a huge responsibility and one that can feel overwhelming. It naturally leads to DSLs using a defence of invincibility and being a saviour to a child.

In one meeting Daniel, a DSL, explained that he had tried to arrange for a social worker to come out when a child was too scared to go home. The social worker told the DSL to call the police if necessary and said she would be in touch the next day. The police were not available immediately and Daniel had to wait with the child, despite having his own children to collect from school. Eventually Daniel decided to drive the child to her house to take her possessions to a friend's house. Daniel had to then drive the child to a friend's house, where eventually the police arrived to talk to them. Daniel had been placed in the role of saviour and hence Daniel spoke of himself as the only one who had cared. The defence placed him in a tricky position, as it appeared to the group that he had taken up a role outside the boundaries of his role. Daniel, however, saw himself as the only active agent in the system.

With careful discussion, the group helped Daniel to see that perhaps he had taken up the role of social worker. Daniel was initially angry and felt he had done the right thing and reiterated, 'But there was nobody else!' It was a challenging conversation in which the group tried to help Daniel to consider whether he had taken up actions that were outside of his role.

As a group, we were then able to discuss how the conversations with other professionals who choose not to take a referral or resist completing an intervention often push us into significant levels of anxiety and agreeing to take on other roles or actions that are not perhaps strictly within our role. The group were able to notice that we all have moments of thinking that we are the only people able to save a child and that this is often when we are feeling most anxious or isolated about a case. Difficult discussions followed about how we need to place boundaries around our role and ensure other agencies take up their roles.

My 'second skin'

Teachers already carrying out such a challenging job are open to a high level of public scrutiny, including the risk of publicly losing one's job. Case reviews indicate the need to support individuals to remain open to questions and challenges (Connor, 2019). Teachers and those who work in schools are often under huge organisational pressure under the mantra of 'need to do better'. The unrelenting pressure to move to outstanding means that school staff are already under pressure to take on an appearance of strength (Tucker, 2015). The perception and role of school staff in safeguarding appear to confuse the government. Statutory guidance indicates all safeguarding leads across all public bodies should have supervision, but the individual guidance for schools reduces it to 'support' for DSLs (HM Government, 2018: Department for Education, 2019). This feeds into the perceived culture of school staff being 'tough' and managing, despite school staff experiencing one of the highest levels of stress, anxiety and depression (Hymans, 2008; Health and Safety Executive, 2019). Lucey (2015) has suggested that the growing performance culture in institutions leads us to focus on technical efficiencies and outcomes, rather than the complexity of the ethical and social dilemmas that complex working requires. When the organisation cannot support adults to think about the more complex aspects of their work, adults unconsciously take on a pseudo-protective layer, which may be seen as becoming rigid in procedures, obsessive in behaviour, appearing to be constantly busy, relying on oneself or discussing only surface level issues (Lucey, 2015)

Esther Bick named this type of defence as 'second skin' defences (Bick, 1968). In order to protect themselves, DSLs unconsciously take on a second skin that acts as a psychic protective layer manifesting itself as rigidity in ways of working, covering up vulnerability, and relying on one's self and not allowing other's in. Many DSLs I would suggest appear on the outside as strong and competent but that this hides a vulnerability (Lucey, 2015). The impermeability of the 'second skin' can result in DSLs appearing judgemental of children, young people and families and/or other professionals. Their need for rigidity can mean they become focused on actions and paperwork rather than people or emotions (Menzies, 1959).

This 'second skin' defence came across most strongly through the countertransference I experienced, especially in the initial few sessions. Countertransference is the feelings and reaction in the individual in response to the behaviour shown towards them by the client. In many sessions it felt like the members were trying to overwhelm me with more shocking stories than the last and that I had to prove my ability to contain them. Often, after such stories, I would ask the DSL how they managed to go home after experiencing an incident and the DSL would frequently shrug and say, 'I'm tough.' Looking back at my notes after the initial sessions, I wrote 'bear it' on many occasions. DSLs appeared to need someone else to take up the challenging content for short period. In addition, it seemed to be an important test of my ability to give them some peace, when others had found such stories painful and difficult to make sense of. The journey together to make sense of it felt important. At the end of such sessions, when asked for feedback, DSLs would not always have any new solutions or ideas but remarked that what had been important was that they knew that they were 'not alone'. Winnicott would perceive this as the relationship being transformative for the individual, to go back out and independently deal with their challenges as their emotions had been held and handled by the group (Kahr, 2016).

Reading back over my notes I have considered how delicate this 'second skin' can be. Many of the cases that are brought involve harrowing information that the adults are struggling to manage. It often felt that stories were hurled out at the group to see whether the facilitator and the group could tolerate the stories. The benefits of a confidential space where such disturbing cases could be talked about was noticed over future sessions, as the cases felt less hurled out but there was more possibility to talk about them. The next vignette explores how even the strongest DSLs need to be held and supported.

Shakira was an experienced deputy DSL who was also a trained counsellor. Shakira worked in an area of high social need and deprivation, including a large number of bed and breakfasts and emergency accommodation units. She presented herself as almost invincible. On a number of occasions, she had been vital in supporting others who were struggling, and her outside appearance was one of confidence and strength. After her school was taken over by a new academy, she was told they could no longer afford for her to attend and I didn't see her for several months. Out of the blue she told me she had persuaded the academy, and she could come back. She returned to supervision and told a story in which she had to tell a child that she would have to return to her mother, when she felt that this was wrong. The child's reaction had been so emotionally difficult for Shakira that she had struggled to deliver the message to her. I struggled to handle her complex emotions around this case, which was difficult and complicated, and I listened

> to my feelings of inadequacy and reflected them back to Shakira. She reflected that she too had those feelings with regards to this case. My vulnerability gave her permission to show her vulnerability before she once again put on her 'second skin' and went to deal with a child and adult waiting for her outside.

In the containing space afforded by the WDG, Shakira was able to reflect on her experiences and make links between the task and the emotions such a task evoked in her. Through this came a better understanding and clarity of her role and how she could helpfully take it up.

Organisational defences

Much of the content of the groups involved content that appeared 'unspeakable'. In both primary and secondary school settings, sexual abuse was frequently brought, including interfamilial, peer-on-peer and child sexual exploitation. Initially the members wanted to have organisation defences to manage these feelings. They asked for exemplar complaints letters from each other, flow charts, discussed how they filed their records and discussed the pros and cons of different systems to log concerns. Initially I wondered if I had got it wrong in trying to address their emotional needs and encouraged and assisted in the sharing of information about systems. After a few sessions the content changed, however, and individuals started to reflect on the limits of systems and records and they began to try to think about individual children. It was interesting that across the groups the same pattern occurred. This is in line with the literature on WDGs, where, as the group becomes accustomed to the process and to each other, individual and organisationally linked defences begin to lower (Jackson, 2008).

At different times, when new members have joined or the balance of members has changed, I have noticed a retreat back to focusing on organisational defences. New members joined one group and we agreed to invite someone from social care to join us following our meeting, so we could be sure about procedures. This felt very different to previous attempts to find an organisational solution, however. Previously this organisational defence had felt like an idealisation. Klein has suggested that individuals under stress will divide things into good or bad (Segal, 1988). It had previously felt that DSLs considered that, if only they had the perfect system or process, then all would be good. Increasingly I experienced the group taking up a more moderate position that recognised that, although we might invite a professional or develop a new system, it wouldn't solve everything. Klein has identified this state as the depressive position, when individuals are able to experience that individuals and systems are integrated, with both bad and good inside them (Segal, 1988; Bibby, 2011). This new state meant I experienced groups in which it felt like the DSLs grew in knowledge together, and through that developed sufficient trust to share the more difficult emotions. Cooper and Lees (2015) identified this as the development of the ability for individuals to learn to bear the complexity, insolubility and pain of such cases and be able to maintain their focus on the child despite the challenges and difficulties that they face.

Being a 'good-enough' DSL

Over time the DSLs spoke of why they wanted to keep coming. Often the response was simple: 'It's nice to know I am not alone.' DSLs explained that in school other adults often left them to manage cases and they appeared to others as strong, and yet here in the safe space they were able to let their exterior down and share. It was alright to admit vulnerability.

Other reflections that were often more painful led DSLs to reflect, 'I just know there isn't anything else I can do, is there?' This often followed insightful, solution-rich reflections by the group, but ultimately all had been tried by the DSL. To let go of the 'saviour' role then enabled the DSL to reflect again on the case and take an alternative perspective or approach. Often, helpful suggestions could then be shared about charities or other agencies that might be able to offer something different.

Thinking about the role of other agencies was often very challenging, especially when DSLs noticed a mistake or error. Over time they began to reflect on the limits of other roles and professional groups. In one meeting the DSLs noticed just how lucky they were compared with another agency, which they reflected was short of money, overworked and overcriticised, and one member said 'It's just so sad, isn't it.' Staying sympathetic to other agencies was an important part of letting down the projective identification, and through it individuals developed new ways of approaching and developing relationships with others. Through

WDG, the individuals had moved towards a more depressive position and individuals began to be able to hold in mind conflicting ideas about cases. Feelings such as impotence and uselessness, which previously may have been projected into others or placed in themselves, were now data that could be used.

I would argue that a key part of the EP job 'is to disrupt the cycle (of defences) by helping to understand and contain the complex feelings evoked' (Music, 2019, p. 183). When EPs can help adults to hold in mind the complexity of situations and manage their feelings towards individuals and organisations, then adults working with children are able to keep the child at the centre of the thinking and focus on what is possible.

Keeping the child at the centre

One example of maintaining focus on the child involved a child who the social worker declared couldn't be trusted to tell the truth. The DSL had been left with conflicting emotions about the case and was overwhelmed with feelings of not knowing what was the correct thing to do. This case was complex and the group unpicked the feelings of those involved and considered the organisational and legal boundaries of the role of the social worker and the responsibilities of the DSL.

Together, the group moved towards thinking about the child and focusing on what was happening for her My process notes included in capital letters 'They bore the pain and the complexity' and felt like a vindication of the decision to adopt this style of supervision. The DSL went away holding in mind the child and aware of both the structural and ethical way forward.

The challenges

The project was not without ethical and practical problems.

Practical problems

The project had to be self-funding and it therefore relied on schools to purchase supervision for their DSLs. Many of the local schools were in a state of flux following government policy to encourage schools to move away from local government control into independently run academy chains. This meant that many schools during this period had significant changes to their leadership and management, as well as their ethos, during this period as they moved into a different accountability structure. A different chain might refuse to pay and the membership therefore inevitably fluctuated. This meant that at times we returned to former defences, and trust needed to be developed again.

Attendance wasn't always consistent. At times DSLs were called away to attend Child Protection conferences or cover for a colleague, and on one occasion the DSL wasn't able to attend as she was in hospital with a pupil who had attempted suicide.

Some leaders refused to let their DSLs attend and responded that they could meet the needs in-house. The fear of the outsider and revealing any vulnerability was difficult to overcome, especially for those schools that were perceived as 'outstanding'. A number of schools in neighbouring boroughs wanted to join, but distance meant it was not always possible to meet their needs. Others, at times, asked to have individual supervision and avoid the group, which at times was appropriate to the individual needs.

Ethical problems

It was my hypothesis that all DSLs would benefit from supervision and ethically it felt unfair that some benefited and others were left to struggle. In one of my schools, the DSL had been refused permission to attend and yet whenever I was present in the school she sought me out for informal supervision. It felt ethically important to allow her to have time to discuss her issues, but it wasn't always clear where the money or time for this support was coming from. I raised the issue several times with her manager but the problem remained unresolved. The willingness of schools to value paying for support for their staff continues to be a significant ethical barrier.

Conclusion

The success of the project was evident, as further groups were added that required new facilitators. As a consequence, guidelines were needed to ensure the well-being of the new facilitators and that 'good-enough' care was provided to those taking part. Facilitating such a group without suitable psychoanalytically informed supervision risked facilitators feeling isolated or holding too much, and so this became an essential part of the model. The supervision provided a space to process the feelings that facilitators faced when dealing with such cases. Facilitators reported feelings of being overwhelmingly sad or angry and wondering whether there wasn't some ideal system we could create to prevent so much pain. It was vital to have the facilitators' feelings managed, to focus the facilitator back on the emotions of the DSLs, so that the groups could keep the focus on trying to keep children safe and improving their outcomes.

The success of the project led to a successful expansion to support additional DSLs during the coronavirus outbreak in 2020, when many DSLs faced considerable challenges and stressors. In addition, headteachers asked for similar groups to support groups of staff working in schools.

This model of psychoanalytic thinking and practice seems to have been useful in processing the stories and emotions in the supervision room. DSLs all agreed that they found supervision supportive and helpful in thinking about children and their own emotions and defences. EPs are well placed to deliver this kind of work, sitting independently from the processes involved in safeguarding and having experience of providing safe and confidential spaces. The success of this project relied on managers valuing the development of the emotional strength and resilience of their DSLs and it is testament to the feedback of the DSLs that managers continue to pay for their DSLs to attend the WDGs. The success of supervision is dependent on the courage and willingness of DSLs to try something new initially and over time develop reflexivity and an ability to bear complexity and pain. Through the work, adults caring for some of the most vulnerable were able to refocus on the children, supporting them, their families and the professionals around them to try to reduce risk and harm. Supervision using a psychodynamic model is of benefit to DSLs and school staff. EPs with the skills and knowledge to provide this format of support can provide a unique package of support to DSLs and other school staff through WDGs.

PART VI

ORGANISATIONAL PERSPECTIVES

CHAPTER 13

Coaching school leaders: a psychoanalytic approach

Beverley Clarke

Introduction

This chapter looks at psychoanalytic ideas in relation to coaching school leaders. It seeks to introduce these ideas to educational psychologists (EPs) who currently coach and those with an interest in exploring psychoanalytic thinking as a tool in coaching.

Leadership (and executive) coaching is no longer a new phenomenon in schools, nor in the wider education sector. However, there is arguably a predominance of cognitive–behavioural approaches in this work, which reflects the strong performance and goal orientation of the education system as well as the strong presence of cognitive–behavioural approaches within the coaching field itself. I argue that most school leaders are strongly cognisant of and often skilled in setting and managing their professional goals and those of their settings. When faced with highly complex or intransigent work dilemmas, however, a deeper, more relational and transformational approach to coaching may be needed.

This chapter looks at psychoanalytic ideas in relation to the psychological function of work for school leaders and their psychological contract with their employing organisation(s). It explores the impact of unconscious dynamics on leadership behaviour, drawing from traditional psychoanalytic theory and transactional analysis, whose roots lie in the psychoanalytic tradition. I propose the establishment of a 'thought partnership' with school leaders that can support them in approaching problem solving in a more in-depth manner.

I argue that coaching creates an opportunity for EPs to work at the organisational level and discusses the benefits this can bring, not only to individual headteachers but to the school system they manage. I also examine the impact of such work on the coach and the importance of self-awareness and supervision in supporting the coach in maintaining appropriate and necessary separation between themselves and their coachees.

The school leadership context

EPs work alongside educators at all levels in a range of schools. This work provides them with a rich insight into the joys and challenges faced by a wide variety of educators, from executive heads to TAs and playground supervisors, currently working in the UK education system. Frequently, staff supporting vulnerable pupils will cite the pressures and obstacles they face in promoting academic progress and social and emotional well-being. Although not unique to the area of special educational needs and disability, these obstacles are often lack of resources, lack of specialist knowledge, lack of professional development opportunities and the demotivating effects of an inspection regime considered insufficiently sensitive to the progress of vulnerable pupils who do not meet expected standards.

For headteachers, these pressures can feel magnified by the unique nature of the role. Although curriculum leads or classroom teachers enjoy shared experiences with others in a similar role in a school, headteachers' experience can often be of loneliness and isolation. The level of accountability in schools – the majority of which are now academies – means that weaknesses in organisational performance are often understood in terms of leadership failure.

These pressures were described in detail in a 2007 study by Bristow, Ireson and Coleman in a National College of School Leadership study, *A Life in the Day of a Headteacher*. An extensive qualitative study revealed:

> *particular issues around contemporary headship and well-being. Amongst others, the constant flow of new initiatives together with an increasing emphasis on output measures has affected the role and remit of headteachers profoundly. Driven by changes of policy and emphasis, the tasks that headteachers are expected to undertake*

have changed significantly in recent years, with their work increasingly being perceived as pressured. The well-being of headteachers is affected by the operational and strategic working environment and the ethos and morale within the education system, as well as opportunities to undertake professional development.

These descriptions showed that participants' working lives are demanding and pressured, with a fast pace and involving long hours.

The least rewarding and satisfying elements of headship included dealing with negative staff and parent issues, and excessive bureaucracy.

When asked what they would change about headship, participants identified accountability, bureaucracy and external demands. Additionally, increased capacity, more professional development opportunities and challenging the culture of headship were also cited. (Bristow et al., 2007, pp. 8–9, 10)

Coaching to support motivation and performance in a high-pressure environment

A relatively recent NFER (National Foundation for Educational Research) study (Lynch, Mills, Theobald and Worth, 2017) further explored what would support headteachers in long-term career sustainability and retention. Qualitative interviews with headteachers indicated that system instability (the pace and nature of policy changes) and mixed experience of support were the main sources of stress and challenge. The report recommended a number of interventions and I have highlighted two here as being relevant to the impact and usefulness of leadership coaching for headteachers.

Clarify the career pathways of headteachers. These pathways should allow effective heads to lead a challenging school without a higher risk to their career and encourage more experienced headteachers into challenging schools. Headteachers should be able to move into different roles that make use of their expertise, before returning to headship. There should be clear opportunities for the future pipeline of heads to develop leadership capabilities. There should also be a clear way for headteachers to develop the skills they may need if moving into system leadership roles.

New heads should have access to formal induction. Leaders need practical and emotional support, as well as opportunities for peer support (such as coaching, mentoring and shadowing). Governors and MATs should foster an open culture where heads can seek support without feeling vulnerable. (Lynch et al., pp. 1–2, emphasis added)

What is coaching and how can it support school leaders?

Coaching, mentoring and shadowing are related but differing mechanisms for providing emotional and technical support for those facing challenges in their professional roles. Mentoring and shadowing usually have a stronger technical focus for professional development, as they are offered by those deemed to have achieved a level of success and expertise in the receiver's specific (or closely related) fields. Coaching stands apart from both these offers in a number of aspects. There are numerous ways in which coaching has been described, but for the purposes of this chapter I have chosen Kilburg's (2000) overview of coaching for managers:

A helping relationship formed between a client who has managerial authority and responsibility in an organisation and a consultant who uses a variety of behavioural techniques and methods to assist the client to achieve a mutually identified set of goals to improve his or her professional performance and personal satisfaction and consequently to improve the effectiveness of the client's organisation within a formally defined coaching agreement. (pp. 65–66)

I have chosen this definition because it highlights three key aspects: the intent to help within the context of a relationship; a focus on improved professional performance at the individual and organisational level; and the use of a 'variety' of (behavioural) techniques. As referenced in the introduction to the chapter, effective coaching techniques can be drawn from many schools of psychological theory and practice. However, in my experience, headteachers have often achieved their current job role through the demonstration of an extensive range of skills and a strong drive and vision to improve social and academic outcomes for pupils.

The most frequently occurring issues raised by school leaders in coaching sessions relate to the creation, management and maintenance of relationships with adult stakeholders who contribute to the complex dynamics of the school, its community and its broader management system. Although headteachers can often feel pride and satisfaction at aspects of a complex job well done, they are equally often subject to guilt, anxiety and self-doubt when faced with challenges to which there are no easy or comfortable answers.

In my experience of coaching education leaders, it is these more relational conflicts that are brought into the coaching session. Thus typical issues can include: balancing the needs of the pupils and the school with those of a staff member with long-term health needs impacting on their attendance and performance; managing the desire to defend and protect staff and the school's reputation in the face of a regularly or severely critical parent/carer; acknowledging their own contribution to a lack of clarity about expectations for staff or about how they see their vision for the school being realised; developing an authoritative presence in one's first headteacher role; maintaining curiosity and openness to learning and acknowledging mistakes when one is an experienced headteacher; managing heavy workloads; and maintaining a work/life balance. School leaders are no strangers to issues such as these.

Feelings of guilt, anxiety, self-doubt and shame are, however, uncomfortable to experience and extremely difficult to name and explore even to oneself, let alone to another. Such feelings are often ignored or repressed, denied and avoided. Nonetheless, psychoanalytic theory holds that they impact on behaviour however far from our conscious minds they may exist. Psychoanalytic approaches to coaching can create a dialogue within the safe and confidential space coaching provides. They can open up the possibility that, in exploring such challenging feelings and understanding their origins and functions, both in the past and now, school leaders can be freed from inner conflicts and preoccupations which inhibit creative solutions and innovation in decision making.

This seems a suitable point to explore the aspects of psychoanalytic thinking I find most useful in my work as a coach, before returning to how EPs might develop their interest and practice in applying these in the workplace.

Leadership coaching from a psychoanalytic perspective

In this part of the chapter I will be giving specific focus to:
- how psychodynamic theory and practice help us understand people's behaviour in work
- how those theories and practices can be applied in each phase of coaching, as described by O'Neill (2000).

I have paid particular attention to the key theoretical aspects of psychodynamic thinking that describe or hypothesise the psychological processes, thoughts and feelings influencing how individuals feel about their work. The rationale for this approach is that knowledge of these theories can support the formation of working hypotheses for the coach when working with clients who hold significant management and leadership roles in organisations. In turn, these hypotheses can support the formation of open, exploratory questions that invite coachees to reflect on the origins and formation of beliefs, values and behaviours impacting on current dilemmas. Such beliefs, values and behaviours may have provided valuable ways in which to negotiate the sometimes complex and challenging world of early childhood and adolescence. They may have been forged under highly challenging circumstances, including trauma, or be the result of consistent 'messaging' and reinforcement from key adults in their lives. Such reinforcement of ideas, or injunctions as transactional analysis would term them, can become articles of faith that have served individuals as guides through life or important explanations of how the world can be. It is only when our long-standing ways of being and doing no longer bring desired results that we need to reconsider them. Coaching using psychoanalytic thinking can explore how lessons and experiences from the past which no longer serve us might be getting in the way of new and different approaches to the issues school leaders face.

Headteacher A runs a successful school. The school is now thriving following several years of unsatisfactory performance and a

previous OFSTED rating of inadequate. The headteacher is proud
of the achievements of her staff and the pupils and committed
to the ongoing improvement journey the school is on. The
headteacher prides herself on high standards of professionalism,
combined with care for her staff, and well-being and morale in
the school are generally high. However, this is not the case for the
head herself. She arrives at school at 6.45 a.m. and, although she
leaves at 4.30 p.m. to ensure she has time with her two children
and her partner, she begins work again once the children are in
bed. She raises her concern that the impact on her family life
is unsustainable, but she feels unable to reduce her hours. She
communicates a strong sense of responsibility and of the 'buck
stops with me'. 'Whatever it takes to do the job, it's down to me
to do it.'

A previous conversation about using a 'dismiss, delegate, do' system
to allocate work brought a small measure of change in behaviour.
The head was able to identify a small number of tasks she could
delegate, but very few that could be dismissed or postponed
as longer-term aspirations. While there was undoubtedly some
reality to this analysis, the head acknowledged that even delegating
tasks her mind told her could be delegated, in her heart of hearts
she believed it to be her responsibility to ensure the delivery of
several tasks or areas of work by doing them herself if necessary.
We explored together if there was ever a time when she had not
worked this hard and what had been the results. I invited her to
tell me more about the place of hard work in her life. Through
this dialogue it emerged that she had always been seen as the
least intellectually able among her siblings. Her parents had always
believed she could achieve her chosen goals, but had repeatedly
told her, 'You're not as quick as your brothers and sisters, but in
the end you will get there – you just have to work that bit longer
and harder.' This experience and the within-family messaging
continued across a range of activities and goals, ultimately resulting
in Headteacher A's profound belief about herself that she could
achieve only if she worked harder and longer than others in her
family. Within the 'family' of the school staff, therefore, the head
could accept that staff might have a work/life balance, since their
skills and talents allowed them to complete work within reasonable
time boundaries. Since her expectation was that she would have

to work harder and longer simply because that was 'who she was' (and not because she had a different level of accountability and responsibility) meant that she accepted her much longer hours as the way the world of work was meant to be.

The notion that she might not have to work harder than everyone else opened up new avenues of discussion linked to outcomes and achievements that were good enough and were achieved within manageable time frames.

Psychodynamic theories and practice

Coaches (from an EP background or any other) can find psychoanalytic literature overwhelming and contradictory. This is partly because psychodynamic thinking has arguably never been one body of theory and related practice (Lemma, 2007). Classic Freudian theories have co-existed and been heavily adapted and developed by Jungian psychoanalysts, object relations theorists such as Melanie Klein and Lacanian psychoanalysts, to name but a (very) few. However, there are key theories with practice implications for coaching, which appear in some form in almost all psychodynamic schools and are referenced by contemporary commentators such as Peltier (2011) in his insightful summary of the range of psychological approaches to coaching, *The Psychology of Executive Coaching*.

The main theoretical concepts I find most useful to frame my thinking are:

- the existence of an unconscious which 'holds' feelings and thoughts too powerful or persecutory for the conscious mind
- the use of defence mechanisms which protect our sense of self from overwhelming feelings of anxiety, guilt and shame
- that social behaviour is an indicator (or symptom) of the individual's inner world.

This inner world is characterised by dynamic forces, often in conflict. These dynamic forces include: a pleasure-seeking drive (understood or referenced as the 'id'); a reality-oriented drive seeking to manage more primitive drives within the individual's current social context (known as the 'ego'); and the 'super-ego', which drives the individual towards ideal (and often unattainable) behaviours. Achievement of the ideal brings pride and self-esteem; significant failure to achieve the ideal results in guilt and shame. Defence mechanisms are employed to defend against the experience of guilt, shame, murderous competitiveness or retaliatory urges (Peltier, 2011).

In addition to these theoretical concepts, psychodynamic schools of thought assert the significance and influence of early child-rearing experiences on the way in which individuals relate to one another as adults. For some psychodynamic theorists, the impact of these early experiences 'play out' in all forms of relationships via the mechanism of transference; that is, where the client re-enacts an earlier relationship (such as with a significant carer) and behaves towards the coach as if he or she were that significant carer. Bowlby's (1973) attachment theory might be understood as a development of this. Attachment theory asserts the significance of early childhood experiences of primary caregivers' ability to 'contain' an infant's primitive, though understandable, anxieties and fears and how the resulting 'attachment styles' or tendencies impact on adult relationships, both in intimate relations and at work.

More controversially, psychodynamic theorists described the existence and influence of countertransference. Thus, coaches are subject to emotional experiences created by the client at the unconscious level. Although rejected as a concept by some psychodynamic thinkers, this concept remains a live, if controversial, idea. For some (Bollas, 1987, quoted by Pelham, 2017), countertransference is an important source of data for the coach but depends upon a high level of self-understanding in the coach in order to separate the coach's own transference from the countertransference.

Psychodynamic theory in the workplace – the function of work

Schools of psychodynamic thought have also paid attention to the role of work in the maintenance of an individual's psychological health and development. The western European, post-industrial workplace is held to be a key element of an adult's social world and successful transition into the workplace is a rite of passage for the majority of this population. Starting with Freud, psychoanalytic thinkers have held such a transition to be a real-world mirror to the developmental and psychological transition from child to adult. Furthermore, psychoanalytic theory proposes that the same unconscious dynamics and defence mechanisms operate in the workplace and at the level of the organisation just as they do within the individual.

Becoming a teacher or educator is often understood to be a vocation – though the terms sometimes feel a little old-fashioned in these days of 'portfolio careers' and a constantly changing work landscape. However, it is not unusual to hear educators talk in terms of vocation or being values led when talking about what drives them to work in this field. The explicit acceptance that being an educator is 'more than just a job' makes coaching conversations rich in the language of feelings, values and beliefs and, in my experience, opens them to in-depth reflection when conflicts arise between inner-world values and real-world pressures. It is for this reason that I have included these key ideas in this chapter.

> Headteacher B worked in a faith-based school. He was keen to explore the usefulness of coaching for developing his leadership authority following a recent move from deputy headship. However, he was not only late for the first two coaching sessions but told me as we started that he could not remember the length of the sessions and, in any case, he could not stay for longer than an hour (the first session had been contracted for 2 hours, the second for 90 minutes). Familiar as I am with the demands of a busy school, I nonetheless wondered aloud why he found it so difficult to protect time for his professional development, which came at a financial cost to the school. His initial response was that 'People need me' and 'It's my job to be supportive. It's only right that I make sacrifices so that my staff can do their jobs.' The use of the word 'sacrifice' seemed important – especially in the context of a (Christian) faith-based school where sacrifice is likely to carry potent and positive meanings. Further discussions allowed us to surface his beliefs about whether his preparedness to sacrifice had limits beyond which he thought it not necessary or useful and whether he was applying these limits in practice. It emerged that he no longer thought beyond the general obligation he felt to put the needs of others before himself, which he realised he had begun to do on taking up the headship. He reflected that the notion of putting on his own oxygen mask before helping others to put on theirs had seemingly fallen by the wayside, allowing us to explore explicitly what and whose needs required a purposeful sacrifice from him, and which did not.

Why work matters

Naturally, if one is to do something in a public health sense about keeping people well, that is most easily done through social systems and primarily, therefore, with those institutions in which people work, inasmuch as their work is of great psychological significance to them.' (H. Levinson, personal correspondence, 1993, quoted by Diamond, (2003, p. 2)

I stumbled upon this quotation from Harry Levinson while immersed in background reading for a doctoral thesis. It seemed then, as now, to encapsulate something obvious and yet undervalued both by those who work (which, after all, is almost all of us) and by those who seek to understand the role and meaning of work for human beings. Work matters not only because it pays the rent, but because it partly defines who we are and how we are seen, heard and understood, both by ourselves and by those around us. Providing coaching within the workplace for those facing challenges creates space and time in which individuals can change their behaviours and approaches, in turn influencing or leading change in their wider organisation.

Czander (1993) quotes Freud: 'On the one hand work is one of the two great pleasures of human activity, [and on the other, it is] not as a pleasurable activity to be sought, but as a painful burden to be endured (p111, Civilisation and Its Discontents)' (Czander, 1993, p. 12).

It seems to me that work is usefully understood as a double-edged sword. It is an undertaking in which humans invest and hope for much but in which they can be subject to intense feelings of stress, loss and anger. For Freud, successful entry into the world of work depends upon an individual leaving behind his or her (childish) preoccupation with living life governed by the 'pleasure principle' and living a life more appropriately influenced by the 'reality principle'. Such internal change and reorientation were viewed as key to being able to form adult relationships with colleagues and with key work tasks required by organisations. There exists a significant body of work exploring and hypothesising on the impact on emotional health, where individuals struggle internally with this development or where the circumstances in play within the workplace interfere with an individual's ability to use work to manage unconscious and inner-world tensions (Ferenczi, 1950). Thus, job loss, long-term unemployment and long-term unsatisfactory work are all held to contribute to poor emotional health (Menninger, 1942, referenced by Czander, 1993; Jahoda, 1966). Hirschhorn (1988) has written eloquently of the human search for connectedness in groups, of which the workplace is a significant example. Work provides opportunities for individuals to adapt their behaviours in the pursuit of relationships that can be repaired, where actual or imagined damage has resulted from regularly occurring competition for reward, recognition and survival through organisational restructure (Hirschhorn, 1988). Braun (2011) has looked more explicitly at the interplay of individual attachment style (Ainsworth) and employee transference to the organisation within which they work. Her proposition is that an individual's attention style influences how employees feel about their employing organisations – in terms of both their expectations of, and the sense they make of, managerial decisions and organisational demands.

Psychological contracts with work

By and large, all workers understand that they have a contract with their employer which is legal in character and lays out a basic exchange. The employee provides time, skills, knowledge and effort, and the employer or employing organisation provides a physically and psychologically safe workplace and financial recompense. However, the notion of a psychological (rather than legal) contract emerged during the mid-twentieth century (Homans, 1961), focusing on a more psychological understanding of what employees and employers believe is expected from one another. Psychoanalytic thinkers have added to this by positing that a significant part of a person's psychological contract may be unconscious and informed by previous or early relationship experiences. Where children have been able to internalise positive models of parenting linked to notions of attachment, competence mastery and curiosity, such individuals are more able to relate to others in adult life, including colleagues in the workplace.

A significant body of work exists that describes the nature and importance of the employee's conscious and unconscious psychological contract with work (Kilburg and Levinson, 2008). The concept of a psychological contract allows the coach to hold in mind questions relating to an individual's expectations and hopes from both his or her employing organisation and more junior staff. This includes beliefs and feelings about mutual obligations and about what is felt when there is a perceived breach or violation of the psychological contract (Morrison and Robinson, 1977). Breaches and violations of the psychological contract refer respectively to the perceptions and feelings of employees who believe that the organisation has 'reneged' on its obligations. This usually occurs when employees' assumptions about exchange and reciprocity, good faith and fair dealings are disappointed. The reader may note that, in this relationship, the 'organisation' is experienced as a 'failed provider or parent' and as if it were a sentient being rather than a collection of individuals in roles. Thus, the psychological contract with work involves what Greenson (1967) describes as a pervasive transference where, over time, employees come (unconsciously) to expect a commitment from the organisation that mirrors that of a containing or protective primary caregiver. Equally, employees can experience negative and positive transference in relation to key managers or leaders in their organisation from whom they may expect specific considerations or care or by whom they may feel let down or betrayed.

Exploring a coachee's conscious expectations from their organisation may lead to a surfacing of their unconscious psychological contract. For school leaders whose commitment to the task of education is intense and often of long duration, disappointments or frustrations in this contract can be fertile areas for work.

The coaching process: application of psychodynamic theory to O'Neill's phases of coaching

Coaching using a psychoanalytic frame is likely to involve the use of associative thinking and analogy to explore coachees' narratives and how these might be influencing their feelings and behaviour. This does not always sit comfortably with coach or coachee expectations of strong goal orientation and problem solving. Consequently, I have outlined here a structure for the coaching process drawn from Mary Beth O'Neill's (2000) book *Coaching with Backbone and Heart*. Her structure owes much more to systemic models of consultation and coaching, but it provides a useful structure within which in-depth, exploratory conversations can take place. There are similarities with Huffington, Cole and Brunning's (1997) model of consultancy, with which many EPs will be familiar. Most EPs will recognise similarities with common approaches to consultation they use with a variety of school staff in their day-to-day work.

However, just a note on associative thinking. It is important that the process of associative thinking and use of analogy is not confused with the technical process of 'free association' used by psychoanalysts and psychodynamic psychotherapists in therapy. This latter is a technique that involves encouragement of the client by the analyst to report thoughts and feelings as they emerge into conscious thought without conscious filtering (Rycroft, 1968). Associative thinking involves the spontaneous linking of ideas, emotions and thoughts, triggered by the experiences described by the coachees and resonating with or contradicting the coach's own.

Contracting

The purpose of the contracting phase is to clarify expectations of how the coach and client will work together. Some of the content will be concerned with logistical issues such as number, location and timing of sessions, fees and reporting. However, the key task here in psychological terms is the identification of the client's goals and the establishing of a rapport with the client, which will serve those goals. The title of O'Neill's (2000) book on approaches to coaching provides an apposite summary of the relational task in coaching: 'with backbone and heart'. This phrase appears to capture the notions of coach independence from the organisation's norms and the ability to challenge. However, it also speaks to me of the emotional warmth, authenticity and connectedness one needs to bring to the coaching process.

At this early point, O'Neill suggests that key tasks to focus on are: establishing one's credibility with the client, being curious, gaining familiarity with the client's challenge(s) and establishing the coaching as a joint enterprise. As a model, this constitutes an accessible, operationally clear route to beginning the relationship. However, like any relationship, the coach–client pairing is likely to be a complex one. A coachee's excitement or anticipation around beginning coaching may be balanced by a number of anxieties about whether his or her vulnerable selves will be 'exposed' or that naming his or her improvement goals will risk being understood as a less than successful leader/employee. It is in this domain that psychodynamic theory has a particularly strong and useful contribution to make to coaching. Sandler's (2011) work on the use of this approach in coaching clearly outlines the likely ambivalence of coaching clients. Sandler reinforces the need for the coach to stay mindful of 'the client's need for psychological safety' (p. 51). There is always a risk that the coach may inadvertently say something which, while intended only as helpful, is experienced by the client as judging, threatening or shaming. Under such circumstances, the client is likely to respond rapidly to a sense of psychological threat in ways which impede the creation or maintenance of a dialogue in which challenging issues can be thought about. In psychodynamic terms, the client may defend against these unwittingly evoked feelings by employing a range of defence mechanisms.

Planning

For O'Neill, this is the phase of coaching concerned with collecting information from the client about how he or she operates and about the multi-layered structures and processes at play in his or her organisation. This information or data allows the identification of:

- behavioural patterns the client uses which may promote or hinder him or her in achieving their goals
- new or different strategies that the client wishes to deploy to achieve those goals
- how the client might manage resistance to these new approaches
- how the client will recognise any signs of success in his or her endeavour.

The range of data may include 'formal' data gathered via observation, interview and questionnaires. It will also include 'informal' or qualitative data emerging during the coaching conversations themselves.

A coach using a psychodynamic approach is likely to be engaged in the process of what Sandler (2011) describes as 'building the working alliance' (p. 52). This process involves creating a relationship or partnership, which Sandler describes as more than the creation of rapport. It is the creation of a psychological bond between the client's desire to learn and change and the coach's desire to support the client and to do so via the process known as coaching. Psychodynamic ideas of transference and countertransference, of the impact of anxiety and defence mechanisms, will be key in supporting the coach to co-create such a partnership. Identifying and working with these often unconscious forces helps to maintain the necessary level of separation and objectivity required to attend not only to the emotional presence of the client but also to the stated goals of the coaching process.

Remaining open to what the coach may represent to a client can help the EP, who coaches in a number of ways:

- An EP employed by the local authority may be experienced as part of a supportive organisation where such coaching has been offered as part of a non-traded intervention linked to the trauma of a critical incident.
- An EP coaching as part of a traded offer may be the recipient of unexpressed but present beliefs about what constitutes value for money or 'getting one's money's worth' and what success should look like – some of which may be more achievable than others.
- An offer of coaching to a school leader as part of a post-OFSTED improvement plan may be experienced as yet more persecutory intervention from a disapproving or judgemental organisation.

Simply asking the client how he or she is feeling about being in the coaching session has usually – in my experience – elicited powerful emotions and beliefs. Bringing these to the explicit coaching conversation is key to creating a relationship based on, and in reality rather than, fantasy.

Coaching

During ongoing coaching sessions, maintaining what O'Neill (2000) terms 'a strong signature presence' is key. Complementary theories, such as systems theory, support this in its clarity and emphasis on roles, boundaries and patterns of behaviour. The coach is supported in holding in mind the importance of exploring the client's understanding of his or her formal and informal roles in the organisation, while maintaining an ability to remain clear about his or her own complementary, though different, role. This differentiation in role contributes to the coach's ability to manage his or her own emotional response to the issues brought by the client.

On occasion, coaching conversations can feel 'stuck' in a pattern of relating which is unusual or feels difficult to understand. This can be the result of parallel processes. Parallel process is a phenomenon originally identified (by Searles, 1955) as a potential aspect of therapeutic supervision. The supervisee relates to the supervisor in a way that parallels the relational challenges of his or her work with clients. In coaching, the coachee relates to the coach in a manner that parallels the relational and organisational challenges he or she describes happening outside the coaching space. This is not a deliberate act by the coachee, but an unconscious one. The impact on the coach may be a countertransferential one – that he or she begins to behave towards the coachee either as the coachee behaves towards his or her colleagues/clients or as those colleagues/clients are described as behaving towards the coachee.

From my coaching experience, examples might include:

School leader C, who brought to a coaching session her frustration with a key staff member she described as judgemental and uninclusive. This was in response to her experience of the staff member demanding the exclusion of a pupil with behavioural challenges but with significantly challenging home circumstances. I explored with the school leader what explanatory narrative she had about the staff member's reluctance to support the pupil's placement in the school. The school leader challenged my questions. Why, she asked, was it not obvious? She had tried everything to support the staff member to change her views when she believed she should not have had to do so given the school's ethos of inclusivity to which she expected staff to adhere. The school leader experienced the questions as suggesting she had not done everything possible to support the staff member and that she was being negatively judged by me. Observing that such a process in the room seemed rather similar to the emotional 'feel' of the head/staff relationship and the staff/pupil relationship allowed both of us to acknowledge the possibility that powerful aspects of the work had entered into the coaching session. In turn, such a possibility allowed me to invite the school leader to help her in finding a more supportive way to explore the issue.

It is also possible that the coach may be subject to strong (unconscious or conscious) identification with a coachee's experiences and feelings. In such a situation, the coach may find him- or herself asking questions or making observations more pertinent to him -or herself than to the coachee. As a coach with more than three decades of experience working in the education field, it is important that any empathy I may feel or exhibit for a school leader facing issues that resonate for me does not result in being unable to hold a position of curiosity about the coachee's aims, and manoeuvring the coachee closer to a solution of my making rather than his or her own.

Being attuned to anxiety and how this plays out for the individual coachee is of particular advantage to the psychodynamically oriented coach. Sandler (2011) reflects that 'Human beings become anxious much more easily than is generally realized' and that 'anxiety manifests itself in a wide range of hidden and indirect ways' (p. 54). Being alert to anxiety and ambivalence can support the coach in maintaining high curiosity and low judgement in the face of anxiety acted out as persistent lateness to sessions or cancellations. Fear of failure or of feeling dependent for support on someone unknown can interfere with the coachee's engagement with the process – especially in highly pressurised and /or competitive work environments.

The psychodynamic concept of containment is hugely useful in working with clients in the grip of anxiety linked to fundamental beliefs about their self-worth and a low expectation of being held benignly in mind by those from whom they seek validation, care and love. This anxiety can be the result of transference, i.e. the client experiencing the coach 'as if' they were an important figure from their past. The client's response can also be influenced by their attachment style or attachment traits.

- A client with experiences of an authoritarian, judgemental parent/carer may come to the coaching process with unconscious expectations that such negative judgement will be repeated in a relationship that feels to him or her reminiscent of their parent–child experiences.
- A client with an early childhood history of inconsistent or unavailable parenting may have developed an anxious or avoidant attachment style. In new or unfamiliar situations, such as a new coaching relationship, he or she may present as needy and dependent and become increasingly anxious and distressed by

failing (unconsciously) to find a sufficiently nurturing parent in the person of the coach.

- Equally, he or she may protect him- or herself from the unbearable disappointment of experiencing the coach as unavailable by remaining emotionally distant from and disengaged by the work – particularly those aspects of the work involving exploring relational aspects of change in the workplace.

Understanding that these behaviours are not directed at the person of the coach, but at what the coach represents, may enable the coach to avoid defensive behaviours of his or her own. It enables the coach to offer consistently warm but boundaried responses (heart and backbone) to the behaviour of the coachee and to support the coachee in separating past experience from those in the present. To do so is not an aim in itself. This separation of past from present or an awareness that difficult feelings in the present reflect past rather than current experiences, can enable the coachee to work with the coach *as he or she is* and not as the coachee fears he or she might be. Furthermore, it can enable the coachee to respond to current work challenges as they are rather than as if they were similar or equivalent to events or relationships in the past.

> A school leader who grew up as an elder child with absent or unavailable parents may have developed a strong sense of responsibility for those younger or with less authority than themselves. Within the school context, this can lead to rescuing rather than facilitative problem solving by the school leader. While staff and parent/carers might be drawn to the possibility of having burdens lifted from them, they may also experience being 'rescued' as signalling they are not trusted to be able to resolve problems themselves and feel deskilled and infantilised.

Debriefing (and ending)

Debriefing and ending occur in each coaching session, but need to be paid particular attention to at the point when the coaching relationship is coming to an end. Regardless of theoretical perspective, this aspect of the coaching process usually involves some form of evaluation of the effectiveness of the coaching in reaching the coachee's goals. It also involves the management of the ending of the coaching relationship.

- Coachees with a history of traumatic or unprocessed grief and loss may find endings difficult or even impossible to bear. The approach of the end of coaching can then trigger a resurgence of issues and worries in an unconscious attempt to justify the need for coaching to continue.
- Equally, some coachees with an avoidant attachment style, stemming from unmet early attachment needs, may avoid acknowledging the end of a coaching contract or may express views as to the lack of impact of the coaching offer even where evaluation has indicated that coaching goals have been met.

Educational psychologists as coaches

Within the EP profession, the proper and most effective role for EPs has been much debated (Dessent, 1994; Mackay, 2002; Ashton and Roberts, 2006). Much of this debate features the relative merits and achievability of a role for EPs outside those defined by special educational needs and disability (SEND) legislation and linked to individual assessment and teacher consultation. (Ashton and Roberts, 2006). Some authors (Mackay, 2002) encourage the pursuit of a role for EPs as researchers within a local authority context and the possibility of a role supporting well-being within the whole school or organisational context:

> It is time for a broader role for educational psychology, and for all of psychology. This may be illustrated with reference to other origins of applied psychology in Britain in the main settings of health, work, the law and education ... Psychologists were employed in these fields to deal, respectively, with disorders and disabilities, meeting the demands of war, the aftermath of crime and special educational needs (i.e. to respond to the problem areas of life). All of this will continue to be needed, but the almost unlimited scope for psychology in these four fields is a much wider and more positive one – promoting health and quality of life, enhancing work satisfaction and motivation, building harmonious communities and, in relation to education, fostering learning and raising achievement. (Mackay, 2002, pp. 248–49, emphasis added)

I would argue that coaching provides an impactful and cost-effective mechanism for supporting all the aims I have highlighted above.

In my experience as an EP of more than 25 years, including roles as a Senior EP and Principal EP, creating opportunities for such work is not easy. Schools and school special educational needs co-ordinators (SENCos) value highly the more 'traditional' role of EPs as providing assessment, consultation and advice – albeit from a psychological perspective – on meeting the needs of individual pupils and supporting the efficacy of those who routinely support them (Ashton and Roberts, 2006). My ambitions for this chapter reflect in part not only my experience as a senior manager within a number of local authorities but also my long-standing commitment to raising the profile of the *psychological* skills and knowledge an EP can deploy across a range of contexts. The much-debated emergence of traded EP service within local authorities has created opportunities to provide services as long as schools and settings are willing to buy them. Coaching is an intervention that is offered directly to school leaders, and as such its impact on culture and ethos and thus well-being can be significant.

Support for EPs who coach: self-reflection and supervision

My experience of coaching is that it can provide immense satisfaction and reward. It is, however, cognitively and emotionally demanding. As coaches, we are no less subject to unconscious dynamics and the impact of anxiety on our behaviour than our coachees. We too have suffered losses, traumas, deprivations. We too have developed and grown into the social world with beliefs and values, fears and preoccupations based on our early experiences. Coachee challenges can trigger responses in us which belong in the past, not the present. How do we ensure that we have the best possible opportunity to maintain our curiosity and objectivity when subject to these dynamics, and to do so while maintaining warm, authentic relationships with school leaders?

Being able to observe ourselves and to reflect on moments of high emotionality in coaching sessions is key to this. Self-reflexivity is not an unknown skill to EPs, but it is not always nurtured in busy, complex workplaces. Supervision is one mechanism through which any coach

– EP or not – can and should seek to maintain reflexivity, objectivity and curiosity. The value of supervision does not depend upon the psychological approach used by the coach. However, for those bringing an awareness of psychoanalytic thinking into the coaching space, it is important to seek out a supervisor who is familiar with the importance of the impact of transference, countertransference and defence mechanisms on both coachee and coach. Attention needs to be paid to a coach's triggers and to those issues likely to lead a coach to behave 'as if' he or she were responding in the past rather than the present. Supervision need not always be individual. Work discussion groups, group supervision and peer supervision are tried-and-tested, as well as economical, ways of delivering an appropriate space in which to share, think, reflect and learn.

Conclusion

In this chapter I have sought to highlight the contribution of psychoanalytic ideas in creating emotionally rich coaching relationships, relationships within which education leaders can address some of the most challenging aspects of their work – that is, those aspects that threaten their sense of competence and efficacy in leading complex and dynamic systems.

I have attempted to describe the key aspects of psychoanalytic theory that are most useful and accessible to non-experts, in order to support the framing of hypotheses, which in turn influence coaching questions and reflections. Such questions and reflections can bring depth to coaching in a way that permits both coach and client to move beyond the transactional aspects of coaching to a more transformational approach.

I believe this is an ambitious chapter, in its invitation to EPs to bring depth and psychoanalytically informed insight into the coaching space. Although coaching is no longer a new offer in schools and education settings, it is not widely offered to school leaders by EPs for the reasons I have discussed. There are arguably more accessible psychological approaches available, some of which more explicitly mirror the results-oriented culture prevalent in our education system today. By encouraging services and individual EPs to promote this offer, and to do so using a psychoanalytic approach, I am aware that I am issuing an invitation to enter unknown territory for many in our profession. Nonetheless, I do so as a result of my own experiences and the feedback that coaching clients have generously provided. Using this approach has supported coaching clients in seeing themselves in new lights and thus as individuals with many more options (or more realistic ones!) than they had previously imagined. Many have commented on the quality of the listening this approach provides and on the positive impact on their levels of anxiety that comes with being understood without judgement. In terms of contributing to a more positive experience of the human condition, as well as supporting individuals engaged in such an important task as leading schools, what more could a coach ask for?

CHAPTER 14

Social defences: managing the anxiety of work

Dale Bartle and Xavier Eloquin

This chapter moves away from the more familiar individual psycho-analytic focus to consider how unconscious processes can dynamically affect organisations, including organisational behaviour and resistance to seemingly commonsense changes and initiatives. An understanding of social defence systems and a wider awareness of unconscious organisational dynamics has, we argue, at least two important implications for educational psychologists (EPs). First, such an awareness can help the EP avoid becoming (too) enmeshed in complex social systems in a way that can lead to experiences of 'stuckness' and role-related impotence; and second, arising from this, is the possibility to help the systems with which we work to recognise some of the less obvious processes at play in them. In this chapter we want to consider the contribution psychoanalytic theory can make to our understanding of organisations, including schools and other learning institutions. We believe that the recognition of unconscious processes at play in organisational life can be useful in determining the roles EPs might take up and how support can be offered to the system-as-a-whole and those that inhabit it: students, teaching staff, parents and so on.

In this chapter, then, we will give a brief outline of the history of psychoanalytic organisational theory and then present some examples from our own experiences of working in schools. This is important: there is a sizeable literature on the contributions of psychoanalysis to wider and whole systems, but little of it that relates to schools.

Occupational emotional hazards

EPs work with and for children and young people with complex needs in often complex and demanding situations. This includes representatives from family and school systems. Such encounters can often evoke a range of tensions and unspoken anxieties: for example, when parents and a school have conflicting accounts of a child's behaviour and the EP, in the act of consultation, must manage both these accounts with some level of impartiality and neutrality (Cecchin, 1987) in the room, at the same time. No amount of theorising can diminish the strains such an activity can place on an individual-in-role.

It is this very tension and conflict in the system that can be attended to – or not. Different perspective may compound complexity, yet there is, in essence, an emotional nub that stimulates behaviour and demands attention. In schools, this is often to do with failure of some sort. Accompanying this failure is a sense of loss of competence that those involved may feel when engaging with those who are struggling to make progress . This may elicit feelings of shame and guilt. Such feelings are hard to bear and generate emotional 'static' in the system that can impair more rational modes of thinking. Indeed, how often has one observed in schools and similar systems that it is impossible to think? This is usually then registered as an occupational reality: life is busy, after all.

In schools, as with many organisations, formal and informal systems and procedures come to act as a buffer between a person-in-role and the emotional realities of the task they are to perform. For example, the way a SENCO or assistant head can end up tasked with meetings with angry parents. As EPs, we may devise procedures that enable us to 'manage' the psychological reality of meeting with a child experiencing profound emotional distress or having to contend with significant barriers and difficulties. We might reflect on the feeling of anxiety, for example, when we realise we have forgotten a specific test and have to 'wing it'.

In thinking about emotions – and how the organisation responds to them – the organization can be conceptualised as an entity, a whole organism, that in part is driven by the unconscious forces manifest in the group engaging with an assigned task. Organisational behaviours emerge which are driven by these unconscious forces, the purpose of which can be more to do with minimising emotional distress than with facing the task at hand. To cope with such painful experiences, a defensive sub-nexus can form.

The system unconsciously finds ways of functioning which help to avoid or ameliorate upset. Splitting can occur, where unpalatable states of mind are cut-off and projected out, allowing the system to regulate emotional energy and regain equilibrium. Over time such customs can crystallise into ways of working that shield those involved from facing, directly, such distress. In psychoanalytic theory, these ways have come to be known as social defences. They can be thought of as unconscious organisational processes that reduce, successfully or not, the psychic distresses of work, the everyday occupational hazard of engaging with difficult emotions.

A metaphor of the defended self and defended system

Imagine wandering across an unfamiliar land. We might feel overwhelmed, we might feel wonderment, fear, joy, a plethora of sensory and emotional bombardment. We may be driven to explore and to survive. We might gather resources to help us survive. In this pursuit, we might in some ways armour ourselves, accumulating protective materials to ward off threats we may sense in the environment.

Imagine, further, that our armoured wandering brings us into contact with others. We may find that by joining together we increase our chances of finding security and development. We may form groups; develop enhanced variations of our protective apparatus. The individual armour and shield transform and evolve into castles and cities. An adaptive and interacting series of mechanisms, emerging in the service of growth and survival. Before long, more energy comes to be given to the preservation and development of our individual and group armouring than to the capacity it allows us to engage – guardedly – with risky and uncertain environments.

This metaphor, a playful reverie, is underpinned by an interplay between human instincts that tap into our sense of opportunities and threats. These instincts may not be known or available to consciousness in the moment-to-moment acts of the individual or the organisation. It is, however, argued that these instincts and the behaviours they generate can be open to scrutiny and which, through a concerted focus of attention, may illuminate our understanding of how an organisation and the individuals who comprise it can ostensibly want one thing and yet act in a way that assures the contrary. This can be thought of as an introductory working definition of a social defence, elaboration of which follows next.

Some central concept of social defences

Object relations

Central to this theoretical development was Klein's development of object relations theory. One foundational idea of the theory is that anxious, envious and aggressive emotions are present in us from infancy. The infant experiences a range of discomforting sensations as he or she is exposed to the world. To a newborn infant the first few experiences of hunger, cold, loneliness are not temporary states that will soon be soothed, but existential threats for which it has no terms of reference to understand. Central to object relations theory is the notion of the paranoid–schizoid (Klein, 1946; Lemma, 2016) state of mind. The 'paranoid' refers to the sense of threat that is experienced in response to a bombardment of stimuli, experienced as persecutory: not 'I am hungry/cold/lonely' but 'Hunger, Cold, Loneliness is out to get me.' The somatic experiences become an externalised attacking force, at first identified in the present absence of a wilfully denying mother figure. The schizoid aspect relates to a mechanism that can help in tolerating the terrifying experience. The 'bad' feelings evoked cannot be tolerated, and a fragmentation (or 'splitting') occurs, where the 'bad' is cut off and put somewhere else, in order to relieve the discomfort. Splitting is a primitive defence (Lemma, 2016), discussed elsewhere in this book, and may be seen as creating a distorted sense of reality, commonly involving an unrealistic sense of 'all good' and 'all bad' in a way that soothes the individual and may give the impression of being released from conflict. In infants, it is their first attempt at making sense of the world and managing complexities that might otherwise overwhelm the infant's sense of self.

In time, the infant mind moves to what is called, sometimes unhelpfully, the depressive position. This is not a reference to a state of depression as a mental health disorder *per se*. Rather, it is an attempt to describe the subdued emotional state that arises out of a recognition that the separate 'good' and 'bad' mother object of the paranoid–schizoid position is actually one and the same person. It is a mental development of some sophistication that responds to the violent, angry and aggressive feelings of the paranoid–schizoid position with a sincere and more mature response of 'Oh dear! I was so angry with one part of mother that I wanted to destroy her and now I see that such a thing would have hurt the whole of her.' In other words, the infant (and subsequently the child, adolescent and adult mind) moves from a position of stark extremes, of black and white, to one of recognition of nuances and shades of grey. Furthermore, it recognises that 'I am an agent in this, not just a passive recipient. Just as others affect me, I can affect them: for good or ill.' We all tend to operate along a moving scale between the two positions. Situations of high stress can shift us back into a paranoid–schizoid position, colouring our view of others and their intentions, and thus mobilising certain energies and behaviours.

Important for our purposes here is a consideration, briefly, of individual defence mechanisms. In simplest terms, defence mechanisms serve to ensure a level of emotional and cognitive equilibrium by minimising and displacing anxiety and its impact on the ego (Bowins, 2004). More extreme anxieties, as experienced in (and because of) the paranoid–schizoid position, beget more extreme defences, while the level of maturity denoted by the depressive position leads to more mature defence types.

Although we do not intend to give a full exposition of defence mechanism theory here (see Vaillant and Vaillant, 1986), what we want to convey is the idea that the more extreme paranoid-schizoid defences become unhelpful in the long term. For example, in the case of projection, if too much of the self is projected out, then one becomes psychologically depleted. In other words, reality becomes too greatly distorted and the defence itself moves from a method of alleviating distress to one that can cause it.

We will now consider how psychoanalytic insights were transferred to a consideration of unconscious group behaviour.

Contributions from group dynamic theory

Group dynamic theory arose out of pioneering work by Bion in the UK and Lewin in the USA during and after the Second World War (Lewin, 1947; Bion, 1961; Stokes, 1994). Group dynamic theorists came to regard the group as an entity, something supraphenomenal to the individual members that constitute it (Wells, 1985). The group-as-a-whole, depending on the emotional ambience at any one time, might mobilise individual members in ways that served to momentarily protect the group from distressing psychological realities: a shift from getting on with the task at hand to ensuring the group survives at any cost. While at one level a group assembles with a stated intent to get on with the stated task, at another level the very same group behaves in ways that, rather than facing difficulty, serve to avoid it.

With Kleinian and Bionian ideas, a system-wide account of group and organisational life was possible, leading to the development of social defences – a concept we will turn to next.

Social defence systems: what organisations do with emotional distress

Part 1: We are crazy and work keeps us sane

One of the pioneers of this exploratory work was Elliot Jaques (1953), a Canadian psychoanalyst, social scientist and management consultant, who formulated the notion that 'unconsciously people can come together in collective support of each other's defensiveness' (Hinshelwood and Chiesa, 2001, p. 150). It is this fundamental concept that describes the essence of what we might refer to as 'social defences'.

His groundbreaking study involved consultation to a metal works company undergoing radical restructuring to the way it paid its workers. From his observations and interviews he came to several conclusions, two of which we share here. The first is that the structure and stability of work (in the 1950s, at least) provided a form of psychological containment for workers, protecting them from paranoid and depressive anxieties. Put another way, individuals import their own anxieties and psychological conflict into the workplace, and it is the relatively containing structure of the workplace (start and finish times, rituals around tea-breaks, work routine, etc.) that manages them more or less well. The routine, rhythm and boundaries of work provide a structure to manage the relatively less structured psychology of individuals who come to work. While we may rail against our place of work, it does give shape and form to our days, as studies of the deleterious effects of long-term unemployment so dismally attest (Abraham, Haltiwanger, Sandusky and Spletzer, 2019).

Jaques' second conclusion was concerned with the manner in which workers and managers related to each other during the period of the pay dispute. On the shop floor and in day-to-day interaction, relations were genuinely cordial. But, during meetings between union representatives and mangers over pay, a very different dynamic evolved in which managers were seen as 'bad'. Jaques conjectured that a social defence was in play to maintain a level of daily equilibrium: the workers effectively split managers into 'good' on the shop floor and 'bad' in union meetings. As a paranoid–schizoid defence this split, while it culminated in stalemated negotiations, permitted the workplace to be – at face value – free of conflict and resentment. The defences of the social system 'managed' discord off the factory floor and into union meetings.

Jaques' study was groundbreaking. It built on contemporary theorising by Lewin (1947) that groups and organisations could be intelligible fields of study and laid the foundation for a more structured psychoanalytic study of organisations. One result was an equally seminal study by Menzies (1960) of student nurse dropout in a training hospital.

Part 2: We may be crazy, but work makes us worse

By the late 1950s the NHS was well established. One result of this was the need for ever greater numbers of nurses, which itself led to an increase in nurse training. At one training hospital, managers were perturbed by the very high dropout rate of trainee nurses (about a third of all student nurses), who also tended to be the more able students. Isabel Menzies, a psychoanalyst, and member of the Tavistock Institute for Human Relations, was commissioned to explore this phenomenon.

Her study of 'obsessive–punitive' defences (Halton, 2015, p. 27) that were inherent in the structure of the hospital's hierarchy offered an staggering insight into the world of work and how workers – individually, in groups and in organisations – develop unconscious systems to manage role related anxiety and emotional distress. Unlike Jaques, who maintained it was the individual who brought anxious psychic material to a work setting, Menzies proposed that something more systemic was at play, which was linked to the task of nursing itself: the structure of the organisation and the way it related to the psychic life of those working within it affected how those individuals engaged with the tasks they were there to perform.

The trainee nurses worked with ill and dying patients and concerned and sometimes resentful relatives. The primitive emotions evoked by proximity to illness, disease and death would be hard to bear at the best of times, with support and supervision. This, however, was not the experience of the nurses. The hospital was heavily hierarchical, with little emotional support, a culture of blame and shame, and very little opportunity for autonomy. In order to manage the double pressures of high anxiety in such a culture, the hospital had developed a complex and interrelated set of social defence mechanisms to minimise them. Menzies enumerated distinct but related social defences that helped nurses manage the stresses and strains of the work in the context of an organisation that did not register how these same stresses impacted on young, novice nurses. Many of these defences involved a splitting up and depersonalisation of nurse–patient relationships: 'nurses often talk about patients, not by name, but by bed numbers or by their diseases or a diseased organ, the liver in bed 10 or the pneumonia in bed 15 ' (Menzies, 1960, p. 102). Others reduced individual nurse autonomy and decision-making need or capacity through an unquestioned culture of 'ritual task performance' (1960, p. 103), which led to oxymoronic behaviours such as waking up patients to give them sleeping pills. Although such defence systems, incorporated at the organisational level, reduced some of the distress arising out of encounters with pain and death, it also reduced a necessary prerequisite for thoughtful work: meaning. And as a result it was the most promising students who quit their training, as individual need for meaning and purpose collided with a social system that tried to dampen down the inevitable difficulties of working with those who are ill.

It should not take us too much effort to make links between hospitals and schools. The sources of pressure in the latter come not from physically ill patients but from the interplay of individual, family, systemic and suprasystemic tensions. One of us, for example, was disturbed by a school's rigid response to a young trans student's managed move to a new secondary school. This intelligent (eligible for MENSA) and thoughtful young person had a history of self-harm and school refusal at previous schools. Despite this, she had settled in the new school and her attendance was significantly better than ever before. The deputy head responsible for school attendance had set 87 per cent as a red line for any student and, despite pleas for flexibility, her lower attendance rate ultimately culminated in the managed move being deemed a failure.

Menzies' study paved the way for looking at how emotions in work can be linked, not solely to the individual, but to the organisational task individuals take up. Her study of social defences showed that institutions can work with or defend against difficult emotions, and this has ramifications for burnout, staff retention and task effectiveness. Since then, her work on social defence systems has been applied in many fields (Armstrong and Rustin, 2015).

Social defences: relevance for EPs?

So far, we have given some examples that are both old and outside the world of the EP. Factories and hospitals are not places we tend to visit. We believe that a knowledge and understanding of social defences are important for EPs for two main reasons. The first is that such knowledge helps to explain organisational behaviour in any setting. Schools are ever more places of anxiety and pressure (Tucker, 2015; Adams, 2018) and we suggest that some of those pressures lead to and are then recursively caused by how the school as a whole reacts to the anxieties it faces. And these anxieties are real, from increased student mental health, to the pressures of OFSTED and the very real risk a poor OFSTED poses to a headteacher's career (Weale, 2016), to say nothing of the pressures classroom teachers, middle leaders and senior leaders also face. EPs enter these complex systems and very quickly have certain emotions projected on to them (Bain, 1979; Eloquin, 2016). Indeed, if not sufficiently aware of these projections and the anxieties they are rooted in, an EP can easily end up unconsciously colluding with the system, further perpetuating the defence system. A trite example might be agreeing to work with a number of students in the same year/gender/race instead of recognising a more systemic/cultural issue, or losing impartiality in favour of a family or school to act out a certain agenda on behalf of either.

Such knowledge can also mean, ultimately, that an EP is well placed to surface some of these unconscious processes in such a way that they can be registered by individuals and groups within the system. We want to be clear here, however, that defences run deep. They are not easily or quickly brought to conscious awareness and they exist to protect. Working psychoanalytically, one does not attempt to remove or 'solve' a problematic defence system. Indeed, it would be unwise and probably impossible. But by bringing them into awareness people are better able to make sense of organisational behaviour and the thoughts and feelings behind it. Organisationally, this can lay a foundation for a genuine change of culture. Individually, it can help one to see that the cause of distress and dysfunction is not (solely) located in the individual, but in a set of assumptions that underlie organisational perspectives and behaviours.

In the following two case studies, we want to give a sense of the workings of a social defence system and describe the ways that they were then communicated to key role holders. It is important to note, however, that defences are notoriously hard to pin down. Shaw's comment on individual defences holds as true for organisational defences too: 'One knows them best, only after the fact, catching them so to speak, by a non-essential tail that breaks loose just as it is grasped' (2002, p. 32). The meaning and function of a behaviour are not immediately obvious or easily inferred. We suspect that many EPs have entered systems somewhat disconcerted by the emotional tone of the place and the practices they observe. Yet some of these practices have a reality-based rationale – they serve the primary task (Roberts, 1994) of the organisation. It is when organisation behaviour *runs counter* to the espoused aim of an institution that one can begin to explore whether systemic defences structures are at play.

Case 1: The mate/monster dilemma

In a therapeutic residential school for adolescents presenting with harmful sexualised behaviours, managers were concerned at the frequent breaking of supervision rules by staff. The school maintained a strict staffing ratio of one residential social worker (RSW) to two students, and students were never to be left unsupervised, as there was a risk of further sexualised behaviour. Despite regular reminders of this need, supervision was continually neglected, culminating in several sexual incidents that were then reported to social services. Organisationally, this placed immense pressure on senior managers, as each incident of sexualised behaviour was reported to the respective social services department, with further ramifications during OFSTED and Care Standards inspections.

Management's response was to act in a harsh and punitive manner to any staff caught breaking supervision rules. This had no effect on the frequency of the phenomenon. Furthermore, such a stance was inimical to the espoused 'therapeutic' aims of the unit. Staff were tense and this was further impacting on the way they related to the students.

As part of a wider range of interventions, the EP was asked to facilitate a workshop on social defences for the staff team. He gave a brief input on defences and introduced them to the concept of hypothesising (see below), seeking to engage staff in actively thinking about this issue. This was followed by a series of goldfish bowl conversations, with staff listening to colleagues discussing their experiences of working and relating with young men who were also dangerous offenders.

Out of these discussions, two main camps or views emerged: those who saw the students as monsters to be watched like hawks and never trusted, and those who saw them as damaged children in need of a therapeutic milieu and deserving of a second chance. These were highly polarised positions and it was difficult for any individual to hold a more balanced view. Intense discussions arose between the groups: those who thought the boy monsters never really developed the warm and easy rapport required to work therapeutically. Interaction with students tended towards direct instruction, with no possibility of reciprocal conversation. Conversely, those who saw the students as damaged children, as much victims of abuse as they were perpetrators, tended to be the ones who talked with the boys, relating to them more and in a warmer and friendlier manner. Although this was therapeutically beneficial, they acknowledged that this view made it more likely that a staff member would 'forget' about the need to keep students under supervision.

What emerged was a dichotomy in how the staff responded to a central fact – the horrific forms of abuse the students had perpetrated on others. This was hard to keep in mind with even a modicum of equanimity, evoking, as it did, very strong feeling and opinion. The stark division of views was indicative of a staff team operating from within a paranoid–schizoid position, in which members struggled to hold a dual perspective of the young men they were working with. Put simply, the unit was home to two different types of students, depending on the outlook of the staff. This split perspective helped defend against awareness that horrific crimes could be committed by people who were – likeable, and who under different circumstances might have grown up just like them. This was a hard thing to bear. One group could barely conceive of the students as human. They had to be watched at all times, lest their monstrousness run free. The other group, in order to relate to the 'boys', had to 'forget' their crimes and, in so doing, the need for watchful supervision was also forgotten, as they began to relate to them as if they were regular adolescents, playing pool, engaging in banter and enjoying their company.

Through a series of staged discussions, with strategic theoretical inputs given by the EP, the staff team were able to reflect on their experiences and views and come to see that, for the students to be appropriately supervised and worked with therapeutically, the opposing views needed reconciling within each member. This was not the end of the problem, far from it, but they had a deeper understanding of why keeping to the supervision requirements was so difficult: it was not simply a case of sloppy work ethics. It helped in their mental preparation at the start of their shifts.

Case 2: The 'life of ease' as a defence against risk of violence

Strathmore House is a residential school for children aged 11–18 years with severe learning disabilities. One year, an OFSTED inspection resulted in an 'Inadequate' rating. Following internal enquiries, the principal left the school. An acting principal was appointed.

One of the identified areas of improvement within the school was the taught curriculum. There was no real implementation of practical numeracy or literacy and a lot of 'chillout' time. One class seemed to be a permanent café, while another embarked on an endless series of minibus trips with no specific objective identified.

The new acting principal, Matt, and Jane, the school manager, identified a new practical literacy and numeracy curriculum, and Jane introduced it at a staff meeting, highlighting the need to improve teaching and learning standards. This meeting did not go well. Jane was mobbed by angry staff, who accused her of not recognising all the work they were doing and the pressures they were under. Concerned, Matt raised the issue with the EP consulting to the school. He was angry with staff, whose behaviour and resistance to the new curriculum signalled laziness and lack of teaching ability. He was determined to get them teaching properly or 'encourage' them to leave. This was an extreme strategy, predicated on equally extreme emotions, hardly surprising given the pressures the school was under. The EP was concerned that such a strategy was coun-terproductive and offered to undertake an exploration of dynamics at play in the school system, promising Matt deeper insight into the moti-vations of the staff.

Gathering information

The EP spent several days in observations and interviews of staff, during which new data emerged, casting a new light on their resistance to the new curriculum. To a person, staff described being left utterly unsup-ported in the past. They had been ostensibly left to manage the teaching, learning and behaviour of their classes on their own.

One striking observation was the low professional self-esteem of teaching staff. With no 'organisational holding environment' (Stapley, 2006) to help them reflect on progress and find meaning in the work they were doing, a pervasive sense of impotence and despondency had arisen. Furthermore, attempts to challenge students and orientate them to tasks not of their choosing frequently led to physical aggression, and staff all presented with bruises and bite marks. At the same time, they spoke of their students with fondness and were determined to play a meaningful role in their education. The same fondness could not be mustered when it came to describing their views of the senior leadership team (SLT) and measures taken to improve the school in general and teaching and learn-ing in particular. The staff uniformly reported an experience of being done to, with no meaningful opportunity to state their point of view or play a role in developing solutions. They described the new curriculum as an imposition, limiting their powers through draconian measures. They told the EP that the curriculum meant that they would 'never be allowed off site' and that 'they [senior management] want students sitting at desks like a mainstream school', statements that were proved false by simply asking Matt. The general supposition was that the SLT were intent on 'taking all positive activities away'.

Analysis

It is clear that projective processes are at play here: there is a split between management and the teachers, with the former experienced as distant, cruel and persecutory. At face value, it might be easy to view the teachers as obstreperous and disengaged. Social defence theory, however, offers a different account of their behaviours, one in which the established pattern of the schoolday was born, not out of laziness or a desire for ease, but as a way of managing distinct dangers and anxieties.

Remember, first, that the teaching staff had been left to their own devices, and that they were confronted with a range of challenging and violent experiences. They had to contend daily with bodily functions and behaviours that, to recall Menzies' (1960) nurse study, evoked primitive emotions such as disgust, impotence and fear. Such experiences would evoke equally primitive anxieties in individuals, which had to be defended against if they were simply to turn up to work. It would be understandable if one were to stay at the level of the individual in analysis of the situation – that staff were overwhelmed, vulnerable, demoralised and so on. But this is to miss the way in which these shared individual concerns meshed into a larger, cultural pattern of behaviour. Just as individual defence systems come to form an aspect of personality, so too can social defence systems come to inform the culture or 'personality' of the organisation (Stapley, 1996).

Social defences and resistance to change

It can become clearer, then, why the objectively trivial curriculum change was met as it was. It threatened the carefully developed network of assumptions and behaviours that led to a 'good-enough' equilibrium: students were happy, staff were not hurt and the day passed well enough. To change this 'life of ease' system would be to return to them the very anxieties they were striving to defend against. Indeed, one can discern some displacement of these fears from students to SLT. It was now not students who were threatening them, but management.

In this case, the key first intervention response by the EP was to produce a working note (Miller, 1995), a document consisting of the observations and hypotheses described above. The aim of a working note is not to produce a definitive account with a set of recommendations, but rather to metabolise organisational data into something that can be thought about: to make psychological sense of it. The working note was sent to Matt several days before they met for their next consultation, giving him time to read and reflect on the stated hypothesis. When they met, it was a chance to consider the 'state of play' in the school system and one result of this was a slowing down of the implementation of change and a deeper registering of the anxieties that stimulated such seemingly unreasonable resistance.

Social defences and EPs: implications for practice

Social defences serve a necessary function in organisations. They can act as a regulating principle and ensure a form of systemic equilibrium. When presented with abrupt organisation change programmes, the resistance they produce can be seen not just as obstreperous 'cussedness' on the part of stakeholders, but as a legitimate political stance that invites further investigation into the dynamic forces that maintain such a position. Defences are there to ensure psychological safety, to protect individuals and system from psychic overwhelm. But if the pressures are too great, the defences evoked begin to distort task engagement in favour of understandable, but illusory and unhelpful, attitudes and behaviours that are orientated to the immediate protection of those individuals and subsystems in which anxieties are located. As we have seen here, this can be teachers expected to manage the brunt of institutional reorganisation, taking on new tasks, duties or ways of working, or staff working with young people whose experiences and behaviours evoke very extreme feelings of disgust, horror and rage, while they are expected to relate in a therapeutic manner. When considered through a psychoanalytic lens, the existence of social defences cannot be a surprise. Rather, they are an organisational prerequisite if challenging and demanding emotional toil is to be undertaken. Knowledge of social defences, we strongly believe, can help EPs to manage their own role-related emotional experiences and help others to make sense of theirs.

What is more, paranoid–schizoid defences risk reducing organisational members to 'part objects', no longer seen as distinct human beings, but as representative functions. This has disastrous consequences for all concerned, as Menzies' (1960) account of nurses and patients attests. Given the pressures schools are under, our fear – and experience – is that all too easily the most vulnerable in any system are the ones worst served by such dynamics. An awareness and understanding of social defences provide EPs with a systemic rationale for some of the sometimes strange behaviours observable in organisational life, and for the cultural conflicts that can take place within them. It further provides a framework for helping such systems come to terms with the emotions they are defending against. This can offer some liberation through increased insight and understanding.

What helps?

The concept of a social defence invites EPs to consider phenomena within an organisation as part of an interrelated network of whole-system unconscious dynamics. Furthermore, it presents a way of understanding organisational behaviours as being either in service to the organisational task (where the dominant position is depressive and reality based) or more orientated to anxiety reduction for individuals or subsystems within the organisation. Here projective and other more primitive defences are mobilised. Although this may seem strange at first, the idea of individuals arranging the psychological furniture so as to minimise psychological threat at an unconscious level is something that a psychoanalytic perspective prepares us for. In the case of social defences, this requires a change of focus, from the individual to the group, the inter-group and the whole system (Wells, 1985), something that is not always easy to do. What, then, can help? Certainly, supervision and training are useful, as is an experience of psychoanalysis in some form. In the daily round of an EP, though, the following are things we have found to be important and helpful.

Observation and attention

Observing others and one's own state, especially when crossing an organisational threshold, is a necessary prerequisite. Isolated behaviours and expressions of attitude need to be contextualised within the wider system of which they are a part. Only then is it possible to ask, 'What purpose do they serve?' This can help throw assumptions into relief: condemnation or judgement of organisational players (for example, the SLT's frustration with the RSWs or Matt's anger at the teachers) can be an indication that defensive processes are in play.

Explore the anxiety

Asking just what anxiety might be being defended against is the beginning of an extended exploration of the system. Observation, interviews – formal and informal – and a working knowledge of the pressures the system faces (both internal and external) serve to develop a whole-system hypothesis about organisational functioning. Such a hypothesis acts as a 'because' clause, linking observed phenomena to unrecognised, unconscious phenomena: essentially, 'behaviour X occurs because of Y (the unconscious anxiety)'. This acts as a rudder in the water, helping the EP to test out interventions based on the hypothesis, which are then – importantly – confirmed or not. For example, the EP in Case 1 explored whether staff tended to hold one or other extreme position, because it is hard to think that a sexual offender can both commit horrific acts and be likeable.

Use one's own subjectivity

The use of one's own subjective experience, one's countertransference, is a powerful source of emotional data. This is an alien concept to many, but emotions occur in an environmental context – in this case, an organisational one (Neumann, 1999). Research on polyvagal theory demonstrates how mammals, particularly higher primates (including humans), use body language, facial expression and vocal tone to communicate threat or safety in groups (Porges, 2011). Armstrong has demonstrated how emotions can be used as data or 'intelligence' (2005, p. 90 ff.) when engaged in organisational consultancy. How, for example, does one's emotional state change upon entering a new system? Are initial encounters with receptionists, teachers, the head welcoming, distant, anxiety-raising? By shifting from an individual to an organisational level of analysis, such emotional responses can offer possible meaning about the emotional 'pH' level of the organisation. Such data must be supported, triangulated, by other forms of information, but to dismiss how one is made to feel (what is projected into one) is to neglect a valuable resource that exists within us.

By extension, it is useful to observe the unofficial and unauthorised roles and tasks one unthinkingly takes up, and that run counter to conscious intention. Upon entering the organisational field, an EP (in this case) is subject to an array of projective processes that often push him or her to take up a role as antidote to the anxieties defended against (Bain, 1979). To acquiesce to this pressure is to engage in a more or less unconscious collusion with the system to *make the problem go away*. Attention to this dynamic helps to avoid such collusive working and allows for the eventuality that the EP may help the organisation face the anxieties it is defending against in a more mature, depressive manner.

A final reflection

This chapter has explored the concept of social defences that may emerge in educational systems. As mentioned at the outset of the chapter, we argue that there is a theme here, and across this book as a whole, that involves the potential for shame and guilt within educational systems. If progress is not demonstrated, there is a raft of consequences that can threaten the survival of organisations and individuals within them. We do not underestimate the force that shame may hold within educational systems. One further link may be considered here. Armstrong (2005) suggested that an unidentified basic assumption within groups may relate to guilt. If Armstrong is correct, and groups may develop ways of behaving under the sway of guilt, we wonder if shame may feed into this group phenomenon. It is perhaps conceivable that the nature of this emotion is more difficult to identify, as the unbearable experience of the group is of necessity buried deeply in order to protect the group from disturbance. We believe that this idea of collective shame and guilt merits further consideration within the educational context.

PART VII

POSTSCRIPT: WIDENING THE HORIZON

CHAPTER 15

The psyche as a complex system: insights from chaos theory

Christopher Arnold

Freud's long-standing ambition was to establish psychoanalysis as a natural science. As early as the 1890s Freud prepared drafts for a paper entitled 'Project for a Scientific Psychology' in which the topic would be grounded in the natural sciences with similar status and disciplines such as physics or biology. The links between these differing schools may still be questioned, but it is worth recalling that Freud's own supervisor for his doctoral studies was Ernst Wilhelm von Brücke, who in turn was a colleague of Helmholtz, an eminent physicist and researcher into the fundamental laws of physics that govern the universe. One such law is the conservation of energy. Energy cannot be created or destroyed, but converted from one form to another. This idea fed Freud's theories about the psyche and is still in use today. There are papers both questioning the appropriateness of the assumptions (Macmillan, 2001, for instance) and providing new possible lines of enquiry (for example, Mechelli, 2010).

The purpose of this chapter is to consider the substance of some of the challenges to the theories on which psychoanalysis is based and to suggest at least one alternative framework that has the potential to both explain and justify the theory as a natural science. In so doing, the reader will note that the epistemological stance in this chapter is different from that in others. This is intentional. As we shall see, the appreciation of positivist natural sciences has developed over the last half-century or so and our application of this to psychodynamic thinking needs to take account of this. As the closing chapter for this book, it aims to provide a context for the contributions and suggest future directions for research.

The Nobel laureate Eric Kandel (1999) remarked that a most disappointing aspect of psychoanalysis is its failure to evolve and progress scientifically, specifically its failure to develop objective methods for testing the ideas it formulates. 'Psychoanalysis', he asserted, 'has traditionally been far better at generating ideas than at testing them' (cited in Taylor and Bagby, 2013). Attempts to encourage students and practitioners to engage in high-quality research have not always been well received, with many finding their structures lacking in relevance for their work. Mechelli (2010) relates a list of concerns in this field, including:

- the failure to demonstrate that mechanical or biological explanations would be capable of making psychological concepts perspicuous and free from contradiction
- a failure to see how a characterisation of the ego as a 'complex of neurons which could hold fast to their cathexis (the concentration of mental energy on one particular person, idea, or object)'
- a failure to be able to demonstrate that psychoanalytic theories could be falsified on the basis of empirical evidence
- the theories cannot be compared, as it is impossible to manipulate the variables. (Mechelli, 2010).

Kandel commented that there was a decline in public enthusiasm for psychoanalytic treatments in favour of less expensive options, although he did offer the idea that modern brain imaging techniques might provide support for the theories.

In line with Kandel's observations are studies such as Van Etten and Taylor's (1998), who offer a meta-analysis of treatments for PTSD (post-traumatic stress disorder). Unfortunately, in an examination of 46 different studies, only one used psychodynamic approaches, thus making evaluation difficult. That said, the indications of efficacy were positive.

Challenges come from other fields, too. Wilson (2010) describes Lacan's doubt that psychoanalysis would ever be relevant in Japan, as the language has such radically different structures as to render the concepts of psychoanalysis incomprehensible. However, psychoanalysis is thriving in Japan, suggesting that its methods and concepts transcend culture.

In a paper directly addressing concerns and doubts about the scientific nature of psychoanalytic thinking, Macmillan (2001) takes the debate to the core issues of validity and reliability when applied to the method of free association. He links Freud's description of free association as being able to prevent patients being led astray by suggestions and expectations. This relates to validity in the sense that the patient is relating ideas purely from his or her own psyche rather than from those of others. As for reliability, Freud dismisses variations between different therapists' observations to be of little consequence, comparing the method to microscopic examination of nature's minutiae. Freud even quotes correlations to support the concept of scientific reliability. The challenge, however, is found in this area. The utility of a theory cannot just be found in its explanatory power, but in its predictive ability. It is this that admits the theory into natural science.

It would be remiss to omit the critics of such stances. Ashworth and Chung (2006) note that psychologists have located their work within the disciplines of natural science, but phenomenologists see the psyche rather differently and set out an alternative line of research. If natural science is advanced through the manipulation of variables, the understanding of lived experience is not. Phenomenological psychology reflects human experience, with its data gathered from people describing their under-standing of natural phenomena including emotion and thought. This can be seen to be at odds with the natural scientific method, in which a researcher is either one or the other.

Such binary options are now even questioned within natural science.

In the 1960s, researchers into weather systems started to publish ideas and models of complex and unstable systems. The name most commonly cited was Edward Lorenz (1972), who produced a paper with the attrac-tive title of 'Predictability: does the flap of a butterfly's wings in Brazil set off a tornado in Texas?' The paper appeared to capture the imagination of many people and the theory he outlined was given the label 'chaos theory', although 'dynamic systems theory' is often used in some publications. Not since the publication of Einstein's theory of relativity did a mathematical theory appear in popular culture. The novelist William Boyd produced a book *Brazzaville Beach*, in which the main character was married to a mathematician working on chaos theory, and the structure of the book has many aspects that reflect phenomena described by the theory. The film *Jurassic Park* has a 'chaotician' as one of the key players in the plot.

Such popularity, however, did lead to some lack of rigour in people's understanding of the theory. Perhaps a better description for the theory is 'deterministic chaos' or 'a theory of unstable deterministic systems'. It does not suggest that there are patterns in events driven purely by random features. When using the term 'deterministic' we are referring to phenomena that follow rules. The complexity comes when multiple factors are involved.

As part of his PhD thesis, this author analysed the use of the term 'chaos' and 'chaos theory' in psychology and suggested the following taxonomy (Arnold, 2002):

- There are applications that apply rigorous mathematical models to psychological phenomena such as language development (for example, Van Geert, 1994).
- There are publications that do analyse the phenomena with some rigour, but do not go as far as producing mathematical models.
- Finally, there are publications that use the term 'chaos' in an informal sense, but with no link to the formal theory (such as, 'The National Health Service is in chaos').

This chapter will consider the nature of psychoanalytic theory through the lens of dynamic systems theory and, in so doing, re-evaluate some of the criticisms described above.

Let us start with a definition of dynamic systems. Van der Maas and Hopkins (1998) offered this from Morrison (1991): 'Dynamics is the study of the ways in which systems change over time in seeking new optimal states of stability.'

Interest in this field is still in evidence, although the number of publications using the term 'chaos' does appear to be declining. The following data (Figure 15.1) were obtained from a university database. The search covered 1988 to 2017, although note that the data for 2017 may not yet be complete. The trend may be downwards, but the number of titles is still large, particularly when compared with some other terms, such as 'dyslexia', which had 7691 titles in 2016 – barely one-tenth of the references to 'chaos' in the same year. Clearly research into 'chaos' is still popular.

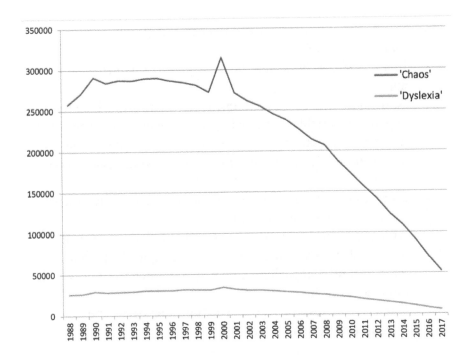

Figure 15.1 'Chaos' and 'dyslexia' titles

The features of chaotic systems

There are four necessary and sufficient conditions to be met for a dynamic system to develop deterministic chaotic patterns:

- There are at least three similarly empowered elements, although there can be many more.
- These elements learn iteratively. In other words, the output from one learning cycle acts as the input to the next.
- The elements exist in an ecology of finite resources: if one element gains resources, it is at the expense of the others.
- There are no large-scale forces or preset architecture applied to the system.

When the above conditions are met, some of the following phenomena may be found (Mandelbrot, 1977, cited in Gleick, 1987):

- Periods of apparent stability, followed by periods of significant change.

- Small changes either side of a large transition – known as 'chaotic markers'.
- Predictability is finite and the term 'prediction horizon' is applied.
- Non-linear change – a relationship in a system in which the dependent variable is affected by the independent variable in a non-proportional way, or a linear increase in one variable corresponds with a non-linear change in another (Van Geert, 1994).
- Bifurcations – the sudden appearance of qualitatively different solutions to the same problem.
- Strange attractors – unseen features that influence elements of the system in systematic ways. For example, the path of a moth around a single light bulb may not touch the bulb, but the influence is clear.
- Fractals – processes or transformations that occur at different level or locations in a system.

It is furthermore important to understand that chaos has been applied to systems with random features. This is not a feature of the kinds of systems being described here. While there may be random events, the systems are subject to deterministic rules. What singles these systems out is their complexity and instability, both of which result in individual (and unique) presentations.

Chaotic systems and the human psyche

The four conditions needed for deterministic chaos to occur were outlined above, with all of the associated phenomena. Let us consider these in turn.

- *Three or more similarly empowered elements*
  At first glance this might seem problematic, but if we consider learning skills, attitudes and behaviours as having discrete features, this condition may be met. If we use Freud's distinction of ego, id and super-ego, again they may be met. However, authors such as Styles (2009) have described neural pathways developing in the brain as a result of experience and learning. If we consider

the neural pathways to be distinct and discrete elements, the conditions are almost certainly met. A clinical example of this could be in the analysis of a person's behaviour which changes over time as a result of experience. Some experiences may reinforce one particular response style (for example, anger) and lead to some reduction in a different response, such as empathy.

- *The elements learn iteratively*
  Learning is primarily an iterative process. There would be few who would take issue with this. Styles (2009) describes the firing of neurons together as creating stronger connections and gene expression, which produces a substance that is essential for the survival of the neuron. This is how we learn and, more importantly, how the neuron survives. Furthermore, the inherited (or genetic) elements interact with experienced phenomena to produce complex (and sometimes unpredictable) outcomes. The example above applies here too. If someone has had a successful outcome from one response style, he or she is likely to repeat it.

- *An ecology with finite resources*
  The firing of neurons requires energy. This is finite. If we change the domain to that of human attention, we find that this too is finite. If you are attending to one thing, you are attending less to another. If learning is influenced by what is attended to, then elements that could be learned could compete for attention. So, for example, if we focus our attention on learning to play the piano, then we probably have less time to learn something else.

- *No preset architecture or large-scale forces*
  This is more contentious. However, the assertions from Styles, Brown, Haist and Jernigan (2015) strongly suggest that, while there is no blank slate, the development of the brain is more plastic than previously thought and subject to complex inter-actions between genes and the environment. Clearly there will be some biological forces influencing aspects of human development, but, in terms of the more sophisticated higher-order aspects of knowledge and behaviour, these may play less of a part than for the purely physical features.

It would not be appropriate to assert definitively that the four conditions above are met for chaotic development of the psyche. However, the possibility remains that they *might*. Let us turn our attention to the observable phenomena and see if there are elements here that match observable human behaviour.

- *Periods of apparent stability, followed by periods of significant change*
  There are many presentations of such events in psychology. People who experience psychotic episodes can exhibit sudden extreme changes in behaviour. Anger is reported to produce different levels of aggression and distress involving sudden changes. Both these can be preceded by periods of stability and can be followed by similar periods of apparently 'normal' experience and behaviour. School teachers describe children with difficulties conforming to behavioural expectations of the class as being 'unstable' but also able to display calmness and stability for significant periods of time.

  We should note that the examples cited come from situations of human difficulty. Many people (perhaps the vast majority) do not display sudden changes or periods of significant change, but we must also recall that the psychoanalytic theories had their origins in helping people with significant neuroses. It may be useful to consider whether people with these experiences are, perhaps, displaying conditions reflecting more unstable mental states that do follow some of the features of dynamic systems.

- *Small changes either side of a large transition – 'chaotic markers'*
  Van Geert (1994) has modelled speech development in young children using dynamic systems theories. He has demonstrated chaotic markers prior to a child progressing from a two-word to a three-word level. In particular he has recorded periods of reduced speech just prior to the transition. He suggests that this corresponds to the changes in cognitive function that occur when the child moves towards the three-word level. He notes that children do not *gradually* change from two- to three-word utterances, but there is a sudden change, preceded by a short period of reduced speech.

Predictability is finite, 'prediction horizon' is applied
This is generally most understood in weather prediction. The original work on dynamic systems found that very small errors in measurement of atmospheric conditions would work through the iterative processes in the evolution of the weather system to lead to very different outcomes later. The 'prediction horizon' is the time during which predictions can be made with some degree of accuracy. For the weather system in the UK, it is between 16 and 23 days (Buizza and Leutbecher, 2015). This is more difficult to describe in human terms, but it has some resonance when working with people with unstable conditions.

One area in psychology that worked to model future actions and development in people was the development of the intelligence quotient (IQ). This modelled cognitive development through a number of dimensions to arrive at a quotient that offered a degree of stability about expected development. On the basis of this, predictions could be made about appropriate careers, partners and some features of the subjects' children. Correlations were produced to show the accuracy of the method. However, correlations between IQ and other, non-psychometric measures rarely exceeded 0.7 (Cripps, 2018) and were often much lower. Such a correlation only accounts for 49 per cent of the variance in a particular population, leaving the other 51 per cent unaccounted for. This suggests that other factors play parts in human development that have not yet been modelled.

The first educational psychologist (EP), Cyril Burt, worked on the selection of 11-year-old pupils leading to different educational systems depending on the results of their performance in the exams. The relatively poor correlation between scores at 11 and 16, when the selection process was widely abandoned, is an example of a prediction horizon with limitations. Pupils who did score higher at the age of 11 did not always do better than others at the age of 16.

A complex and potentially unstable system can react to changed circumstances in ways that are impossible to anticipate. The reaction can be delayed, missed or even not in evidence.

Non-linear change
This is a relationship in a system in which the dependent variable is affected by the independent variable in a non-proportional
way, or a linear increase in one variable corresponds with a
non-linear change in another (Van Geert, 1994).

This area is difficult to justify in people. It is rare that studies
are able to create situations with dependent and independent
variables that can be manipulated in the same way that other
scientific disciplines can. EPs are applied psychologists who
rarely have the opportunity to manage variables.

- *Bifurcations which are the sudden appearance of qualitatively
  different solutions to the same problem*
  There are a number of examples we could cite here. Perhaps
  the most relevant for psychodynamic theories is the concept of
  'splitting' as described by Melanie Klein. A child can project
  unpleasant aspects of experience on to objects in the outer
  world, thus creating a comforting and pleasant sense of distance
  between the individual and the unpleasant experience. In
  accounts of schizophrenia, discussion of alternative versions of
  reality are suggested. People can categorise artefacts as 'good'
  or 'bad' and maintain these views for extended periods of time.
  Situations that engender cognitive dissonance display bifurcations when the dissonance reaches a critical point.

  A more concrete example of this in educational psychology
  would be the suggestion that a student transfer school rather
  than continue in his or her existing one. Transfer to a special
  school (or unit) can be suggested quite quickly in situations of
  great instability for children.

- *Strange attractors*
  These are unseen features that influence elements of the system
  in systematic ways, and there are many examples that fit this
  description. If we start with the tripartite model of the human
  psyche – id, ego and super-ego – we get a good sense of the
  match. In Freud's time, brain imaging was not able to explore
  neuropsychology. The concept of the three elements came from

observation of behaviour and utterances. It became clear to Freud that there were unseen influences and forces at work, and he hypothesised the three parts. Human drives cannot be seen directly, yet their influence is clear. These could all be examples of 'strange attractors'.

- *Fractals*
  These are processes or transformations that occur at different levels or locations in a system, and are harder to define in human terms unless we consider comparison as a fractal. We compare and allocate a category to different elements of ourselves. The category 'best/worst' (or 'successful/least successful') can be applied to genes, organs, people, groups, populations and probably species. Thus comparison is a fractal process.

Implications for psychology

Within psychology, the terms 'validity' and 'reliability' are often used to justify particular approaches, whether to assessment or intervention methods. There is a framework published by the European Federation of Psychological Associations (EFPA) for evaluating tests used in psychology, and which includes the thresholds for allocating star ratings. These are expressed as correlation coefficients (Tables 15.1 and 15.2).

Table 15.1 Reliability (stability)

R value	Category
$r < 0.60$	Inadequate
$0.60 < r < 0.70$	Adequate
$0.70 < r < 0.80$	Good
$r > .80$	Excellent

Table 15.2 Validity thresholds

R value	Category
$r < 0.55$	Inadequate
$0.55 \leq r < 0.65$	Adequate
$0.65 \leq r < 0.75$	Good
$r \geq 0.75$	Excellent

The mathematics behind correlation coefficients are linear. The formulae used to calculate the coefficients are robust, but depend on linear systems. If we conceptualise psychodynamic systems as dynamic rather than linear, then the application of conventional evaluative methods is inappropriate. We do not eliminate weather forecasting as a waste of time simply because the predictions cannot exceed a couple of weeks. Instead, we understand the limitations of the approach and work within them. Similarly, with other complex systems, the ability to look backwards to understand how a position has been arrived at is useful to a certain extent. Kierkegaard's oft-cited quote that 'life can only be understood backwards, but it must be lived forwards' (1957, pp. 79–80) summarises the situation well.

Evaluating dynamic systems within a natural science framework

Clearly if conventional methods of justifying approaches are not appropriate, we must consider alternatives. Let us start with well-recognised tools that are still relevant in these situations.

Reliability is not simply robustness across time. Inter-observer reliability measures determine the agreement between two or more observers commenting on the same events. These techniques apply to dynamic systems and can be established in the usual ways. Researchers evaluate a situation independently and the extent of agreement can be expressed as a coefficient. This is not a particularly new suggestion, as Macmillan (2001) makes similar observations and refers back to Freud's original sources.

Validity measures the extent to which an assessment evaluates what it says it does. Face validity is highly applicable to dynamic systems. To what extent does the account of the phenomena arising from the theory make sense to those using it? Again there is some discussion of this in Macmillan (2001), albeit using a small range of examples.

The danger inherent in applying either of these measures is clear. To establish inter-observer reliability both the observers must use the same framework when describing their observations. If one observer is using a behavioural observation schedule and the other a more systemic version, it is unlikely that there will be a high degree of match; however, if both are skilled in the same observation techniques the descriptions should be amenable to meaningful comparison. For measures of validity the danger of explanatory fictions is ever present. An explanatory fiction is a circular argument without triangulation that appears to be an explanation. For example:

Statement 1   This child has attention deficit hyperactivity disorder (ADHD).

Question 1   How do you know?

Statement 2   Because he is always active.

Question 2   Why is he always active?

Statement 3   Because he has ADHD (that is, the same as Statement 1).

This is different from triangulated explanations. For example:

Statement 1   This child has appendicitis.

Question 1   How do you know?

Statement 2   Because he has acute pains in his abdomen.

Question 2   How do you know that he hasn't got indigestion?

Statement 3   Because his blood contains higher numbers of white blood cells and an ultrasound indicates an infected appendix.

This last statement acts as a way of triangulating the hypothesis.

Within psychology, similar dangers of explanatory fiction exist. Triangulation is an essential safeguard to avoid this.

Areas for future research

Two areas seem ripe for research: evidence of cyclicity and prediction horizons.

Evidence of cyclical behaviour

Complex systems can have homeostatic features that are not obvious at first sight. Two mathematical tools exist to reveal underlying cyclical behaviour in complex systems. The tool for analysing phenomena that are continuous is Fourier analysis. This starts from a theorem, originally developed by Joseph Fourier, which found that any complex waveform can be created by the addition of different simple waves with defined amplitudes and frequencies. If an element of human behaviour or experience can be expressed by continuous data, then the technique can be applied. One example would be level of anxiety. A time sequence can be generated from such data and the analysis would describe underlying cycles. This has some predictive power and offers positive insights for treatment.

Prediction horizons

Not all data are continuous, but discrete. For example, an annual survey of particular behaviours produces a value for the year as a whole rather than continuous sequences during the time under consideration. There exists the maximum entropy spectral method to cover these situations (Hamilton and West, 2000). However, the outcomes are similar to the application of Fourier analysis, in that underlying frequencies of recurring events are uncovered, if they exist.

In circumstances where they do appear, again there is some predictive power, although it is subject to a prediction horizon. This author applied this technique to reading survey data in 98 junior schools in an urban authority. There was clear evidence of cycles of attainment in all but two schools, and running the models forwards revealed a predictive power for the following two years. This was based purely on the data presented for the previous 20 years (Arnold, 2002).

The use of these analytical techniques is helpful when working to understand complex systems and represent valuable tools for those working in these areas. I am not aware of their application in psychoanalytic research so far. For those seeking to explore these ideas further, they may offer new insights and support for the assumptions under examination.

Summary

This chapter has set out to reconsider some criticisms raised about the nature of psychodynamic theory and its status as a science in the way that the founders proposed. In so doing, it proposes that the framework offered by dynamic systems theory (also known as chaos theory) offers an alternative model for the phenomena under examination. The conditions for the appropriate application of this theory *may* be met, but the phenomena under consideration do appear to display most of the features associated with this model. The weather is well understood to be a complex, deterministic, dynamic system with finite predictability, yet no one questions the scientific nature of weather patterns. The same may be true for the human psyche. Rejection of the scientific nature of psychodynamic theories on the basis of the application of linear models may miss a valuable resource when considering human behaviour.

REFERENCES

Foreword

Dutton, R. (1995). *Clinical Reasoning in Physical Disabilities*. London: Williams and Wilkins.

Introduction

Bell, D. (2010). 'Psychiatry and Psychoanalysis: A Conceptual Mapping', in A. Lemma and M. Patrick (eds), *Off the Couch: Contemporary Psychoanalytic Applications*. Hove: Routledge.

Devereux, G. (1967). *From Anxiety to Method in the Behavioural Sciences*. The Hague: Mouton.

Farrell, P., Woods, K., Lewis, S., Squires, G., Rooney, S. and O'Connor, M. (2006). *A Review of the Functions and Contribution of Educational Psychologists in England and Wales in Light of 'Every Child Matters: Change for Children*. Nottingham: DFES Publications.

Hellerstein, D. J. (2008). 'Practice-Based Evidence Rather Than Evidence-Based Practice in Psychiatry'. *Medscape Journal of Medicine*, 10(6), 141.

Lemma, A. (2016). *Introduction to the Practice of Psychoanalytic Psychotherapy*. Chichester: John Wiley & Sons Ltd.

Lewin, K. (1945). 'The Research Centre for Group Dynamics at Massachusetts Institute of Technology'. *Sociometrics*, 8, 128–35.

Chapter 1

American Psychological Association (APA) (2017, December). 'How Psychoanalysis Got a Bad Rap'. *Monitor on Psychology*, 48(11). Retrieved from www.apa.org/monitor/2017/12/psychoanalysis-bad-rap [accessed 28.05.2020].

Bartle, D. (2015). 'Deception and Delusion: The Relational Aspect of Supervision Explored Through Greek Mythology'. *Educational & Child Psychology*, 32(3), 41–50.

Bazeley, E.T. (1928). *Home Lane and the Little Commonwealth*. London: Allen & Unwin.

Bhaskar, R. (1975). *A Realist Theory of Science*. Brighton: Harvester.

Bion, W.R. (1961). *Experiences in Groups*. London: Tavistock Publications.

Bion, W.R. (1962). 'A Theory of Thinking'. *International Journal of Psychoanalysis*, 43, 306–10.

Bion, W.R. (1963). *Elements of Psychoanalysis*. London: Karnac.

Bion, W. R. (1976) Evidence. In Bion, W.R. & Bion, F. *Clinical Seminars and Other Works*. London: Karnac Books, 1994. [Reprinted in *Clinical Seminars and Other Works*. Oxon: Routledge, 2018].

Bion, W.R. (1990). *Brazilian Lectures: 1973 São Paulo; 1974 Rio de Janeiro/São Paulo*. London: Karnac.

Burden, R.L. (1978). 'School's Systems Analysis: A Project-Centered Approach', in W. Gillham (ed.), *Reconstructing Educational Psychology*. London: Croom Helm.

Cioffi, F. (1998). *Freud and the Question of Pseudoscience*. Chicago, IL: Open Court.

Corvath. D. (2016). 'Introduction to Kleinian Theory 2'. Retrieved from www.youtube.com/watch?v=yxKRC6HzPA0&t=2041s [accessed 15.04.2020].

Crews, F. (2017). *Freud: The Making of an Illusion*. London: Profile.

Dallos, R. and Draper, R. 2000. *An Introduction to Family Therapy: Systemic Theory and Practice*. Buckingham: Open University Press.

Dennison, A., McBay, C. and Shaldon, C. (2006). 'Every Team Matters: The Contribution Educational Psychologists Can Make to Effective Teamwork'. *Educational & Child Psychology*, 23(4), 80–90.

Devereux, G (1967). *From Anxiety to Method in the Behavioural Sciences*. The Hague: De Gruyter Mouton.

Dockar Drysdale, B. (1993). *Therapy and Consultation in Child Care*. London. Free Association Books.

Ellenberger, H.F. (1970). *The Discovery of the Unconscious*. New York: Basil Books.

Eloquin, X. (2016a). 'Systems-Psychodynamics in Schools: A Framework for EPs Undertaking Organisational Consultancy'. *Educational Psychology in Practice*, 32(2), 163–79.

Eloquin, X. (2016b). 'The Tyrant-in-the-Mind: Influences on Worker Behaviour in a Post-Totalitarian Organisation'. *Management Forum*, 4(3), 41–51.

Eysenck, H.J. (1991). *Decline & Fall of the Freudian Empire*. New Brunswick, NJ: Transaction Publishers.

Fairbairn, W. (1954). *An Object Relations Theory of Personality*. New York: Basic Books.

Fox, M. (2002) 'A Question of Survival: Who Cares for the Carers?' *Journal of Social Work Practice*, 16(2), 185–90.

Fox, M. (2003). 'Opening Pandora's Box: Evidence-Based Practice for Educational Psychologists'. *Educational Psychology in Practice*, 19(2), 91¬–102.

Fraher, A. (2004). *A History of Group Study and Psychodynamic Organizations*. London: Free Association Books.

Freud, A. and Dann, S. (1951). 'An Experiment in Group Upbringing'. *Psychoanalytic Study of the Child*, 6, 127–68.

Freud, S. (1922). *Group Psychology and the Analysis of the Ego*. London: International Psychoanalytic Press.

Freud, S. (1923). *The Ego and the Id*. Standard Edition, Vol. 19. London: Hogarth Press.

Freud, S. (1927/2010). *The Future of an Illusion*. Seattle, WA: Pacific Publishing Studio.

Freud, S. (1930/2002). *Civilisation and its Discontents*. London: Penguin.

Freud, S. (2002). *Wild Analysis*. London: Penguin.

Frosh, S. (2003). Psychosocial Studies and Psychology: Is a Critical Approach Emerging? *Human Relations*, 56(12), 1545–1567.

Gilmore, T.N. and Krantz, J. (1985). 'Projective Identification in the Consulting Relationship: Exploring the Unconscious Dimensions of a Client System'. *Human Relations*, 38(12), 1159–77.

Gameson, J., Rhydderch, G., Ellis, D. and Carroll, H. C. M. (2003). Constructing a flexible model of integrated professional practice part 1-conceptual and theoretical issues. *Educational and Child Psychology*, 20(4), 96-115.

Gomez, L. (2005). *The Freud Wars: An Introduction to the Philosophy of Psychoanalysis*. New York: Taylor & Francis.

Heimann, P. (1950). 'On Counter-Transference'. *International Journal of Psychoanalysis*, 31, 81–4.

Hinshelwood, R.D. (1991). *A Dictionary of Kleinian Thought*. London: Free Association Books.

Hinshelwood, R.D. (1994). *Clinical Klein*. London: Free Association Books.

Hinshelwood, R.D. (1995). 'Psychoanalysis in Britain: Points of Cultural Access, 1893–1918'. *International Journal of Psychoanalysis*, 76, 135–51.

Hoffman, D.D., Singh, M. and Prakash, C. (2015). 'The Interface Theory of Perception'. *Psychonomic Bulletin & Review*, 22(6), 1480–1506.

Hollway, W. (2008). 'The Importance of Relational Thinking in the Practice of Psycho-social Research: Ontology, Epistemology, Methodology and Ethics', in S. Clarke, P. Hoggett and H. Hahn (eds), *Object Relations and Social Relations*. London: Karnac, pp. 137–62.

Hollway, W. and Jefferson, T. (2013). *Doing Qualitative Research Differently*. London: Sage.

Hulusi, H. and Maggs, P. (2015). 'Containing the Containers: Work Discussion Group Supervision Foot Teachers – A Psychodynamic Approach'. *Educational & Child Psychology*, 32(3), 30–40.

Isaacs, S. (1952). *The Educational Value of the Nursery School*. London: Headly Brothers Ltd.

Isaacs, S. (1971). *The Nursery Years: The Mind of the Child from Birth to Six Years*. London: Routledge.

Jacobs, T.J. (2001). 'On Misreading and Misleading Patients: Some Reflections on Communications, Miscommunications and Countertransference Enactments'. *International Journal of Psychoanalysis*, 82(4), 653–69.

Joseph, B. (1985). 'Transference: The Total Situation'. *International Journal of Psychoanalysis*, 66, 447–54.

Kelley, B., Woolfson, L.M. and Boyle, J. (eds) (2016). 'Integrated Framework: An Executive Framework for Service Wide Delivery', in *Frameworks for Practice in Educational Psychology: A Textbook for Trainees and Practitioners*, 2nd edn. London: JKP.

Kirsner, D. (1990). 'Mystics and Professionals in the Culture of American Psychoanalysis'. *Free Associations*, 20, 85–105.

Klein, M. (1935). 'A Contribution to the Psychogenesis of Manic Depressive States'. *International Journal of Psychoanalysis*, 16, 145–74. Notes: reprinted in M. Klein, *Love, Guilt and Reparation and Other Works, 1921–1945*. London: Hogarth Press.

Klein, M. (1946). 'Notes on Some Schizoid Mechanisms'. *International Journal of Psychoanalysis*, 27(3–4), 99–110.

Klein, M. (1975). *Envy and Gratitude and Other Works 1949–1963*. London: Hogarth Press.

Langer, W.C. (1972). *The Mind of Adolf Hitler*. New York: Basic Books.

Lemma, A. (2016). *Introduction to the Practice of Psychoanalytic Psychotherapy*. Chichester: John Wiley & Sons Ltd.

Mohr, G. (1966). 'August Aichhorn. Friend of the Wayward Youth', In F. Alexander, S. Eisenstein and M. Grotjahn (eds), *Psychoanalytic Pioneers*. New York: Basic Books.

Moscovici, S. (1984). 'The Phenomenon of Social Representations', in R.M. Farr and S. Moscovici (eds), *Social Representations*. Cambridge: Cambridge University Press, pp. 3–69.

Moustaki-Smilansky, E. (1994). 'Glossary', in S. Box (ed.), *Crisis at Adolescence: Object Relations Therapy with the Family*. Northvale, NJ/London: Jason Aronson.

Neill, A.S. (1962). *Summerhill: A Radical Approach to Education*. London: Victor Gollancz.

Newton, J., Long, S. and Sievers, B. (2006). *Coaching in Depth: The Organizational Role Analysis Approach*. London: Karnac.

Nietzsche, F.W. (1997). *Twilight of the Idols, or, How to Philosophize with the Hammer*, trans R.F.H. Polt. Indianapolis, IN: Hackett Publishing.

Obholzer, A. and Roberts, V.Z. (1994). *The Unconscious at Work: Individual and Organizational Stress in the Human Services*. London: Routledge.

Ogden, T.H. (1982). *Projective Identification and Psychotherapeutic Technique*. New York: Jason Aronson.

Pellegrini, D. (2010). 'Splitting and Projection: Drawing on Psychodynamics in Educational Psychology Practice'. *Educational Psychology in Practice*, 26(3), 251–60.

Pepper, R.S. (1992). 'Psychoanalytic Training Institutes as Cults: An Example of Entropy'. *Journal of Contemporary Psychotherapy*, 22(1), 35–42.

Rachman, J. (2003). 'Eysenck and the Development of CBT'. *Psychologist*, 16(11), 588–611.

Redl, F. (1966). *When We Deal With Children*. New York: The Free Press.

Sharpe, C. (1985) 'Fritz Redl and the Life Space Interview'. Retrieved from www.goodenoughcaring.com/the-journal/who-am-i-an-account-of-my-childhood-and-teenage-years-in-the-1930s-and-1940s-and-my-discovery-at-the-age-of-63-that-i-was-an-adopted-child/fritz-redl-and-the-life-space-interview/ [accessed 09.01.2020].

Sharpe, C. (2007). 'In Care in Therapy ? A Consideration of the Usefulness of Psychoanalytic Theory for the Care of Young People Living in Children's Homes'. Retrieved from www.goodenoughcaring.com/writings/in-care-in-therapy-a-consideration-of-the-usefulness-of-psychoanalytic-theory-for-the-care-of-young-people-living-in-childrens-homes/ [accessed 09.01.2020].

Shaw, M. (2002). *The Object Relations Technique*. New York: ORT Institute.

Smith, L.A.H. (1985). *To Understand and to Help: The Life and Work of Susan Isaacs (1885–1948)*. Cranbury, NJ: Associated University Presses.

Stapley, L.F. (2006). *Individuals, Groups and Organizations Beneath the Surface*. London: Karnac.

Steiner, J. (1993). *Psychic Retreats: Pathological Organisations in Psychotic, Neurotic and Borderline Patients*. London: Routledge.

Steiner, J. (2011). *Seeing and Being Seen: Emerging from a Psychic Retreat*. London: Routledge.

Sutoris, M. (2000). 'Understanding Schools as Systems: Implications for the Management of Pupil Behaviour'. *Educational & Child Psychology*, 17(1), 51–62.

Symington J. and Symington, N. (1996). *The Clinical Thinking of Wilfred Bion*. Routledge: London.

Waddell, M. (1998). *Inside Lives: Psychoanalysis and the Growth of the Personality*. London: Karnac.

Waismann, F. (1968). 'Verifiability', in R. Harré (ed.), *How I See Philosophy*. London: Palgrave Macmillan, pp. 39–66.

Webster, R. (1995). *Why Freud Was Wrong: Sin, Science and Psychoanalysis*. London: Orwell Press.

Westen, D. (1998). 'The Scientific Legacy of Sigmund Freud: Toward a Psychodynamically Informed Psychological Science'. *Psychological Bulletin*, 124, 333–71.

Westen, D. (1999). 'The Scientific Status of Unconscious Processes', Paper presented on 13 June 1999 at the Annual Meeting of the Rapaport-Klein Study Group. Retrieved from www.psychomedia.it/rapaport-klein/westen99.htm. ('The Scientific Status of Unconscious Processes: Is Freud Really Dead?' appeared in the *Journal of the American Psychoanalytic Association*, 47(4), 1061–106.)

Westen, D. and Gabbard, G.O. (1999). 'Psychoanalytic Approaches to Personality', in L.A. Pervin and O.P. John (eds), *Handbook of Personality: Theory and Research*. New York: Guilford Press, pp. 57–101.

Whitman, W. (1855/2017). *Leaves of Grass*. Harmondsworth: Penguin.

Young-Bruehl, E. (2008). *Anna Freud: A Biography*. London: Yale University Press.

Chapter 2

Bartle, D. (2015). 'Deception and Delusion: The Relational Aspect of Supervision Explored Through Greek Mythology'. *Educational & Child Psychology*, 32(3), 41–50.

Billington, T. (2006). 'Psychodynamic Theories and the Science of Relationships (Bion): A Rich Resource for Professional Practice in Children's Services'. *Educational & Child Psychology*, 23(4), 72–9.

Briggs, S. (2008). *Working with Adolescents and Young Adults: A Contemporary Psychodynamic Approach*, 2nd edn. Basingstoke: Palgrave Macmillian.

Copley, B. (1993). *The World of Adolescence. Literature, Society and Psychoanalytic Psychotherapy*. London: Free Association Books.

Copley, B. and Forryan, B. (1987). *Therapeutic Work with Children and Young People*. London: Cassell.

Darlington, Y. and Scott, D. (2002). *Qualitative Research in Practice: Stories from the Field*. Buckingham: Open University Press.

Diamant, E. (2009). 'Understanding Korina. How Can Psychodynamic Observation Support the Role of a Class Teacher Teaching Special Needs Children in a Mainstream School?' *Infant Observation*, 12(3), 319–33.

Eloquin, X. (2016). 'Systems-Psychodynamics in Schools: A Framework for EPs Undertaking Organisational Consultancy'. *Educational Psychology in Practice*, 32(2), 163–79.

Fonagy, P. (2003). 'The Research Agenda: The Vital Need for Empirical Research in Child Psychotherapy'. *Journal of Child Psychotherapy*, 29(2), 129–36.

Fox, M. (2003). 'Opening Pandora's Box: Evidence-Based Practice for Educational Psychologists'. *Educational Psychology in Practice*, 19(2), 91–102.

Fraiberg, S.H. (1980). 'Ghosts in the Nursery: A Psychoanalytic Approach to the Problem of Impaired Infant–Mother Relationships', in S.H. Fraiberg, (ed.), *Clinical Studies in Infant Mental Health, the First year of Life*. London: Tavistock Publications, pp. 164–96.

Hinshelwood, R.D. (1994). *Clinical Klein: From Theory to Practice*. Basic Books.

Hulusi, H. and Maggs, P. (2015). 'Containing the Containers: Work Discussion Group Supervision for Teachers – A Psychodynamic Approach'. *Educational & Child Psychology*, 32(3), 30–40.

Kennedy, E.K., Keaney, C., Shaldon, C. and Canagaratnam, M. (2018). 'A Relational Model of Supervision for Applied Psychology Practice: Professional Growth Through Relating and Reflecting'. *Educational Psychology in Practice*, 34(3), 282–99.

Lanman, M. (1998). 'The Human Container; Containment as an Active Process'. *Psychodynamic Counselling*, 4(4), 463–72.

Maltby, J. (2008). 'Consultation in Schools: Helping Staff and Pupils with Unresolved Loss and Mourning'. *Journal of Child Psychotherapy*, 34(1), 83–100.

Midgley, N. (2004). 'Sailing Between Scylla and Charybdis: Incorporating Qualitative Approaches into Child Psychotherapy Research'. *Journal of Child Psychotherapy*, 30(1), 89–111.

Midgley, N. (2006). 'The Inseparable Bond Between Cure and Research : Clinical Case Study as a Method of Psychoanalytic Inquiry'. *Journal of Child Psychotherapy*, 32(2), 122–47.

Mintz, J. (2007). 'Psychodynamic Perspectives on Teacher Stress'. *Psychodynamic Practice*, 13(2), 153–66.

Mychailyszyn, M.P., Beidas, R.S., Benjamin, C.L., Edmunds, J.M., Podell, J.L., Cohen, J.S. and Kendall, P.C. (2011). 'Assessing and Treating Child Anxiety in Schools'. *Psychology in the Schools*, 48(3), 223–32.

Pellegrini, D.W. (2010). 'Splitting and Projection: Drawing on Psychodynamics in Educational Psychology Practice'. *Educational Psychology in Practice*, 26(3), 251–60.

Price, H. (2002). 'The Emotional Context of Classroom Learning: A Psychoanalytic Perspective'. *European Journal of Psychotherapy, Counselling and Health*, 5(3), 305–20.

Rustin, M. (2003). 'Research in the Consulting Room'. *Journal of Child Psychotherapy*, 29(2), 137–45.

Salzberger-Wittenberg, I. (1970). *Psycho-Analytic Insights and Relationships: A Kleinian Approach*. London: Routledge & Kegan Paul.

Salzberger-Wittenberg, I., Henry, G. and Osbourne, E. (1983). *The Emotional Experience of Learning and Teaching*. London: Routledge.

Segal, H. (1994). 'Salman Rushdie and the Sea of Stories: A Not-So-Simple Fable About Creativity'. *International Journal of Psycho-Analysis*, 75, 611–19.

Soloman, M. and Nashat, S. (2010). 'Offering a Therapeutic Presence in Schools and Education Settings'. *Psychodynamic Practice*, 16(3), 289–304.

Swisher, A. K. (2010). 'Practice-Based Evidence'. *Cardiopulmonary Physical Therapy Journal*, 21(2), 4.

Waddell, M. (2002). *Inside Lives: Psychoanalysis and the Growth of Personality*. London: Karnac.

Youell, B. (2006). *The Learning Relationship. Psychoanalytic Thinking in Education*. London: Karnac.

Chapter 3

Annan, M., Chua, J., Cole, R., Kennedy, E., James, R., Markúsdóttir, I. *et al.* (2013). Further Iterations on Using the Problem-Analysis Framework, *Educational Psychology in Practice*, 29(1), 79–95. Retrieved from https://doi.org/10.1080/0 2667363.2012.755951

Bion, W.R. (1962a). 'A Theory of Thinking', in W.R. Bion, *Second Thoughts: Selected Papers on Psycho-Analysis*. Bath: Pitman Press, pp. 110–19.

Bion, W.R. (1962b). *Learning from Experience*. London: Karnac.

British Psychological Society (2010). *Standards for the Accreditation of Doctoral Programmes in Educational Psychology in England, Northern Ireland and Wales*. Leicester: British Psychological Society.

British Psychological Society (2011). *Good Practice Guidelines on the Use of Psychological Formulation*. Leicester: British Psychological Society.

British Psychological Society (2017). *Practice Guidelines*, 3rd edn. Leicester: British Psychological Society.

Denicolo, P., Long, T. and Bradley-Cole, K. (2016). *Constructivist Approaches and Research Methods. A Practical Guide to Exploring Personal Meanings*. London. Sage.

Department for Education (2019). *Statements of SEN and EHC Plans: England, 2019*. Retrieved from https://assets.publishing.service.gov.uk/government

Edwards, J. (2015). 'Teaching, Learning and Bion's Model of Digestion'. *British Journal of Psychotherapy*, 31(3), 376–89. Retrieved from https://doi.org/10.1111/BJP.12158

Frosh, S. (2010). *Psychoanalysis Outside the Clinic: Interventions in Psychosocial Studies*. Basingstoke: Palgrave Macmillan.

Gameson, J., Rhydderch, G., Ellis, D. and Carroll, H.C.M. (2003). 'Constructing a Flexible Model of Integrated Professional Practice: Part 1, Conceptual and Theoretical Issues'. *Educational & Child Psychology*, 20, 96–115.

Health and Care Professions Council (2015). *Standards of Proficiency for Applied Psychologists*. London. HCPC.

Johnstone, L. (2014). *A Straight Talking Introduction to Psychiatric Diagnosis*. Monmouth: PCCS Books.

Johnstone, L. and Boyle, M., with Cromby, J., Dillon, J., Harper, D., Kinderman, P., Longden, E., Pilgrim, D. and Read, J. (2018). *The Power Threat Meaning Framework: Towards the Identification of Patterns in Emotional Distress, Unusual Experiences and Troubled or Troubling Behaviour, as an Alternative to Functional Psychiatric Diagnosis*. Leicester: British Psychological Society.

Kelly, B. (2008). 'Frameworks for Practice in Educational Psychology. Coherent Perspectives for a Developing Profession', in B. Kelly, L. Woolfson and J. Boyle (eds), *Frameworks for Practice in Educational Psychology: A Textbook for Trainees and Practitioners*. London: JKP, pp. 15–30.

Klein, M. (1959). 'Our Adult World and its Roots in Infancy'. *Human Relations*, 12(4), 291–303.

Monsen, J., Graham, B., Frederickson, N. and Cameron, R.J. (1998). Problem Analysis and Professional Training in Educational Psychology: An Accountable Model of Practice'. *Educational Psychology in Practice*, 13(4), 234–49.

Neri, C. (2015). 'The Go-Between', in M. Williams (ed.), *Teaching Bion: Modes and Approaches*. London: Karnac.

Newman, D.S. and Rosenfield, S.A. (2019). 'Consultation Relationships: Building Working Relationships', in D.S. Newman and S.A. Rosenfield (eds), *Building Competence in School Consultation: A Developmental Approach*. New York: Routledge, pp. 40–53.

O'Shaughnessy, E. (1981). 'A Commemorative Essay on W.R. Bion's Theory of Thinking'. *Journal of Child Psychotherapy*, 7(2), 181–92. Retrieved from https://doi.org/10.1080/00754178108255031

Ogden, T. (2004). 'An Introduction to the Reading of Bion'. *International Journal of Psychoanalysis*, 85(2), 285–300. Retrieved from https://doi.org/10.1516/3TPR-AXTL-0R8M-7EQ0

Ruch, G. (2018). 'Theoretical Frameworks Informing Relationship-Based Practice', in G. Ruch, D. Turney and A. Ward (eds), *Relationship-Based Social Work. Getting to the Heart of Practice*, 2nd edn. London: JKP, pp. 37–54.

Sandoval, J. (2011). 'Constructivism, Consultee-Centered Consultation, and Conceptual Change'. *Journal of Educational and Psychological Consultation*, 7(1), 36–62. Retrieved from https://doi.org/10.1207/s1532768xjepc0701_8

Sandoval, J. (2014). *An Introduction to Consultee-Centered Consultation in the Schools*. London. Routledge.

Waddell, M. (2002). *Inside Lives: Psychoanalysis and the Growth of the Personality*. London: Karnac.

Wagner, P. (2000). 'Consultation: Developing a Comprehensive Approach to Service Delivery'. *Educational Psychology in Practice*, 16(1), 9–18.

Wicks, A. (2013). 'Do Frameworks Enable Educational Psychologists to Work Effectively and Efficiently in Practice? A Critical Discussion of the Development of Executive Frameworks'. *Educational Psychology in Practice*, 29(2), 152–62. Retrieved from https://doi.org/10.1080/02667363.2013.796444

Chapter 4

Bion, W.R. (1959). 'Attacks on Linking'. *International Journal of Psycho-Analysis*, 43, 308–15.

Bion, W.R. (1978). *Four Discussions with W.R. Bion*. The Roland Harris Educational Trust, Scotland. Blairgowrie Printers for Clunie Press, Ballechin House.

Bion, W.R. (1984). *Learning from Experience*. London: Karnac.

Box, S., Copley. B., Magagna, J. and Moustaki, E. (1981). *Psychotherapy with Families: An Analytic Approach*. London: Routledge & Kegan Paul.

Cooper, A. (2018). *Conjunctions: Social Work, Psychoanalysis, and Society*. Abingdon: Routledge.

Greenson, R. (1967). *The Technique and Practice of Psycho-Analysis*, Vol. 1. Madison, CT: International Universities Press and Institute of

Psycho-Analysis (1967). In J. Mattinson (1975), *The Reflection Process in Casework Supervision*. London: Institute of Marital Studies/Tavistock Institute of Human Relations.

Hinshelwood, R.D. (1991). *A Dictionary of Kleinian Thought*. London: Free Association Books.

Howell, D.D. (1992). 'Style or Method', in *The Practice of Supervision: Some Contributions*. Paper presented at Conference, March 1992. London: British Association of Psychotherapists, monograph 4.

Klein, M. (1959). 'Our Adult World and Its Roots in Infancy'. *Human Relations*, 12, 291–303.

Mattinson, J. (1975). *The Reflection Process in Casework Supervision*. London: Institute of Marital Studies/Tavistock Institute of Human Relations.

Mollon, P. (2002). *Shame and Jealousy: The Hidden Turmoils*. London and New York: Karnac.

Searles, H. (1955). 'The Informational Value of the Supervisor's Emotional Experience', in H. Searles (1965) *Collected Papers on Schizophrenia and Related Subjects*. London: Karnac, pp. 157–75.

Trowell, J. (1995). 'Key Psychoanalytic Concepts', in J. Trowell and M. Bower (eds), *The Emotional Needs of Young Children and their Families Using Psychoanalytic Ideas in the Community*. Hove and New York: Routledge, pp. 12–21.

Winnicott, D.W. (1982). *Through Paediatrics to Psycho-Analysis*. London: Hogarth Press.

Chapter 5

Armstrong, D. (2005). *Organization in the Mind. Psychoanalysis, Group Relations and Organisational Consultancy*. Occasional papers 1989–2003. London: Karnac.

Bion, W.R. (1962). 'A Theory of Thinking'. *International Journal of Psychoanalysis*, 53.

Hirschhorn, L. (1988). *The Workplace Within: Psychodynamics of Organizational Life*. Cambridge, MA: MIT Press.

Hutton, J., Bazalgette, J. and Reed, B. (1997) 'Organisation-in-the-Mind', in J.E. Neumann, K. Kellner and A. Dawson-Shepherd (eds), *Developing Organisational Consultancy*. London: Routledge, pp. 113–26.

Jackson, E. (2015). 'Work Discussion Groups as a Container for Sexual Anxieties in School', in D. Armstrong and M. Rustin (eds), *Social Defences Against Anxiety: Explorations in a Paradigm*. London: Karnac, pp. 269–83.

Chapter 6

Bellak, L. (1954). *The Thematic Apperception Test and the Children's Apperception Test in Clinical Use*. Oxford: Grune & Stratton.

Bion, W.R. (1967). *Second Thoughts: Selected Papers on Psychoanalysis*. London: Heinemann.

Burns, R.C. and Kaufman, S.H. (1970). *Kinetic Family Drawings (KFD): An Introduction to Understanding Children Through Kinetic Drawings*. New York: Brunner/Mazel.

Division of Education & Child Psychology (2002) *Professional Practice Guidelines*. Leicester: British Psychological Society.

Dowling, E. (1990). 'Children's Disturbing Behaviour – Whose Problem Is It?' *Tavistock Clinic Paper*, 112. London: Tavistock Library.

Hawkins, P. and Shohet, R. (2000). *Supervision in the Helping Professions*, 2nd edition. Maidenhead: Open University Press.

Heimann, P. (1950). 'On Countertransference'. *International Journal of Psychoanalysis*, 31, 81–85.

Huffington, C., Cole, C. and Brunning, H. (1997). *A Manual of Organizational Development*. London: Karnac.

Jacobs, L. (2012). 'Assessment as Consultation: Working with Parents and Teachers'. *Journal of Infant, Child and Adolescent Psychotherapy*, 11(3), 257–71.

Jaffe, L. (1990). 'The Empirical Foundations of Psychoanalytic Approaches to Psychological Testing'. *Journal of Personality Assessment*, 55, 746–55.

Klein, M. (1940). 'A Contribution to the Psychogenesis of Manic-Depressive States', in M. Klein, *Love, Guilt and Reparation and Other Works 1921–1975: The Writings of Melanie Klein*, Vol. 1. London: Hogarth, 1975.

Meersand, P. (2011). 'Psychological Testing and the Analytically Trained Child Psychologist'. *Psychoanalytic Psychology*, 28(1), 117–31.

Satterly, D. (1981). *Assessment in Schools*. Oxford: Blackwell.

Sugarman, A. and Kanner, K. (2000). 'The Contribution of Psychoanalytic Theory to Psychological Testing:'. *Psychoanalytic Psychology*, 17(1), 3–23.

Weiss, S. (2002a). 'How Teachers' Autobiographies Influence Their Responses to Children's Behaviors: The Psychodynamic Concept of Transference in Classroom Life. Part 1'. *Emotional & Behavioural Difficulties*, 7(1), 9–18.

Weiss, S. (2002b). 'How Teachers' Autobiographies Influence Their Responses to Children's Behaviors: The Psychodynamic Concept of Transference in Classroom Life. Part 2'. *Emotional & Behavioural Difficulties*, 7(2), 109–27.

Winnicott, D.W. (1989). *Playing and Reality*. London: Routledge.

Chapter 7

American Psychological Association (2006). 'Evidence-Based Practice in Psychology'. *American Psychologist*, 61(4), 271–85.

Bellak, L. and Bellak, S.S. (1949). *Children's Apperception Test: Manual*, 8th revised edn. Larchmont, NY: CPS, 1991.

Billington, T. (2006). 'Psychodynamic Theories and the Science of Relationships

(Bion): A Rich Resource for Professional Practice in Children's Services'. *Educational & Child Psychology*, 23(4), 72–79.

Bowlby, J. (1969). 'Attachment', in J. Bowlby, *Attachment and Loss*, Vol. 1. New York: Basic Books.

Brewin, C.R. and Andrews, B. (2000). 'Psychological Defence Mechanisms: The Example of Repression'. *Psychologist*, 13(12), 615–17.

Buck, J.N. (1948). 'The H–T–P Technique: A Qualitative and Quantitative Scoring Manual'. *Journal of Clinical Psychology*, 4(4), 317 *et passim*.

Burnham, J. (1992). 'Approach–Method–Technique: Making Distinctions and Creating Connections'. *Human Systems: The Journal of Systemic Consultation & Management*, 3, 3–26.

Burns, R.C. and Kaufman, S.H. (1970). *Kinetic Family Drawings*. New York: Brunner/Mazel.

Burns, R.C. and Kaufman, S.H. (1972). *Actions, Styles and Symbols in Kinetic Family Drawings (K-F-D): An Interpretive Manual*. New York: Brunner/Mazel.

Chandler, L.A. (2003). 'The Projective Hypothesis and the Development of Projective Techniques for Children', in C.R. Reynolds and R.W. Kamphaus (eds), *Handbook of Psychological and Educational Assessment of Children: Personality, Behavior, and Context*. New York: Guilford, pp. 51–65.

Cunliffe, A.L. (2009). 'The Philosopher Leader: On Relationalism, Ethics and Reflexivity – A Critical Perspective to Teaching Leadership'. *Management Learning*, 40(1), 87–101.

Denborough, D. (2008). *Collective Narrative Practice: Responding to Individuals, Groups, and Communities Who Have Experienced Trauma*. Adelaide: Dulwich Centre Publications.

Department for Education/Department of Health and Social Care (DfE/DoH and SC) (2018). *Government Response to the Consultation on Transforming Children and Young People's Mental Health Provision: A Green Paper and Next Steps*. London: DfE/DoH and SC. Retrieved from https://assets.publishing.service.gov.uk/government/uploads/system/uploads/attachment_data/file/728892/government-response-to-consultation-ontransforming-children-and-young-peoples-mental-health.pdf

Eloquin, X. (2016). 'Systems-Psychodynamics in Schools: A Framework for EPs Undertaking Organisational Consultancy'. *Educational Psychology in Practice*, 32(2), 163–79.

Frosh, S. (2002). *Key Concepts in Psychoanalysis*. London: British Library.

Goodenough, F. (1926). *Measurement of Intelligence by Drawings*. New York: World Book Co.

Groth-Marnat, G. (1999). *Handbook of Psychological Assessment*. New York: John Wiley & Sons, Inc.

Hammer, E. (1958). *The Clinical Application of Projective Drawings*. Springfield, IL: C. Thomas.

Handler, L. and Habenicht, D. (1994). 'The Kinetic Family Drawing Technique: A

Review of the Literature'. *Journal of Personality Assessment*, 62(3), 440–64.

Hojnoski, R.L., Morrison, R., Brown, M. and Matthews, W.J. (2006). 'Projective Test Use Among School Psychologists: A Survey and Critique'. *Journal of Psychoeducational Assessment*, 24, 145–59.

Holaday, M., Smith D. and Sherry, A. (2000). 'Sentence Completion Tests: A Review of the Literature and Results of a Survey of Members of the Society for Personality Assessment'. *Journal of Personality Assessment*, 74(3), 371–83.

Kennedy, E.K. and Monsen, J.J. (2016). 'Evidence-Based Practice in Educational and Child Psychology: Opportunities for Practitioner-Researchers Using Problem-Based Methodology'. *Educational & Child Psychology*, 33(3), 11–24.

King, R. (2017). 'An Exploration of the Use of Projective Techniques by Educational Psychologists in the UK', unpublished PhD thesis, University of Manchester.

Knoff, H.M. (2003). 'Evaluation of Projective Drawings'. In C.R. Reynolds and R.W. Kamphaus (eds), *Handbook of Psychological and Educational Assessment of Children: Personality, Behavior, and Context*. New York: Guilford, pp. 91–158.

Koppitz, E.M. (1975). *The Bender Gestalt Test for Young Children*, Vol. 2, *Research and Application 1963–1973*. New York: Grune & Stratton.

McCallister, R. (1983). 'Usefulness of the Kinetic Family Drawing in the assessment of Aggression Among a Population of Juvenile Offenders', unpublished PhD thesis, Aubern University.

MacKay, T. (2007). 'Educational Psychology: The Fall and Rise of Therapy'. *Educational & Child Psychology*, 24(1), 7–18.

Mason, B. (2012). 'The Personal and the Professional: Core Beliefs and the Construction of Bridges Across Difference', in Inga-Britt Krause (ed.), *Culture and Reflexivity in Systemic Psychotherapy: Mutual Perspectives*. London: Karnac, pp. 163–79.

Midgen, T. and Theodoratou, T. (2020). 'Ethical Selfhood and Team Awareness: The Role of Reflexivity in Leadership', in J. Hardy, M. Bham and C. Hobbs (eds), *Leadership for Educational Psychologists: Principles and Practicalities*. Hoboken, NJ: Wiley & Sons Ltd, pp. 35–49.

Miller, D. and Nickerson, A. (2006). 'Projective Assessment and School Psychology: Contemporary Validity Issues and Implications for Practice'. *California School Psychologist*, 11, 73–84.

Murray, H.A. (1943). *Thematic Apperception Test: Manual*. Cambridge, MA: Harvard University Press.

Pellegrini, D.W. (2010). 'Splitting and Projection: Drawing on Psychodynamics in Educational Psychology Practice'. *Educational Psychology in Practice*, 26(3), 251–60.

Piotrowski, C. (2015). 'Projective Techniques Usage Worldwide'. *Journal of the Indian Academy of Applied Psychology*, 41(3), 9–19.

Rotter, J.B., Lah, M.I. and Rafferty, J.E. (1992). *Rotter Incomplete Sentences Blank Manual*, 2nd edn. San Antonio, TX: Psychological Corporation.

Sobel, H. and Sobel, W. (1976). 'Discriminating Adolescent Male Delinquents

Through Kinetic Family Drawings'. *Journal of Personality Assessment*, 40, 91–94.

Winnicott, D. (1964). *The Child, the Family and the Outside World.* Harmondsworth: Penguin.

Youell, B. (2006). *The Learning Relationship: Psychoanalytic Thinking in Education.* London: Karnac.

Chapter 8

Armstrong, D. and Huffington, C. (2004). 'Introduction'. In C. Huffington, D. Armstrong, W. Halton, L. Hoyle and J. Pooley (eds), *Working Beneath the Surface: The Emotional Life of Contemporary Organisations.* London: Karnac, pp. 1–10.

Bergan, J. and Kratochwill, T. (1990). *Behavioural Consultation and Therapy.* New York: Plenum.

Borden, W. and Clark, J. (2012). 'Contemporary Psychodynamic Theory, Research, and Practice: Implications for Evidence-Based Intervention', in T. Rzepnicki, S. McCracken and H. Briggs (eds), *From Task-Centred Social Work to Evidence-Based and Integrative Practice: Reflections on History and Implementation.* Chicago, IL: Lyceum, pp. 65–87.

British Psychological Society (BPS) (2017). *Practice Guidelines*, 3rd edn. Leicester: BPS.

Britton, R. (1989). 'The Missing Link: Parental Sexuality in the Oedipus Complex', in R. Britton, M. Feldman and E. O'Shaughnessy (eds), *The Oedipus Complex Today: Clinical Implications.* London: Karnac, pp. 83–101.

Burden, R. (2015). 'All That Glitters is not Gold: Why Randomised Controlled Trials (RCTs) Are of Limited Value in Judging the Effectiveness of Literacy Interventions'. *Educational & Child Psychology*, 32(1), 11–20.

Campbell, D., Draper, R. and Huffington, C. (1991). *A Systemic Approach to Consultation.* London: Karnac.

Campbell, D. and Huffington, C. (2008). 'Six Stages of Systemic Consultation', in D. Campbell and C. Huffington (eds), *Organisations Connected: A Handbook of Systemic Consultation* . New York: Routledge, pp. 1–14.

Caplan, G., Caplan, R.B. and Erchul, W.P. (1994). 'Caplanian Mental Health Consultation: Historical Background and Current Status'. *Consulting Psychology Journal*, 44(4), 2–12.

Caplan-Moskovich, R. (1982). 'Gerald Caplan: The Man and His Work', in H.C. Schulberg and M. Killilea (eds), *The Modern Practice of Community Mental Health: A Volume in Honor of Gerald Caplan.* San Francisco: Jossey-Bass, pp. 1–39.

Curtis, H. (2015). *Everyday Life and the Unconscious Mind.* London: Karnac.

Daly, J., Willis, K., Small, R., Green, J., Welch, N., Kealy, M. and Hughes, E. (2007).

'A Hierarchy of Evidence for Assessing Qualitative Health Research'. *Journal of Clinical Epidemiology*, 60(1), 43–49.

Davies, H. (2010). *The Use of Psychoanalytic Concepts in Therapy with Families: For All Professionals Working with Families*. London: Karnac.

Davison, P. and Duffy, J. (2017). 'A Model for Personal and Professional Support for Nurture Group Staff: To What Extent Can Group Process Consultation Be Used as a Resource to Meet the Challenges of Running a Nurture Group?' *Educational Psychology in Practice*, 33(4), 387–405.

Dennis, R. (2004). 'So Far so Good? A Qualitative Case Study Exploring the Implementation of Consultation in Schools'. *Educational Psychology in Practice*, 20(1), 17–29.

Department for Education (DfE) (2019). *Research on the Educational Psychologist Workforce Research Report*. London: DfE.

Eddleston, A. and Atkinson, C. (2018). 'Using Professional Practice Frameworks to Evaluate Consultation'. *Educational Psychology in Practice*, 34(4), 430–49.

Erchul, W. (2009). 'Gerald Caplan: A Tribute to the Originator of Mental Health Consultation'. *Journal of Educational and Psychological Consultation*, 19, 95–105.

Erchul, W. (1993). 'Reflections on Mental health Consultation: An interview with Gerald Caplan', in W. Erchul (ed.), *Consultation in Community, School, and Organizational Practice: Gerald Caplan's Contributions to Professional Psychology*. Washington, DC: Taylor & Francis, pp. 57–72.

Erchul, W. and Fischer, A. (2018). 'Consultation', in S.L. Grapin and J.H. Kranzler (eds), *School Psychology: Professional Issues and Practices*. New York: Springer, pp. 181–95.

Erchul, W.P. and Martens, B.K. (2012). *School Consultation: Conceptual and Empirical Bases of Practice*, 3rd edn. New York: Springer.

Farouk, S. (2004). 'Group Work in Schools: A Process Consultation Approach'. *Educational Psychology in Practice*, 20(3), 207–20.

Fox, M. (2003). 'Opening Pandora's Box: Evidence-Based Practice for Educational Psychologists'. *Educational Psychology in Practice*, 19(2), 91–102.

Frank, J. and Kratochwill, T. (2014). 'School-Based Problem-Solving Consultation: Plotting a New Course for Evidence-Based Research and Practice in Consultation', in W. Erchul and S. Sheridan (eds), *Handbook of Research in School Consultation*, 2nd edn. New York: Routledge, pp. 18–39.

Frosh, S. (2002). *Key Concepts in Psychoanalysis*. New York: New York University Press.

Gutkin, T.B. (2012). 'Ecological Psychology: Replacing the Medical Model Paradigm for School-Based Psychological and Psychoeducational Services'. *Journal of Educational and Psychological Consultation*, 22, 1–20.

Gutkin, T.B. and Curtis, M.J. (2009). 'School-Based Consultation: The Science and Practice of Indirect Service Delivery', in C.R. Reynolds and T.B. Gutkin (eds), *The Handbook of School Psychology*, 4th edition. New York: Wiley, pp. 591–635.

Hanko, G. (1999). *Increasing Competence Through Collaborative Problem-Solving*. London: David Fulton.

Hayes, M. and Stringer, P. (2016). 'Introducing Farouk's Process Consultation Group Approach in Irish Primary Schools'. *Educational Psychology in Practice*, 32(2), 145–62.

Ingraham, C. (2000). 'Consultation Through a Multicultural Lens: Multicultural and Cross-Cultural Consultation in Schools'. *School Psychology Review*, 29, 320–43.

Ingraham, C. (2014). 'Studying Multicultural Aspects of Consultation', in W. Erchul and S. Sheridan (eds), *Handbook of Research in School Consultation*, 2nd edn. New York: Routledge, pp. 323–48.

Kelly, B. (2006). 'Exploring the Usefulness of the Monsen Problem-Solving Framework for Applied Practitioners'. *Educational Psychology in Practice*, 22(1), 1–17.

Kelly, B. (2017). 'Frameworks for Practice in Educational Psychology: Coherent Perspectives for a Developing Profession', in B. Kelly, L. Woolfson and J. Boyle (eds), *Frameworks for Practice in Educational Psychology*, 2nd edn. London: JKP, pp. 11–28.

Kennedy, E.K., Frederickson, N. and Monsen, J. (2008). 'Do Educational Psychologists Walk the Talk When Consulting?' *Educational Psychology in Practice*, 24(3), 169–87.

Kennedy, E.K. and Monsen, J.J. (2016). 'Evidence-Based Practice in Educational and Child Psychology: Opportunities for Practitioner-Researchers Using Problem-Based Methodology'. *Educational & Child Psychology*, 33(3), 11–24.

Kennedy, E.K., Keaney, C., Shaldon, C., & Canagaratnam, M. (2018). A Relational Model of Supervision for Applied Psychology Practice: professional growth through relating and reflecting. *Educational Psychology in Practice*, 34 (3), 282-299

Knotek, S.E. and Hylander, I. (2014). 'Research Issues in Mental Health Consultation and Consultee-Centred Approaches', in W. Erchul and S. Sheridan (eds), *The Handbook of Research in School Consultation*, 2nd edn. New York: Routledge, pp. 153–79.

Knotek, S.E. and Sandoval, L. (2003). 'Introduction to the Special Issue: Consultee Centred Consultation as a Constructivistic Process'. *Journal of Educational and Psychology Consultation*, 14, 243–50.

Kraemer, S. (2017). 'Narrative Matters: The Eternal Triangle – A Century of Family Psychology for Clinicians'. *Child & Adolescent Mental Health*, 22(2), 113–14.

Kratochwill, T., Altschaefl, M. and Bice-Urbach, B. (2014). 'Best Practices in School-Based Problem Solving Consultation: Applications in Prevention and Intervention Systems', in A. Thomas and P. Harrison (eds), *Best Practices in School Psychology: Data-Based and Collaborative Decision-Making*. Bethesda, MA: National Association of School Psychologists, pp. 461–82.

Kratochwill, T. and Bergan, J. (1990). *Behavioural Consultation in Applied Settings:*

An Individual Guide. New York: Plenum.

Kratochwill, T. and Pittman, P. (2002). 'Expanding Problem-solving Consultation Training: Prospects and Frameworks'. *Journal of Educational and Psychological Consultation*, 13(1/2), 69–95.

Larney, R. (2003). 'School-Based Consultation in the United Kingdom: Principles, Practice and Effectiveness'. *School Psychology International*, 24(1), 5–19.

Lee, K. and Woods, K. (2017). 'Exploration of the Developing Role of the Educational Psychologist Within the Context of Traded Psychological Services'. *Educational Psychology in Practice*, 33(2), 111–25.

Lopez, E. and Nastasi, B. (2014). 'Process and Outcome Research in Selected Models of Consultation', in W. Erchul and S. Sheridan (eds), *Handbook of Research in School Consultation*, 2nd edn. New York: Routledge, pp. 304–20.

Lowe, F. (2014). (Ed.) *Thinking Space: Promoting Thinking About Race, Culture and Diversity in Psychotherapy and Beyond*. London: Karnac.

MacHardy, L., Carmichael, H. and Proctor, J. (1995). *School Consultation: It Don't Mean a Thing if it Ain't Got That Swing*. Aberdeen: Aberdeen City Council Psychological Service.

McLoughlin, C. (2010). 'Concentric Circles of Containment: A Psychodynamic Contribution to Working in Pupil Referral Units'. *Journal of Child Psychotherapy*, 36(3), 225–39.

Monsen, J. and Frederickson, N. (2017). 'The Monsen Problem-Solving Framework – Problem Analysis as a Guide to Decision-Making, Problem Solving and Actions Within Applied Psychological Practice', in B. Kelly, L. Woolfson and J. Boyle (eds), *Frameworks for Practice in Educational Psychology*, 2nd edn. London: JKP, pp. 95–122.

Monsen, J., Graham, B., Frederickson, N. and Cameron, R. (1998). 'An Accountable Model of Practice'. *Educational Psychology in Practice*, 13(4), 234–49.

Mosse, J. (2019). 'Making Sense of Organisations – The Institutional Roots of the Tavistock approach', in A. Obholzer and V. Roberts (eds), *The Unconscious at Work*, 2nd edn. New York: Routledge, pp. 1–8.

Newman, D., Hazel, C., Barrett, C., Chaudhuri, S. and Fetterman, H. (2017). 'Early-Career School Psychologists' Perceptions of Consultative Service Delivery: The More Things Change, the More They Stay the Same'. *Journal of Educational & Psychological Consultation*, 28(2), 105–36.

Newman, D., McKenney, E., Silva, A., Clare, M., Salmon, D. and Jackson, S. (2017). 'A Qualitative Metasynthesis of Consultation Process Research: What We Know and Where to Go'. *Journal of Educational and Psychological Consultation*, 27(1), 13–51.

Newman, D. and Rosenfield, S. (2019). *Building Competence in School Consultation*. New York: Routledge.

Obholzer, A. and Roberts, V. (2019). 'The Troublesome Individual and the Troubled Institution', in A. Obholzer and V. Roberts (eds), *The Unconscious at Work*, 2nd edition. New York: Routledge, pp. 144–53.

Rittel, H. and Webber, M. (1973). 'Dilemmas in a General Theory of Planning'. *Policy Sciences*, 4, 155-169.

Roberts, V. (2019). 'The Organisation of Work: Contributions from Open Systems Theory', in A. Obholzer and V. Roberts (eds), *The Unconscious at Work*, 2nd edn. New York: Routledge, pp. 37–48.

Rosenfeld, J.M. and Caplan, G. (1954). 'Techniques of Staff Consultation in an Immigrant Children's Organisation in Israel'. *American Journal of Orthopsychiatry*, 24(1), 42–62.

Ruch, G. (2018). 'The Contemporary Context of Relationship-Based Practice', in G. Ruch, D. Turney and A. Ward (eds), *Relationship-Based Social Work*, 2nd edn. London: JKP, pp. 19–36.

Saltzman, C. (2006). 'Introducing Educators to a Psychodynamically Informed Teaching Practice'. *Psychodynamic Practice*, 12(1), 67–86.

Sapountzis, I. and Hyman, S. (2012). 'Introduction'. *Journal of Infant, Child & Adolescent Psychotherapy*, 11, 172–76.

Schein, E. (1999). *Process Consultation Revisited*. Reading, MA: Addison-Wesley.

Schön, D. (1991). *The Reflective Practitioner: How Professionals Think in Action*. Aldershot: Ashgate.

Shedler, J. (2010). 'The Efficacy of Psychodynamic Psychotherapy'. *American Psychologist*, 65(2), 98–109.

Sheridan, S., Bovird, J., Glover, T., Garbacz, A., Witte, A. and Kwon, K. (2012). 'A Randomised Trial Examining the Effects of Conjoint Behavioural Consultation and the Mediating Role of the Parent–Teacher Relationship'. *School Psychology Review*, 41, 23–46.

Sheridan, S. and Kratochwill, T. (2008). *Conjoint Behavioural Consultation: Promoting Family–School Connections and Interventions*. New York: Springer.

Sheridan, S., Welch, M. and Orme, S.F. (1996). 'Is Consultation Effective? A Review of Outcome Research'. *Remedial & Special Education*, 17, 341–54.

Vailliant, G. (2012). *Triumphs of Experience*. Cambridge, MA: Harvard University Press.

Waddell, M. (2002). *Inside Lives: Psychoanalysis and the Growth of Personality*. London: Karnac.

Wagner, P. (1995). *School Consultation: Frameworks for the Practicing Educational Psychologist*. London: Kensington & Chelsea EPS.

Wagner, P. (2000). 'Consultation: Developing a Comprehensive Approach to Service Delivery'. *Educational Psychology in Practice*, 16(1), 9–19.

Wagner, P. (2017). 'Consultation as a Framework for Practice', in B. Kelly, L.M. Woolfson and J. Boyle (eds), *Frameworks for Practice in Educational Psychology*, 2nd edn. London: JKP, pp. 194–216.

Warshaw, S. (2012). 'Application of Psychodynamic Thinking in the Practice of School Psychology'. *Journal of Infant, Child and Adolescent Psychotherapy*, 11(3), 169–71.

Wicks, A. (2013). 'Do Frameworks Enable Educational Psychologists to Work

Effectively and Efficiently in Practice? A Critical Discussion of the Development of Executive Frameworks'. *Educational Psychology in Practice*, 29 (2), 152–62.

Chapter 9

Al-Khatib, B. and Norris, S. (2015) 'A Family Consultation Service: Single Session Intervention to Build the Mental Health and Wellbeing of Children and Their Families'. *Educational & Child Psychology*, 32(4), 7–20.

Armstrong, D. (2005). *Organization in the Mind: Psychoanalysis, Group Relations, and Organizational Consultancy: Occasional Papers 1989–2003*. London: Karnac.

Bateson, G. (1973). *Steps to an Ecology of Mind: Collected Essays in Anthropology, Psychiatry, Evolution and Epistemology*. London: Paladin/Granada.

Bion, W.R. (1963). *Elements of Psycho-analysis*. London: Karnac.

Bollas, C. (1987). *The Shadow of the Object: Psychoanalysis of the Unthought Known*. London: Free Association Books.

Booker, R. (2005). 'Integrated Children's Services – Implications for the Profession'. *Educational Psychology in Practice*, 22(4), 127–42.

Brunning, H., Cole, C. and Huffington, C. (1997). *A Manual of Organizational Development: The Psychology of Change*. London: Karnac.

Caplan, G. (1970). *The Theory and Practice of Mental Health Consultation*. New York: Basic Books.

Caplan, G. and Caplan, R. (1993). *Mental Health Consultation and Collaboration*. Prospect Heights, IL: Waveland Press.

de Rementeria, A. (2011). 'How the Use of Transference and Countertransference, Particularly in Parent–Infant Psychotherapy, Can Inform the Work of an Education or Childcare Practitioner'. *Psychodynamic Practice*, 17(1), 41–56.

Department for Education and Employment (DfEE). (2000). *Educational Psychology Services (England): Current Role, Good Practice and Future Directions: The Research Report*. London: DfEE.

Dowling, E. and Osborne, E. (1994). *The Family and the School: A Joint Systems Approach to Problems with Children*. London: Karnac.

Eloquin, X. (2016). 'Systems-Psychodynamics in Schools: A Framework for EPs Undertaking Organisational Consultancy'. *Educational Psychology in Practice*, 32(2), 163–79.

Emmanuel, L. (1997). 'The Nature and Function of Projection and Projective Identification: From Evacuation to Communication'. *Projective Psychology*, 42(1), 39–54.

Farouk, S. (2004) 'Group Work in Schools: A Process Consultation Approach'. *Educational Psychology in Practice*, 20(3), 207–20.

Farrell, P.T., Woods, K., Lewis, S., Squires, S., Rooney, S. and O'Connor, M., and Department for Education and Skills (DFES) (2006). *A Review of the Function and Contribution of Educational Psychologists in the Light of 'Every Child*

Matters: Change for Children. Research report 792. London: DFES.

Gilmore, T.L. and Krantz, J. (1985). 'Projective Identification in the Consulting Relationship: Exploring the Unconscious Dimensions of a Client System'. *Human Relations*, 38(12), 1159–77.

Hanko, G. (1985). *Special Needs in Ordinary Classrooms: From Staff Support to Staff Development*, 3rd edn. London: David Fulton.

Hanko, G. (1999). *Increasing Competence Through Collaborative Problem Solving*. London: David Fulton.

Haynal, A. (2002). *Disappearing and Reviving: Sandor Ferenczi in the History of Psychoanalysis*. London: Karnac.

Health and Care Professions Council (HCPC) (2012). *Standards of Proficiency for Practitioner Psychologists*. Retrieved from www.hcpc-uk.org/assets/documents/ 10002963SOP_Practitioner_psychologists.pdf [accessed 06.12.2014].

Hinshelwood, R.D. (1994). *Clinical Klein*. London: Free Association Books.

Joseph, B. (1985). 'Transference: The Total Situation'. *International Journal of Psychoanalysis*, 66, 447–54.

Klein, M. (1935). 'A Contribution to the Psychogenesis of Manic Depressive States'. *International Journal of Psychoanalysis*, 16, 145–74. Reprinted in M. Klein (1975). *Love, Guilt and Reparation and Other Works, 1921–1945*. London: Hogarth Press.

Klein, M. (1946). 'Notes on Some Schizoid Mechanisms'. *International Journal of Psycho-Analysis*, 27(3/4), 99–110. Reprinted in M. Klein (1987), *Envy and Gratitude and Other Works, 1946–1963*. London: Hogarth Press.

Leadbetter, J. (2000). 'Patterns of Service Delivery in Educational Psychology Services: Some Implications for Practice'. *Educational Psychology in Practice*, 16(4), 449–60.

Matte-Blanco, I. (1975). *The Unconscious as Infinite Sets*. London: Duckworth.

Monsen, J.J. and Frederickson, N. (2008) 'The Monsen et al. Problem-Solving Model Ten Years On. The Problem Analysis Framework: A Guide to Decision Making, Problem Solving and Action Within Applied Psychological Practice', in B. Kelly, L. Wolfson and J. Boyle (eds), *Frameworks for Practice in Educational Psychology: A Textbook for Trainees and Practitioners*. London: JKP, pp. 69–93.

Moustaki-Smilansky, E. (1994). 'Glossary', in S. Box (ed.), *Crisis at Adolescence: Object Relations Therapy with the Family*. Northvale, NJ and London: Jason Aronson.

Nolan, A. and Moreland, N. (2014). 'The Process of Psychological Consultation'. *Educational Psychology in Practice*, 30(1), 63–77.

Pellegrini, D. (2010). 'Splitting and Projection: Drawing on Psychodynamics in Educational Psychology Practice'. *Educational Psychology in Practice*, 26(3), 251–60.

Schein, E.H. (1969). *Process Consultation*, Vol. 1. Reading, MA: Addison-Wesley.

Schein, E.H. (1987). *Process Consultation*, Vol. 2, *Lessons for Managers and Consultants*. Reading, MA: Addison-Wesley.

Symington, J. and Symington, N. (1996). *The Clinical Thinking of Wilfred Bion*. London: Routledge.

Wagner, P. (2000). 'Consultation: Developing a Comprehensive Approach to Service Delivery'. *Educational Psychology in Practice*, 16(1), 9–18.

Wilson, Reinhard, Westgate, Gilbert and Ellerbeck (2014). 'Just Think: The Challenges of the Disengaged Mind'. *Science*, 345, 75–7.

Chapter 10

Benjamin, J. (2004). 'Beyond Doer and Done To: An Intersubjective View of Thirdness'. *Psychoanalytic Quarterly*, 73(1), 5–46.

Bibby, T. (2010). *Education – An 'Impossible Profession'? Psychoanalytic Explorations of Learning and Classrooms*. London: Routledge.

Bion, W.R. (1963). *Elements of Psychoanalysis*. London: Karnac.

Bion, W.R. (1984). *Learning from Experience*. London: Karnac.

British Psychological Society (BPS) (2017). *Professional Practice Guidelines*, 3rd edition. Leicester: BPS.

Carroll, M. (2007). 'One More Time: What Is Supervision?' *Psychotherapy in Australia*, 13(3), 34–40.

Constantine, M.G. and Sue, D.W. (2007). 'Perceptions of Racial Micro-Aggressions Among Black Supervisees in Cross-Racial Dyads'. *Journal of Counselling Psychology*, 54(2), 142–53.

Creaner, M. (2014). *Getting the Best out of Supervision in Counselling and Psychotherapy: A Guide for the Supervisee*. London: Sage.

Curtis, H. (2015). *Everyday Life and the Unconscious Mind*, 2nd edition. London: Karnac.

Dickson, J.M., Moberly, N.J., Marshall, Y. and Reilly, J. (2011). 'Attachment Style and Its Relationship to Working Alliance in the Supervision of British Clinical Psychology Trainees'. *Clinical Psychology & Psychotherapy*, 18(4), 322–30.

Dunsmuir, S. and Leadbetter, J. (2010). *Professional Supervision: Guidelines for Practice for EPs*. Leicester: British Psychological Society.

Ferenczi, S. (1994). *First Contributions to Psycho-analysis*. London: Karnac.

Freud, S. (1905). *Three Essays on the Theory of Sexuality*. Standard Edition, Vol. 7. London: Hogarth Press.

Freud, S. (1915). *The Unconscious*. Standard Edition, Vol. 14. London: Hogarth Press.

Freud, S. (1917). *Mourning and Melancholia*. Standard Edition, Vol. 14. London: Hogarth Press

Freud, S. (1923). *The Ego and the Id*. Standard Edition, Vol. 19. London: Hogarth Press.

Freud, S. (1962). *Two Short Accounts of Psychoanalysis* (trans. J. Strachey). Harmondsworth: Penguin. London: Hogarth Press.

Gibbs, S., Atkinson, C., Woods, K., Bond, C., Hill, V., Howe, J. and Morris, S. (2016). 'Supervision for School Psychologists in Training: Developing a Framework from Empirical Findings'. *School Psychology International*, 37, 410–31.

Grant, J., Schofield, M.J. and Crawford, S. (2012). 'Managing Difficulties in Supervision: Supervisors' Perspectives'. *Journal of Counselling Psychology*, 59 (4), 528–41.

Hawkins, P. and Shohet, R. (1989). *Supervision in the Helping Professions*. London: Open University Press.

Hawkins, P. and Shohet, R. (2006). *Supervision in the Helping Professions*, 3rd edn. London: Open University Press.

Hawkins, P. and Shohet, R (2012). *Supervision in the Helping Professions*, 4th edn. London: Open University Press.

Health and Care Professions Council (2016). *Standards of Conduct, Performance and Ethics*. Retrieved from www.hcpcuk.org/globalassets/resources/standards/standards-of-conduct-performance-and-ethics.pdf

Hill, V., Bond, C., Atkinson, C., Woods, K., Gibbs, S., Howe, J. and Morris, S. (2015). 'Developing as a Practitioner: How Supervision Supports the Learning and Development of Trainee Educational Psychologists in Three-Year Doctoral Training'. *Educational & Child Psychology*, 32(3), 118–30.

Kaufman, J., Hughes, T.L. and Riccio, C.A. (eds) (2010). *Handbook of Education, Training, and Supervision of School Psychologists in School and Community*, Vol. 2, *Bridging the Training and Practice Gap: Building Collaborative University/Field Practices*. New York: Routledge.

Kennedy, E., Keaney, C., Shaldon, C. and Canagaratnam, M. (2018). 'A Relational Model of Supervision for Applied Psychology Practice: Professional Growth Through Relating and Reflecting'. *Educational Psychology in Practice*, 34(3), 282–99.

Kennedy, E. and Laverick, L. (2019). 'Leading Inclusion in Complex Systems: Experiences of Relational Supervision for Headteachers'. *Support for Learning*, 34(4), 443–59.

Klein, M. (1940). 'Mourning and Its Relation to Manic-Depressive States'. *International Journal of Psychoanalysis*, 21, 125–53.

Klein, M. (1952). 'Some Theoretical Conclusions Regarding the Emotional Life of the Infant', in M. Klein, *Envy and Gratitude and Other Works 1946–1963*. London: Hogarth Press, pp. 61–94.

Klein, M. (1975). *Love, Guilt and Reparation and Other Works 1921–1945*, Vol. 1. New York: Simon & Schuster.

Le Fevre, D., Robinson, V. and Sinnema, C. (2015). 'Genuine Inquiry: Widely Espoused Yet Rarely Enacted'. *Educational Management, Administration and Leadership*, 43(6), 883–99.

Lizzio, A., Wilson, K. and Que, J. (2009). 'Relationship Dimensions in the Professional Supervision of Psychology Graduates: Supervisee Perceptions of Processes and Outcome'. *Studies in Continuing Education*, 31(2), 127–40.

Lunt, I. (1993). 'Fieldwork Supervision for Educational Psychologists in Training: The 1984–5 Survey and the State of the Art at That Time'. *Educational & Child Psychology*, 10(2), 4–11.

Lunt, I. and Sayeed, Z. (1995). 'Support for Educational Psychologists in Their First Year of Professional Practice: Induction and Supervision Arrangements for Newly Qualified Educational Psychologists'. *Educational & Child Psychology*, 12(2), 25–30.

Mangione, L., Mears, G., Vincent, W. and Hawes, S. (2011). 'The Supervisory Relationship When Women Supervise Women: An Exploratory Study of Power, Reflexivity, Collaboration, and Authenticity'. *Clinical Supervisor*, 30(2), 141–71.

Meltzer, D. (1978). *The Kleinian Development*. Perthshire: Clunie Press.

Page, S. and Wosket, V. (2015). *Supervising the Counsellor and Psychotherapist: A Cyclical Model*, 3rd edn. Hove: Routledge.

Pomerantz, M. (1990). 'Fieldwork Supervision: A Personal Perspective on the State of the Art'. *Educational & Child Psychology*, 7(3), 53–58.

Pomerantz, M. (1993). 'The Value and Purpose of Supervision for Educational Psychologists'. *Educational & Child Psychology*, 10(2), 31–34.

Pomerantz, M. and Lunt, I. (1993). 'Investigating Supervision Practice: History and Methodology of the Enquiry'. *Educational & Child Psychology*, 10(2), 12–15.

Sandler, J. and Davidson, R.S. (1973). *Psychopathology: Learning Theory, Research, and Applications*. New York: Harper & Row.

Sanford, L.A. (1999). 'Learning Psychotherapy Through Connection: A Self-in-Relation Model of Supervision', unpublished PhD thesis, Antioch University.

Scaife, J. (1993). 'Application of a General Supervision Framework: Creating a Context of Co-operation'. *Educational & Child Psychology*, 10(2), 61–71.

Segal, H. (1973). *Introduction to the Work of Melanie Klein*. London: Hogarth Press.

Simon, D J., Cruise, T.K., Huber, B.J., Swerdlik, M.E. and Newman, D.S. (2014). 'Supervision in School Psychology: The Developmental/Ecological/Problem-Solving Model'. *Psychology in the Schools*, 51, 636–46.

Spillius, E.B., Milton, J., Garvey, P., Couve, C. and Steiner, D. (2011). *The New Dictionary of Kleinian Thought*. London: Taylor & Francis.

Waddell, M. (2002). *Inside Lives: Psychoanalysis and the Growth of the Personality*. London: Karnac.

Winnicott, D. (1953). 'Transitional Objects and Transitional Phenomena'. *International Journal of Psychoanalysis*, 3(4), 89–97.

Winnicott, D.W. (1971). *Playing and Reality*. London: Tavistock Publications.

Woods, K., Atkinson, C., Bond, C., Gibbs, S., Hill, V., Howe, J. and Morris, S. (2015). 'Practice Placement Experiences and Needs of Trainee Educational Psychologists in England'. *International Journal of School & Educational Psychology*, 3(2), 85–96.

Chapter 11

Adamo, S.M.G., Serieri, S.A., Gusti, P. and Contarini, R.T. (2008). 'Parenting a New Institution', in M. Rustin and J. Bradley (eds), *Work Discussion: Learning from*

Reflective Practice in Work with Children and Families. London: Karnac, pp. 233–52.

Anthony, E.J. (1983). 'The Group-Analytic Circle and Its Ambient Network', in M. Pines (ed.), *The Evolution of Group Analysis*. London: Routledge and Kegan Paul.

Bartle, D. (2015). 'Deception and Delusion: The Relational Aspect of Supervision Explored Through Greek Mythology'. *Educational & Child Psychology*, 32(3), 41–51.

Bartle, D. and Trevis, A. (2015). 'An Evaluation of Group Supervision in a Specialist Provision Supporting Young People with Mental Health Needs: A Social Constructionist Perspective'. *Educational & Child Psychology*, 32(3), 78–90.

Bion, W.R. (1962). *Learning from Experience*. London: Karnac.

Brown, M. (2019). 'David Hockney Rescued After Being Trapped in an Amsterdam Lift'. *Guardian*, 28 February. Retrieved from www.theguardian.com

Cooper, A. (2018). *Conjunctions: Social Work, Psychoanalysis, and Society*. Abingdon: Routledge.

Dunsmuir, S. and Leadbetter, J. (2010). *Professional Supervision: Guidelines for Practice for Educational Psychologists*. Leicester: British Psychological Society.

Dutton, R. (1995). *Clinical Reasoning in Physical Disabilities*. London: Williams & Wilkins.

Foulkes, S.H. (1948). *Introduction to Group-Analytic Psychotherapy: Studies in the Social Integration of Individuals and Groups*. Abingdon: Heinemann.

Garland, C. (1982) 'Group Analysis: Taking the Non-Problem Seriously', *Group Analysis*, 15, 4–14.

Grotstein, J. (2018). 'Bion's Transformations in 'O' and the Concept of the Transcendent Position ', in *WR Bion*. Abingdon: Routledge, pp. 129–44.

Harding, B. (dir.) (2019). 'Nature', in M. Springfield (prod.), *The Art of Japanese Life*. BBC Four, ep. 1, 13 March.

Kennedy, E., Keaney, C., Shaldon, C. and Canagaratnam, M. (2018). 'A Relational Model of Supervision for Applied Psychology Practice: Professional Growth Through Relating and Reflecting'. *Educational Psychology in Practice*, 34(3), 282–99.

Klein, M. (1961). *Narrative of a Child Analysis: The Conduct of the Psychoanalysis of Children as Seen in the Treatment of a Ten-Year-Old Boy*. New York: Random House.

Nitschke, G. (1993). 'MA – Place, Space, Void', in G. Nitschke, *From Shinto to Ando: Studies in Architectural Anthropology in Japan*. London: Academy Editions, pp. 48–61.

Nitsun, M. (1996). *The Anti-Group: Destructive Forces in the Group and Their Creative Potential*. Hove: Routledge.

Ogden, T. H. (1999). ' The Music of What Happens in Poetry and Psychoanalysis'. *International Journal of Psychoanalysis*, 80, 979–94.

Oliver, M. (1998). *Rules for the Dance: A Handbook for Writing and Reading*

Metrical Verse. Boston, MA: Houghton Mifflin Harcourt.

Roberts, J. (1983) 'Foulkes' Concept of the Matrix'. *Group Analysis*, 15(2), 111–26.

Schapobersky, J. (1994). 'The Language of the Group: Monologue, Dialogue and Discourse in Group Analysis', in D. Brown and L. Zinkin (eds), *The Psyche and the Social World*. London: Routledge.

Schlachet, P. (1986). 'The Concept of Group Space'. *International Journal of Group Psychotherapy*, 36, 33–53.

Waddell, M. (2002). *Inside Lives: Psychoanalysis and the Growth of the Personality*, revised edn. London: Duckworth.

Wason, S. (dir.) (1999). 'Anish Kapoor', in S. Wason (prod.), *The South Bank Show*. London Weekend Television, series 22, ep. 12, 21 February.

Winnicott, D. W. (1953). 'Transitional Objects and Transitional Phenomena – A Study of the First Not-Me Possession'. *International Journal of Psychoanalysis*, 34, 89–97.

Chapter 12

Armstrong, D. and Rustin, M. (2015). 'Introduction: Revisiting the Paradigm', in D. Armstrong and M. Rustin (eds), *Social Defences Against Anxiety: Explorations in a Paradigm*. London: Karnac, pp. 1–23.

Bedford, A. (2015). *Serious Case Review into Child Sexual Exploitation in Oxfordshire: From the Experiences of Children A, B, C, D, E, and F*, 26 February. Retrieved from www.oscb.org.uk/wp-content/uploads/SCR-into-CSE-in-Oxfordshire-FINAL-FOR-WEBSITE.pdf [accessed 18.02.2017].

Bibby, T. (2011). *Education - An 'Impossible Profession'?: Psychoanalytic Explorations of Learning and Classrooms*. Abingdon: Routledge.

Bick, E. (1968). 'The Experience of the Skin in Early Object Relations'. *International Journal of Psychoanalysis*, 49, 484–86.

Child Welfare Information Gateway (2019). *Mandatory Reporters of Child Abuse and Neglect*. Retrieved 10.05.20 from www.childwelfare.gov/pubPDFs/manda.pdf#page=5&view=Summaries%20of%20State%20laws

Connor, D.C. (2019). *Serious Case Review: Child KN15: Review Report*, 11 March. Nottingham: Nottinghamshire Safeguarding Children Board.

Cooper, A. and Lees, A (2015). 'Spotlit: Defences in Human Service Organizations', in D. Armstrong and M. Rustin (eds), *Social Defences Against Anxiety: Explorations in a Paradigm*. London: Karnac, pp. 239–55.

De Board, R. (2006). *The Psychoanalysis of Organizations*. London: Routledge.

Department for Education (2019). *Keeping Children Safe in Education: Statutory Guidance for Schools and Colleges*. Retrieved from https://assets.publishing.service.gov.uk/government/uploads/system/uploads/attachment_data/file/835733/Keeping_children_safe_in_education_2019.pdf

Health and Safety Executive (2019). *Work Related Stress, Anxiety and Depression*

Statistics in Great Britain 2019. Retrieved from www.hse.gov.uk/statistics/causdis/stress.pdf

HM Government (2004). *Children Act*. Retrieved 17.02.2017 from www.legislation.gov.uk/ukpga/2004/31/pdfs/ukpga_20040031_en.pdf

HM Government (2018). *Working Together to Safeguard Children: A Guide to Inter-Agency Working to Safeguard and Promote the Welfare of Children*, July. Retrieved from https://assets.publishing.service.gov.uk/government/uploads/system/uploads/attachment_data/file/779401/Working_Together_to_Safeguard-Children.pdf

Hulusi, H. and Maggs, P. (2015). 'Containing the Containers: Work Discussion Group Supervision for Teachers – A Psychodynamic Approach'. *Educational & Child Psychology*, 32(3), 30–40.

Hymans, M. (2008). 'How Personal Constructs About Professional Identity Might Act as a Barrier to Multi-Agency Working'. *Educational Psychology in Practice*, 24(4), 279–88.

Jackson, E. (2008). 'The Development of Work Discussion in Educational Settings'. *Journal of Child Psychotherapy*, 34(1), 62–83.

Jackson, E. (2015). 'Work Discussion Groups as a Container for Sexual Anxieties in Schools', in D. Armstrong and M. Rustin (eds), *Social Defences Against Anxiety: Explorations in a Paradigm*. London: Karnac, pp. 269–83.

Kahr, B. (2016). *Tea with Winnicott*. London: Karnac.

Lucey, A. (2015). 'Corporate Cultures and Inner Conflicts', D. Armstrong and M. Rustin (eds), *Social Defences Against Anxiety: Exploration in a Paradigm*. London: Karnac, pp. 213–21.

Menzies, I. (1959). 'A Case-Study in the Functioning of Social Systems as a Defence Against Anxiety'. *Human Relations*, 13, 95–121.

Music, G. (2019). *Nurturing Children: From Trauma to Growth Using Attachment Theory, Psychoanalysis and Neurobiology*. Abingdon: Routledge

Riesenberg-Malcolm, R. (2009). 'Bion's Theory of Containment', In C. Bronstein (ed.), *Kleinian Theory: A Contemporary Perspective*. London: Whurr, pp. 165–92.

Rosenfeld, H. (2008). 'A Clinical Approach to Psychoanalytic Theory of the Life and Death Instincts: An Investigation of the Aggressive Aspects of Narcissism', in J. Steiner (ed.), *Rosenfeld in Retrospect: Essays on His Clinical Excellence*. Hove: Routledge, pp. 116–21.

Rustin, M. (2008). 'Work Discussion: Some Historical and Theoretical Observations', in M.E. Rustin and Bradley (eds), *Work Discussion: Learning from Reflective Practice in Work with Children and Families*. London: Karnac .

Segal, H. (1988). *Introduction to the Work of Melanie Klein*. London: Karnac.

Tucker, S. (2015). 'Still Not Good Enough! Must Try Harder: An Exploration of Social Defences in Schools', in D. Armstrong and M. Rustin (eds), *Social Defences Against Anxiety: Explorations in a Paradigm*. London: Karnac, pp. 256–68.

Chapter 13

Ashton, R. and Roberts, E. (2006). 'What is Valuable and Unique About the Educational Psychologist?' *Educational Psychology in Practice*, 22(2), 111–23.

Bollas, C. (1987) *The Shadow of the Object: Psychoanalysis of Unknown Thought.* London: Free Association Books.

Bowlby, J. (1973) *Separation: Anxiety and Anger*, Vol. 2, *Attachment and Loss.* New York: Basic Books.

Braun, G. (2011). 'Organisations Today: What Happens to Attachment?' *Psychodynamic Practice*, 17(2), 123–29.

Bristow, M., Ireson, G. and Coleman, A. (2007). *A Life in the Day of a Headteacher: A Study of Practice and Well-being.* Nottingham: National College for School Leadership.

Czander, W.M. (1993). *The Psychodynamics of Work and Organizations: Theory and Application.* New York: Guilford Press.

Dessent, T. (1994). 'Educational Psychology: What Future?' *Educational & Child Psychology*, 11(3), 50–54.

Diamond, M.A. (2003). 'Organisational Immersion and Diagnosis: The Work of Harry Levinson'. *Organisational and Social Dynamics*, 3(1), 1–18.

Ferenczi, S. (1950) 'Sunday Neuroses 1918', in S. Ferenczi, *Further Contributions to the Theory and Technique of Psycho-Analysis*, 2nd edn. New York: Basic Books.

Greenson, R. (1967). *The Technique and Practice of Psychoanalysis.* New York: International Universities Press.

Hirschhorn, H. (1988). *The Workplace Within.* Cambridge, MA: MIT Press.

Homans, G. (1961). *Social Behaviour: Its Elementary Forms.* New York: Harcourt Brace Jovanovich.

Huffington, C., Cole, C.F. and Brunning, H. (1997). *A Manual of Organizational Development: The Psychology of Change.* London: Karnac.

Jahoda, M. (1966). 'Notes on Work', in R.M. Loewenstein, L.M. Newman, M. Schur and A.J. Solnit (eds), *Psychoanalysis: A General Psychology: Essays in Honor of Heinz Hartmann.* New York: International Universities Press, pp. 622–33.

Kilburg, R.R. (2000). *Executive Coaching: Developing Managerial Wisdom in a World of Chaos.* Washington, DC: American Psychological Association.

Kilburg, R.R. and Levinson, H. (2008). 'More About Executive Coaching: Practice and Research'. *Consulting Psychology Journal: Practice and Research*, 60(1), 7–32.

Lemma, A. (2007) 'Psychodynamic Therapy: The Freudian Approach', in W. Dryden (ed.), *Dryden's Handbook of Individual Therapy*, 5th edn. London: Sage, pp. 27–55.

Lynch, S., Mills, B., Theobald, K. and Worth, J. (2017). *Keeping Your Head: NFER Analysis of Headteacher Retention.* Slough: National Foundation of Educational Research.

Mackay, T. (2002). 'Discussion Paper – The Future of Educational Psychology'. *Educational Psychology in Practice*, 18(3), 245–53.

Menninger, K. (1942). 'Work as Sublimation'. *Bulletin of the Menninger Clinic*, 6(6), 170–82.

Morrison, E.W. and Robinson, S. (1997). 'When Employees Feel Betrayed: A Model of How Psychological Contract Violation Develops'. *Academy of Management Review*, 22(1), 226–56.

O'Neill, M.B. (2000). *Coaching with Backbone and Heart*. San Francisco, CA: Jossey Bass.

Pelham, G. (2017). Presentation to Leeds Beckett University Postgraduate Diploma in Coaching Psychology Group, October.

Peltier, B. (2011). *The Psychology of Executive Coaching: Theory and Application*. Abingdon: Taylor & Francis.

Rycroft, C. (1968). *A Critical Dictionary of Psychoanalysis*. London: Nelson.

Sandler, C. (2010). 'Working with Business Leaders and Their Teams'. *British Journal of Psychotherapy*, 26(2), 186–91.

Sandler, C. (2011). *Executive Coaching: A Psychodynamic Approach*. Maidenhead: McGraw-Hill Education.

Searles, H. (1955). 'The Informational Value of the Supervisor's Emotional Experience'. *Psychiatry*, 18, 135–46.

Chapter 14

Abraham, K.G., Haltiwanger, J., Sandusky, K. and Spletzer, J. (2019). 'The Consequences of Long-Term Unemployment: Evidence from Linked Survey and Administrative Data'. *ILR Review*, 72(2), 266–99.

Adams, R (2018). 'Why Teachers in England are Suffering from So Much Stress'. *Guardian*, 11 January. Retrieved from www.theguardian.com/education/2018/jan/11/teachers-england-suffering-from-so-much-stress-explainer [accessed 07.04.2020].

Armstrong, D. (2005). *Organization in the Mind: Psychoanalysis, Group Relations and Organizational Consultancy; Occasional Papers 1989–2003*. London: Karnac.

Armstrong, D. and Rustin, M. (2015). *Social Defences Against Anxiety: Explorations in a Paradigm*. London: Karnac.

Bain, A. (1979). 'Presenting Problems in Social Consultancy'. *Human Relations*, 29, 643–65.

Bion, W.R. (1961). *Experiences in Groups and Other Papers*. London: Tavistock Publications.

Bowins, B. (2004). 'Psychological Defence Mechanisms: A New Perspective'. *American Journal of Psychoanalysis*, 64(1), 1–26.

Cecchin, G. (1987). 'Hypothesizing, Circularity, and Neutrality Revisited: An Invitation to Curiosity'. *Family Process*, 26(4), 405–13.

Eloquin, X. (2016). 'Systems-Psychodynamics in Schools: A Framework for EPs

Undertaking Organisational Consultancy'. *Educational Psychology in Practice*, 32(2), 163–79. Retrieved from https://doi.org/10.1080/02667363.2016.11395 45

Halton, W. (2015). 'Obsessional-Punitive Defences in Care Systems', in D. Armstrong and M. Rustin (eds), *Social Defences Against Anxiety: Explorations in a Paradigm*. London: Karnac.

Hinshelwood, R. and Chiesa, M. (2001). *Organisations, Anxieties and Defences*. Hove: Brunner-Routledge.

Jaques, E. (1953). 'On the Dynamics of the Social Structure: A Contribution to the Psychoanalytical Study of Social Phenomena'. *Human Relations*, 6(1), 3–24.

Klein, M. (1946). 'Notes on Some Schizoid Mechanisms'. *International Journal of Psycho-Analysis*, 27(3/4), 99–110. Reprinted in M. Klein, *Envy and Gratitude and Other Works, 1946–1963*. London: Hogarth Press, 1987.

Lemma, A. (2016). *Introduction to the Practice of Psychoanalytic Psychotherapy*. Chichester: Wiley.

Lewin, K. (1947) 'Frontiers in Group Dynamics: Concept, Method and Reality in Social science; Socia Equilibria and Social Change'. *Human Relations*, 1(1), 5–41.

Menzies, I.E.P. (1960). 'A Case Study in the Functioning of Social Systems as a Defence Against Anxiety: A Report on a Study of the Nursing Service of a General Hospital'. *Human Relations*, 13, pp. 95–121. Reprinted in *Containing Anxiety in Institutions: Selected Essays*, Vol. 1. London: Free Association Books, 1988.

Miller, E. (1995). 'Dialogue with the Client System: Use of the Working Note in Organizational Consultancy'. *Journal of Managerial Psychology*, 10(6), 27–30.

Neumann, J.E. (1999). 'Systems Psychodynamics in the Service of Political Organisational change', in R. French and R. Vince (eds), *Group Relations, Management and Organisation*. Oxford: Oxford University Press.

Porges, S.W. (2011). *The Polyvagal Theory: Neurophysiological Foundations of Emotions, Attachment, Communication, and Self-Regulation*. New York: Norton.

Roberts, V.Z. (1994). 'The Organization of Work: Contributions from Open-Systems Theory', in A. Obholzer and V.Z. Roberts (eds), *The Unconscious at Work: Individual and Organisational Stress in the Human Services*. London: Routledge.

Shaw, M. (2002). *The Object Relations Technique*. New York: ORT Institute.

Stapley, L. (1996). *The Personality of the Organisation*. London: Free Association Books.

Stapley, L.F. (2006). *Individuals, Groups and Organizations Beneath the Surface*. London: Karnac.

Stokes, J. (1994). "The unconscious at work in groups and teams". In Obholzer, A. and Roberts, V. Z. (eds.) *The unconscious at work. Individual and organisational stress in the human services.* London: Routledge

Tucker, S. (2015). 'Still Not Good Enough. Must Try Harder', in D. Armstrong and M. Rustin (eds), *Social Defences Against Anxiety: Explorations in a Paradigm.* London: Karnac.

Vaillant, G.E. and Vaillant, C.O. (1986). 'An Empirically Validated Hierarchy of Defence Mechanisms'. *Archives of General Psychiatry*, 73, 786–94.

Weale, S. (2016). 'English Schools Struggling to Recruit Headteachers, Research Finds'. *Guardian*, 26 January. Retrieved from www.theguardian.com/education/2016/jan/26/english-schools-struggling-to-recruit-headteachers-research-finds [accessed 12.03.2017].

Wells, L. (1985). 'The Group-as-a-Whole Perspective', in A. Colman and M. Geller (eds), *Group Relations Reader 2.* Jupiter, FL: A.K. Rice.

Chapter 15

Arnold, C. (2002). 'The Dynamics of Reading Acquisition: Applications of Chaos Theory to Literacy Acquisition'. PhD thesis, University of Wolverhampton.

Ashworth, P. and Chung, M. (eds) (2006). *Phenomenology and Psychological Science: Historical and Philosophical Perspectives.* New York: Springer.

Buizza, R. and Leutbecher, M. (2015). 'The Forecast Skill Horizon'. *Quarterly of the Journal of the Royal Meteorological Society*, 141(693), 3366–82.

Cripps, B. (2018). *Psychometric Assessment: A Critical Guide.* London: Wiley/BPS.

Gleick, J. (1987). *Chaos: Making a New Science.* London: Penguin.

Hamilton, P. and West, B.J. (2000). 'Chaos Data Analyzer, Professional Version. By J. Sprott and G. Rowlands'. *Nonlinear Dynamics Psychology, and Life Sciences*, 4(2), 195–99.

Kandel, E.R. (1999). 'Biology and the Future of Psychoanalysis: A New Intellectual Framework for Psychiatry Revisited'. *American Journal of Psychiatry*, 156, 505–24.

Kierkegaard, S. (1957). *The Concept of Dread*, ed. W. Lowrie. Princeton, NJ: Princeton University Press.

Lorenz, E. (1972) 'Predictability: Does the Flap of a Butterfly's Wings in Brazil Set Off a Tornado in Texas?' Address to the American Association for the Advancement of Science, 29 December 29, Massachusetts Institute of Technology.

Macmillan, M (2001). 'The Reliability and Validity of Freud's Methods of Free Association and Interpretation'. *Psychological Enquiry*, 12(3), 167–75.

Mandelbrot, B.B. (1977). *Fractals: Form, Chance and Dimension.* San Francisco, CA: W.H. Freeman.

Mechelli, A. (2010). 'Psychoanalysis on the Couch: Can Neuroscience Provide the

Answers?' *Medical Hypotheses*, 75, 594–99.

Morrison, F. (1991). *The Art of Modeling Dynamic Systems*. Cambridge, MA: Harvard University Press.

Styles, J. (2009). 'On Genes, Brains and Behaviour: Why Should Developmental Psychologists Care About Brain Development?' *Child Development Perspectives*, 3, 196–202.

Styles, J., Brown, T.T., Haist, F. and Jernigan, T.L. (2015). 'Brain and Cognitive Development', in J. Carpendale, C. Lewis and U. Müller (eds), *The Development of Children's Thinking: Its Social and Communicative Foundations*. London: Sage.

Taylor, G. and Bagby, R. (2013). 'Psychoanalysis and Empirical Research: The Example of Alexithemia'. *Journal of the American Psychoanalytic Association*, 61(1), 99–133.

van der Maas, H. and Hopkins, B. (1998). 'Developmental Transitions: So What's New?' *British Journal of Developmental Psychology*, 16(1), 1–13.

Van Etten, M.L. and Taylor, S. (1998). 'Comparative Efficacy of Treatments for Post Traumatic Stress Disorder: A Meta-Analysis'. *Clinical Psychology & Psychotherapy*, 5, 126–44.

Van Geert, P. (1994). *Dynamic Systems of Development: Change Between Complexity and Chaos*. London: Harvester Wheatsheaf.

Wilson, S. (2010). 'Braindance of the Hikikomori: Towards a Return to Speculative Psychoanalysis'. *Paragraph*, 33(3), 392–409.

INDEX